Life-Study

experiencing Creative Lives by
the *Intensive Journal* Method

BOOKS BY IRA PROGOFF

At A Journal Workshop: The Basic Text and Guide
for Using the Intensive Journal Process, 1975

Life Study: Experiencing Creative Lives by the
Intensive Journal Method, 1983

The Practice of Process Meditation: The
Intensive Journal Way to Spiritual Experience, 1980

The Symbolic and the Real, 1963

Depth Psychology and Modern Man, 1959

The Death and Rebirth of Psychology, 1956

The Cloud of Unknowing, 1957

The Image of an Oracle, 1964

Jung's Psychology and Its Social Meaning, 1953

Jung, Synchronicity and Human Destiny, 1973

The Star/Cross, 1971

The White Robed Monk, 1972

The Well and The Cathedral, 1971, 1977

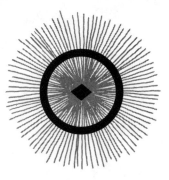

Life-Study

experiencing Creative Lives by
the *Intensive Journal*® Method

by
Ira Progoff

DIALOGUE HOUSE LIBRARY | NEW YORK

Published by
Dialogue House Library
80 East 11th Street
New York, New York 10003

Library of Congress Catalog Card Number: 83-72877

ISBN 0-87941-012-4

Printed in the United States of America

FIRST PRINTING 1983

Table of Contents

1   **Introduction: Toward the Education of Persons**   9

2   **Fundamentals of Life-Study**   23
    From *Holistic* Depth Psychology
    Subjective Process and Creativity
    The Instrument of the Workbook
    The Journal Workshop

3   **Being a Journal Trustee**   47
    The Persons We Choose
    A Human Resource
    Collecting Information: Life-Study Research

4   **The Twilight Atmosphere of a Workshop**   65

5   **The Steppingstones of a Life**   70

CONTENTS

6 **The Primary Steppingstones** 75
Feeling the Flow of the Life
The Readback Experience
From the Life-Study Journals
    Pablo Casals
    Eleanor Roosevelt
    Abraham Lincoln
    Jan Christian Smuts
    Vincent Van Gogh
    Thomas Jefferson
    Queen Victoria of England

7 **The Extended Steppingstones** 89
The Continuity and the Content
From the Life-Study Journals
    Pablo Casals
    Abraham Lincoln
    Eleanor Roosevelt

8 **The Focus Periods** 104
Vertical and Horizontal Time
Choosing Two Life/Time Units
Naming the Focus Periods

9 **Overview Statements** 114
From the Life-Study Journals
    Pablo Casals
    Abraham Lincoln
    Eleanor Roosevelt

10 **The Open Moment Image** 119
Twilight Envisioning at the Start of a Period
From the Life-Study Journals
    Pablo Casals
    Abraham Lincoln
    Eleanor Roosevelt

11 **Signpost Events**   127
     The Unfoldment of a Life/Time Unit
     From the Life-Study Journals
         Pablo Casals
         Abraham Lincoln
         Eleanor Roosevelt

12 **Reconstructing a Focus Period**   139
     Setting a Base for Journal Feedback
     Log and Feedback Entries

13 **Nine Questions for a Life/Time Unit**   152

14 **Excerpts from the Life-Study Journal
     of Pablo Casals: I**   157
     An Early Focus Period: "Preparing for a Career"

15 **Excerpts from the Life-Study Journal
     of Pablo Casals: II**   176
     A Later Focus Period: "Exile in Prades"

16 **Excerpts from the Life-Study Journal
     of Eleanor Roosevelt: I**   196
     An Early Focus Period: "Lucy and Polio"

17 **Excerpts from the Life-Study Journal
     of Eleanor Roosevelt: II**   218
     A Later Focus Period: "A Widow and a Person"

18 **After the Nine Questions**   233
     In the Journal Trustee Log
     The Earlier Focus Period
     The Later Focus Period
     A Private Workplace

CONTENTS

19 In a Journal Relationship   **241**
    The Place of *Meetings*
    The Twilight Dialogue Exercise

20 The Basic Steps in Life-Study: A Review   **249**

Appendix A: The *Intensive Journal* Life-Study
              Workbook   **257**

Appendix B: Entrance Meditations for Life-Study
    Introductory Note   **288**
    The Well and the Cathedral
        Sharing the Underground Stream
    The White Robed Monk
        The Silent Work of the Monks
    The Star/Cross
        Breathing the Breath of Mankind

Chapter 1

Introduction:
Toward the Education
of Persons

In Life-Study we do not work in our own life as we do at other *Intensive Journal* workshops. Here we apply the *Intensive Journal* process to lives that have been lived in an earlier generation. We seek to draw additional understanding from the experience of those who have been here before us. It is someone else's life that we study, but the effect is to clarify the goals and conduct of our own life. Depending on the person to whom we choose to give our *studied attention*, Life-Study leads us to reflect more deeply on the larger purpose and meaning of our life. At that point our practice of Life-Study can become an education for values as well as a stimulus to creativity, whatever our profession or special area of activity in life.

For each Life-Study experience we choose a person to whom we feel drawn on the basis of the general knowledge that we have of their life. This is a preliminary knowledge. That we choose a person does not mean that we agree with their opinions, nor that we consider them to be an ideal figure on whom we wish to model ourselves. Quite the contrary: there are many individuals whom we may choose for Life-Study in order to learn from their mistakes, or to meet them at the intersections of their life where we can learn more about the road they did not take. We may wish to come to know a person more closely just because we are well aware of the profound difficulties in their life, or because of the way they coped with the ambiguities and uncertainties of their existence. We may choose a person for a wide range of reasons, but ultimately it is because we feel, mainly on the basis of a personal intuition, that something in the experiences through which they lived contains a message for our life.

When we choose a person, we designate ourselves to be a Journal Trustee for them. This is a commitment that we make primarily to ourselves. It means that we will set up a Life-Study workbook in their name, and that we will carry out the basic Life-Study exercises in it in such a way as to reconstruct the movement of their life. In Life-Study, however, we do not reconstruct the life as an outsider to it. We are not content to be an observer of the life. We seek to re-experience it as a participant, and we do this by means of our Journal work. When we set up the Life-Study workbook of the person for whom we are Journal Trustee, we treat it as *their* workbook even though it is we who will do the actual writing of the Journal entries. We will write in the first person on their behalf. As their Journal Trustee we are their representative. In that capacity we make the responses, the brief and extended Journal statements that carry out the Life-Study exercises.

We write "I" as we speak for them in their workbook. This sets the tone and the feeling of the Journal work that we do in their name. As we respond for them to each of the exercises, we gradually reconstruct their life from within their perception of what took place. We are re-entering their experiences for them. Our role as Journal Trustee takes us outside our own skin and places us inside their life where we can share not only their emotions but their insights and understandings. We move with them through each of the phases of their life-span, participating in the cycles of frustration and achievement through which they passed. In this way we are able to learn from their weaknesses as well as from their strengths, from their fears as well as from the principles of belief that gave them courage. Of particular importance is the fact that we are able to retrace the steps by which they made their decisions, for this takes us inside their conflicts. Seeing their choices, we can also consider the possibilities of the roads not taken in their lives. Even though their life may have been lived in another culture and in another time of history, we can see the relevance of their experiences for equivalent decisions that we must make in the context of our own life. As their lives speak to ours, they become increasingly *significant persons* to us, for their experiences in the past help us clarify the personal goals and values by which we conduct our life in the present.

Life-Study does not mean studying a life by analyzing it. It means directing our *studied attention* to the whole life of a person, the background out of which it grew and the sequence of events by which it developed. We focus all the capacities of our cognition—our thoughts for understanding, our feelings for empathy, our intuitions for larger awareness—toward that life. We direct our attention to the contents and the movement of our person's life. We give our *studied attention* to the whole of it, including its goals and private purposes, in order that we can feel its inner process and know the person from within. As a Journal Trustee we do not judge the persons we study; we do not diagnose them. But we try to re-experience their life from within its own point of view. We study the life but we do not analyze it. We do not reduce it to this or that analytical factor, not to its sexual feelings nor to its inferiority feelings, not to its psychological type nor to its archetype, nor to any other analytical category. Instead we reconstruct the life in all its aspects, one event and circumstance after another, by means of the *Intensive Journal* method, and we let the contents of the life show us where its main concerns and issues lie. Since the reconstructions of the life within the *Intensive Journal* workbook, by means of the range and special points of focus in its method, direct us to the significant areas of the life, it is not necessary for us to make analytic interpretations. We can concentrate on giving our *studied attention* to the person as a whole as we seek an empathy of understanding.

The *Intensive Journal* process serves as the medium through which we establish our working contact with the life for which we are a Journal Trustee. The first and basic way that it does this is by means of the Journal exercises for establishing the context of the life as a whole. We build a perspective of the changes and developments that took place in the course of the full life-span of the person. Within that context, and with the support of particular exercises in the framework that it gives us, we then use the sections within the *Intensive Journal* structure as these correspond to the specific small processes (the *mini-processes*) that move within each individual's life. As we draw these together, life content by life content, using the *Intensive Journal* techniques, we are able to see from the data recorded in the workbook the areas of experience in which the major portion of the life-activity has been taking place. The way the data come together tells us the information about the life that we need to know. More than that, since the *Intensive Journal* procedures bring life-data together in relation to the period of time in which they happened, the continuity of process in a life becomes directly apparent to us. As the Journal entries form their patterns of movement we are able to see how disparities and paradoxes, events that seemed to contradict one another, all are part of the encompassing unity of process by which a life unfolds.

The separate Journal sections in the *Intensive Journal* workbook give us an avenue of contact with the small processes that move at the subliminal levels of the life; and the integrative structure of the workbook as a whole carries the larger movement through the several cycles of experience in a full life-span. The parts of the life and the self-integrating whole of it are reflected respectively in the individual sections of the workbook and the totality of its structure. The essence of the *Intensive Journal* process, and the key to the effectiveness of its methods, lie in the fact that each workbook embodies a life and is the cumulative carrier of the transitions and developments that take place in the course of a person's life-experience.

In operation, the Journal Feedback exercises feed the material of the small sections of the workbook back and forth into one another, forming and reforming new combinations. These provide the active procedures for ongoing life-development in the personal use of the *Intensive Journal* process. We are able to apply these techniques in Life-Study, although it is necessary to make some alterations in order to accommodate the fact that here we are working in a life other than our own. We use Journal Feedback particularly in the second phase of Life-Study after we have assembled the main data of the person's life-span. At that point the Journal Feedback procedures draw the events and experiences of the life together in a way that highlights the unity of process that is working at the deep levels of a life, whatever facades a person may be showing on the surface. When we reconstruct a life within the framework of the *Intensive Journal* workbook we are brought into contact with this unity of process. While it is an intangible factor in a person's life, our Life-Study work makes it tangible to us. We see it as we mark off the lines of inner development in the life of the person for whom we are a Journal Trustee. And then we progressively work with it as the experiences of their life tell us their messages and open their implications to us.

Working as a Journal Trustee in Life-Study, we write in the first person in the workbook of the person we represent. This has the effect of positioning us *inside the process* of the life. It places us inside the sequence of events by which that life has unfolded. Being inside the movement of the life we can feel its emotions, the plans and the anxieties of the person. We are close enough to share them. This is not an identity with the person, but it makes possible an empathy that can be felt from inside the process of the life. In Life-Study we enter the life. We go back in time within it to re-experience the emotions of the original events as they were happening. As much as we can, we place ourselves where the person was back in time. We do this gradually, one event and situation at a time, as we carry out the Life-Study exercises in the first person. It draws us into contact with the inner process of the life. This connection with the continuity of the interior movement enables us to *know* the person in a non-analytical way.

The equivalent of this experience that we have as a Journal Trustee is the experience that we have when we place ourselves before a work of art, seeking to attune ourselves to it, to enter it, to know it. At such a time, whether it be a painting, a sculpture, a symphony, a novel, we give the work of art our *studied attention* as we let the parts come together to form a whole. And with the exercises of Life-Study we continue giving our *studied attention* to the whole of the life until we feel that we have made contact with the process moving within it. By *studied attention* in Life-Study we connect ourselves with the process moving within the life of a human being.

In the case of the fine arts, we undertake to relate ourselves to the work of art by means of the capacities of perception and intuition that we have developed over the years by our study and interest in that field of art. When we are seeking to relate ourselves to the work of art, flawed though it may be, of another human being's life, we do so by giving it our *studied attention* within the framework of the *Intensive Journal* process. By the method of drawing forth and interrelating Journal entries, we establish a process in written form contained in a workbook that moves on the outer level parallel to the interior continuity of the subjective contents that comprise a person's life. Making our contact with this inner process in the person for whom we are a Journal Trustee is a specific goal of Life-Study. It gives us the direct understanding of a human life that is the equivalent of the experience to which we reach when we place ourselves face to face with a work of art.

Something further takes place in Life-Study as a result of the parallel between a work of art and a human life. When we have the personal experience of connecting inwardly with a work of art, in whatever field of art it may be, we find that it activates a flow of emotions, thoughts and sensitivities in the depth of us. That is one characteristic of a work of art: it has an evocative effect on human beings other than the person who created it. Sometimes, in fact, its power to evoke is so great that it stimulates recognitions of truth in the viewer that are greater and more profound than the artist originally conceived. But that only underscores the power of a work of art. It is able to go beyond itself. The process of creativity continues working in and through it after its own specific creation has been completed. The work of art has been completed,

14

but its life is not finished. It retains a capacity of self-extending creativity that continues as an active factor in the world.

As this is true of works of art, it is also true of human beings. When we re-enter the life of the person for whom we are a Journal Trustee and experience the process within it, a further experience may take place in us that resembles our becoming profoundly attuned to a work of art. When we experience our inner connections to a work of art, feelings and awarenesses may be evoked in us that we had not known before. Something new has been created in us by our contact with it. Comparably, something new may be evoked and created in us when we come by means of Life-Study to an experience of connection with the inner process of the life of a person who is significant to us.

As a work of art can do, a human life can continue and extend its creativity through the persons who re-enter it and re-experience its meaning. Like a work of art that has been completed, the life of a person of earlier generations has also been physically completed. But the experiences that it still can evoke and can bring into the world by its stimulating effects have not been exhausted. These may, indeed, be illimitable and have no end. The life may have more and more to contribute as its suggestive implications open from one to the other. Its creativity may not only continue but enlarge itself as time moves on. In the case of a work of art this *extra* of ongoing creativity can take place only after the work itself has been completed. Once that has been done, whenever we attune ourselves to it something further can happen within us to extend its creative life. The same can be true of a person. When the physical life is over, the life can become a source of new creativity for those who have become attuned to it.

Becoming attuned to the inner process of a life is the purpose underlying the *studied attention* that we give to a person by means of the *Intensive Journal* methods in Life-Study. It takes us in two directions of time. On the one hand it takes us into the past to connect us with the lives of those who have been here before us. And it also leads us into the future as the life of the person whom we study in our role as Journal Trustee becomes, like a work of art, a source of new creativity in us.

With respect to a work of art, the fact that we admire it does not cause it to have a creatively stimulating effect on us. Admiration by itself is not sufficient. It is necessary also to give our *studied attention* to the artwork, considering its background and its development as fully and as profoundly as we can, until we have become one with the process by which it came into being. At that point the artwork is able to extend its creative life through us as it becomes part of our experience.

Again we find that what is true of a work of art is also true of a human being. Admiring a person is not enough. It is necessary also to possess a disciplined method based on valid principles by which we can enter the inner process of the person's experience, not only understanding it but reconstructing the life from within. Possessing a disciplined method, it is necessary for us also to follow the procedures. If we carry out the discipline, we can re-experience the work of art, whether it be a painting or a poem or a human life, to the point where it extends its creative life in our experience.

The principles and exercises of Life-Study that are described in this volume provide a method for giving our *studied attention* to a human life as we would to a work of art. It leads to an educational discipline that draws its lessons from the experience of persons who have lived in past times while it builds capacities of creativity in present-day lives. The conception of education underlying the *Intensive Journal* program is that we develop persons best by expanding the capacities and breadth of consciousness within them.

The specific means by which we do this in Life-Study is by establishing a point of contact as individuals with the actualities of experience in other person's lives regardless of the culture and the period of history in which they lived. We use the Life-Study methods to help us re-enter and share the experience of persons who have lived before us. Participating in their lives, we learn from them despite the differences in the circumstances. We find that the growth that takes place in us is expressed in our outer experiences, but it has an interior source. It is activated by the contents of our Life-Study and it is expressed in the contents of our lives, but its roots are more fundamental than outer events. It is the varied forms in which we build our *inner muscles* that is important.

The Life-Study procedures for entering another person's life and reconstructing that life from within its own conceptions of truth can stretch our own inner perspective. As we retrace the experiences in another person's life, the fact that we perceive the events from within their point of view has an effect on us. We develop a feeling for the rhythms of change as they occur in the continuity of a full human existence. As a result also of the even-handedness with which Life-Study reconstructs a person's life, we re-enter the times of creativity equally with the times when creativity seems to have been absent. We thus acquire an inner view of both the times of blockage and the times of inspiration, building in ourselves a sensitivity to the rhythms and variations of creativity. The practice of Life-Study develops these two capacities, sensitivity to the rhythms of change in human life and sensitivity to the rhythms of creativity.

Those of us who will eventually serve as Journal Trustee for more than one person will be able to develop an additional capacity that tends toward what may be called a wisdom in life. The perspective that we gain from giving our *studied attention* to two or more lives builds the range of intuition with which we can respond to the often inexplicable variations in individual destiny. Our knowledge of life grows, then, drawing on the experiences of persons for whom we are Journal Trustee, but the effect is to add a quality of wisdom to the conduct of our own life. Placing ourselves inside the lives of persons who have struggled through times of difficulty tends to expand our capacity for compassion. It gives us a greater empathy in our perception of other human beings. It enables us to understand that, while some works of art may be perfect, the artwork of a human life depends upon its imperfections. We live with the paradox that difficulties are necessary in human experience as part of the process that draws forth

17

creativity and establishes meaning in life. In this perspective we can understand how Life-Study serves as a method of education. Since its particular contribution is in the area of creativity and human values, it conveys a type of learning that is gradually acquired by practice and cumulative inner experience rather than by being directly taught and memorized fact after fact.

In the *Intensive Journal* program Life-Study is the second of the two major components. The first is the Personal Component of *Intensive Journal* work, which has been the core of the National Program. It has made the *Intensive Journal* method available at varied social and economic levels, from prisons and ghettos to universities and the theatrical professions. In this form the special value of the *Intensive Journal* program is that it provides a tangible tool that individuals can use, especially when they are in times of transition, to draw their lives together and to make constructive decisions within the framework of their own values and goals. After the basic workshops, the method is a means of self-development that can be used in privacy and in a person's own timing. It contains the fundamentals of the *Intensive Journal* process.

In Life-Study as the second component of the *Intensive Journal* program, the Journal process is adapted in order to be applied to the lives of individuals from other times and places to whom we feel personally drawn. We re-experience their lives by means of the *Intensive Journal* format, using methods that have been developed and refined in the course of the many hundreds of workshops in the National Program. Some variations, however, have been necessary in order to meet the special requirements of working in a life other than our own. As a consequence the techniques of Life-Study are not the same in every case as those used in the Personal Component of *Intensive Journal* work. But the principles are the same; and essentially it is the same process that is used throughout. The *Intensive Journal* process is at the heart of the program and of the steps toward the education of persons that it makes possible.

Both of these components, the Personal and the Life-Study uses of the *Intensive Journal* program, follow a parallel sequence.

Each requires a basic workshop experience in which the techniques are learned and the fundamental life-data are collected in a usable form. In the case of the Personal Component this is done in the course of a variety of workshop formats in the National Program. In essence the Life Context workshop gathers the data of the life as a whole and teaches the basic procedures; the Process Meditation workshop deepens the experiences of meaning and creativity in a person's life; and the Journal Feedback workshop focuses on the use of the active *Intensive Journal* techniques. In the case of the Life-Study Component there is a single extended workshop format that establishes the foundation of the method and builds a framework into which data can be added from time to time. The basic Life-Study workshop provides the *foundation and framework* for the further experiences in which the techniques of Journal Feedback will be used in Life-Study. Participation in all these workshops is available nationwide in the United States and in many other countries through the Dialogue House headquarters in New York City. The core exercises are also available in book form. The Personal Component is described in *At a Journal Workshop* and in *The Practice of Process Meditation.*★ The Life-Study Component is described in this volume.

The two components of the *Intensive Journal* work fit together and complement each other in their larger educational effect, but each can be utilized apart from the other. Those individuals who wish to work only with the Personal Component can do so; and those who wish to work only with the Life-Study Component can do so. As much as possible, I have written this volume in such a way that persons who are entering Life-Study without previous *Intensive Journal* experience will not be at a disadvantage. In many cases, where a reference to other aspects of *Intensive Journal* work is essential, I have tried to give the necessary explanations at a basic level.

There are some additional points to bear in mind. One is that the Personal Component includes, in addition to the perspective

★ Available from Dialogue House Library, 80 East 11th Street, New York, NY 10003.

and basic exercises of the Life Context workshop, the transpersonal experiences of Process Meditation and the introductory steps to the holistic, integrative procedures of Journal Feedback. Persons who are interested in the larger educational role of the *Intensive Journal* program may find it meaningful that the reason Life-Study could not be formulated before this relatively late date in the development of the *Intensive Journal* system is that it was first necessary to have the full structure of the Journal sections available, defined and described—at least in relation to their main exercises—before the *Intensive Journal* process could be adapted to Life-Study. This was particularly true of the Journal sections and the exercises for Process Meditation. The transpersonal material that is the main content of Process Meditation deals largely with experiences of meaning, especially with those *ultimate concerns* that are expressed in a person's beliefs and works. These play a very large role in the lives of the persons who tend to be chosen as subjects for Life-Study.

It is a fact that persons in whose lives the issues of Process Meditation have played a large role, whatever the cultural and doctrinal framework of their experiences, are attractive persons for the purposes of Life-Study, and they tend to be chosen by Journal Trustees. These persons do not necessarily have a religious emphasis in their lives, although they may. Their Process Meditation concerns tend more to be related to questions in their professional or artistic work, as for example in the lives of Vincent Van Gogh, Albert Einstein, Frank Lloyd Wright, William Osler, Marie Curie, Florence Nightingale, Ludwig Wittgenstein, Honoré de Balzac, Charles Dickens, Benjamin Cardozo. There are also many individuals in whom the concerns of Process Meditation are of a much more obvious importance than in the lives of the above persons. It was therefore an absolute necessity for me to have a careful formulation of Process Meditation, its Journal sections and exercises, available before presenting the Life-Study Component. Although the principles of Process Meditation have been part of the *Intensive Journal* work since its beginning I was not able to make the necessary formulations and descriptions until 1980.★ Life-Study had to wait for that. But now this second component of the *Intensive Journal* process, complementing the personal use of the method, is ready and in place.

There is a further development of the *Intensive Journal* process that still lies in the future, but of which I must speak here in introducing Life-Study. It concerns the eventual use of the two components in a practical method for the educational development of persons at the level of creativity and human values. When we have carried out the basic Life-Study exercises on behalf of the person for whom we are a Journal Trustee, the question will arise of whether there are issues and awarenesses which that person's experiences stimulate in us as individuals. If there are, and if we have already carried out the Personal Component of *Intensive Journal* work, we will be in a position to engage in an *Interplay* between the Life Study Journal of the person for whom we are a Journal Trustee and our own *Intensive Journal* workbook. On one level it will be an Interplay of Journals. At another level it will be an Interplay of lives represented by their Journals and by the material in particular Journal sections. The *Journal Interplay* that can then take place will be a bridge across the generations, drawing upon the past to stimulate the future in our own present experience.

There are a number of specific procedures that are already clear for taking the steps of *Journal Interplay*. But first things first. Before we can proceed to Journal Interplay we have to do the work of Life-Study in order that the material of both components will be in place when the time for Journal Interplay comes.

I must add that I feel free now to speak of Journal Interplay ahead of its time because I have more than a small feeling that many persons, having done the work in both the Life-Study Component and the Personal Component, will not need my specific guidance as to how to proceed in Journal Interplay. Their

★ Ira Progoff, *The Practice of Process Meditation*, Dialogue House Library, New York, NY, 1980.

experiences will carry their own light. At that point we will see how the further steps of Journal Interplay make possible a self-reliant way in education that can develop persons of creativity with a sensitivity to wisdom in the conduct of life.

The practice of Life-Study enlarges our consciousness in a specific way. Comparable to the way that practicing artists tend to develop a sharper sense of color and form in the course of their work, serving as Journal Trustee for another person tends to develop in us a stronger sense of *life/time*. Re-entering the transitions of a life and moving from cycle to cycle within it builds a sensitivity to the inner rhythms of change. It enlarges our interior perspective of human experience and gives a larger understanding of how creative integrations take shape, often as though spontaneously, beneath the surface of events. Translated into each individual's circumstances, this understanding leads to a more developed capacity of judgment and timing, a capacity of wisdom in the conduct of life by the light of our personal values. It is a main goal of our work in Life-Study as a self-educative process.

Chapter 2

Fundamentals of Life-Study

From HOLISTIC *Depth Psychology*

The present development of Life-Study draws upon material that was one of the research sources from which the original conception of the *Intensive Journal* process was developed. When depth psychology went beyond its earlier analytical phase,* and the formulation of a *holistic* depth psychology had taken place,** the question arose of what would be an appropriate and fruitful subject matter for further research. The concepts of the new *holistic* depth psychology led to hypotheses regarding integrative processes in human experience. The new framework of thought pointed particularly toward lines of development that were inherent in individuals in the sense that, although they were hidden from view, they were present as potentials. They were natural in the way that a seed is natural, and they were inherent as factors that were actively working even though they were not visible. The problem with the potentials of a seed is that they are not only hidden from view, they are reserved for the future. Until the time when they

* Ira Progoff, *The Death and Rebirth of Psychology*, McGraw-Hill, New York, 1956.
** Ira Progoff, *Depth Psychology and Modern Man*, McGraw-Hill, New York, 1959.

are fulfilled, they are nothing more than possibilities. In the case of species other than the human, the potentials for the species as a whole are the same for all its individuals. That is to say, once they reach their mature development, all squirrels possess the potential for burying nuts. Since depth psychology deals with persons, however, its task is to identify the potentials of individuals within the human species, rather than the potentials of the species as an undifferentiated whole. In this regard depth psychology faces the difficulty that, while the potentials of an animal species tend to be generic and apply to all its members, potentials in the human species are unique for each person. In addition, they are hidden in the depth of the personal seed and are difficult to identify because they may be combined with other potentials of which the individual is not aware.

Given this task and the difficulty of its subject matter, the *holistic* point of view in depth psychology directed its attention to the formation of new integrations, or wholes, in the lives of persons. The focus of research in *holistic* depth psychology was to identify those aspects of the depth processes that move toward the formation of new units of experience in a person's life. To do this, it needed to reconstruct the various paths, including the obstacles, to wholeness as these emerge from the seed and reveal themselves in the actualities of human lives. Previous research work in depth psychology, however, did not deal with the type of material in which the integrative processes were visible. Since the days of Breuer and Freud in the nineteenth century when depth psychology first established itself in Europe, its research data have been drawn primarily from its cases in psychotherapy. Since the fundamental quality of this material was pathology, it was inevitable that pathology set the tone of its research and of the concepts that it developed. Occasionally literary materials were used in addition to cases, as when Freud analyzed the novel, *Delusion and Dream,*★ or when Jung analyzed the writings of Schiller.★★ It is generally

★ Sigmund Freud, *Delusion and Dream,* Beacon Press, Boston, 1956. Based on *Gradiva* by Wilhelm Jensen, published in 1903.
★★ C. G. Jung, *Psychological Types in Collected Works,* Bollingen Series XX, Vol. 6., Part I, Pantheon Books, New York.

correct to say, however, that when novels or the writings of philosophical authors have been drawn upon in the history of depth psychology, it has been to help articulate concepts that had already been decided upon. The literary material that has been used in depth psychology cannot be considered to be empirical data since it has served more as a platform for exposition than as a source of information.

When the framework of concepts had been formed in *holistic* depth psychology, a number of new hypotheses emerged. Primarily these involved the nature of the processes that move and unfold in the depths of an individual's life. What were their beginnings, their impulses and energies, their obstacles, their rhythms? How could they be nurtured and assisted in forming their new integrations? It soon became clear that for this purpose the old type of data in depth psychology—the case histories drawn from past and present practice—was not adequate. These contained, even if only implicitly, the influence of earlier diagnostic doctrines, and they could not provide the empirical data with which to build an understanding of human experience in a holistic perspective.

A new source of empirical data was required in order to check the hypotheses of *holistic* depth psychology and to fill in the details of information. The question arose of what type of raw material was necessary, considering that the purpose of the new *holistic* depth psychology was to trace the unfoldment of human lives from birth to death and to open channels for further development along the way. The study of abstract philosophical or sociological tracts could not be a source for this; neither could the pathology of patients in psychotherapy. *Holistic* depth psychology required as its source data the whole lives of persons, drawing on human beings of all circumstances and eliminating no one. As the work proceeded it became apparent that the empirical data for *holistic* depth psychology are to be found not in case histories but in life histories. The question was how to collect the relevant information.

Not having a definite guideline, the gathering of data at the outset was generalized and haphazard. The goal was clear and definite, however: it was to gather data regarding the whole life development for as broad a range of persons as possible. At the Institute for Research in Depth Psychology in the early nineteen-sixties, information was brought together on the lives of persons who were considered to be creative, and those who were considered to be neurotic; persons who were living and those who had died; persons from modern times and those from earlier periods of history; persons from western civilization and those from other cultures. As the information accumulated, there was, however, no cohering principle that would make it possible to sort out the data and work with them. At that point, the *Intensive Journal* process was not in existence.

Looking at the varieties of life-data did, however, lead to the formation of a pertinent question which, in turn, led to the *Intensive Journal* process. The question was:

> When, out of the mass of contents in a person's life, particular experiences come together in a way that brings something new into existence, whatever the form and content may be, we can say that a creative event has taken place at that time. What is the process by which this creativity occurs?

Responding to that question could have involved an answer given in conceptual and analytical terms. It was important, however, to avoid that. A conceptual answer would have been the analytical way of depth psychology since the days of Freud and Adler and Jung. Trying to state what the process of creativity is would have required an interpretive description of creativity. And any description, whatever its theoretic and analytical content, would necessarily be *about* creativity rather than *be* creativity. But creativity is real only when it is an event that is in the act of happening.

The alternative to answering the question with concepts was to take an experiential approach. At that point, however, since the structure of the *Intensive Journal* workbook had not yet been developed, there was no specific instrument available to serve as a vehicle for creative experience. As the data were considered, the observation was made that, of the many persons about whom information had been gathered, there were some whose experiences had come together to form creative events, and others whose experiences had simply not coalesced. In those, nothing creative seemed to have happened. Could we draw upon the experiences of the first group and not the second? Would it be possible to structure the sections of a Journal in a way that would follow the sequence and would carry the accumulation of material of those people in whom creative events had in fact taken place?

If that was the goal, the task was not to describe the creative events but to set up the Journal sections in a format that would parallel the sequence of experiences that took place in those persons in whom creative events did occur. The particular difficulty lay, first, in identifying the specific types of events that were intrinsic to the process by which new integrations were formed, and then in setting these events in an accurately parallel sequence with the exercises that accompany the Journal sections. Many trials and errors were involved in carrying out this project and getting it into working order. Eventually, however, it provided the model on which the structure of the *Intensive Journal* workbook was formed and by which the *Intensive Journal* process was brought into being.

Specific Journal sections were set up to carry the movement of the small processes in a life, the *mini-processes*. A group of Journal sections was set up to collect the events that reflect the movement of the life as a whole. These are the red sections in the workbook. Another group of Journal sections was set up to carry the nonconscious experiences, particularly the dreams and twilight imagery. These are the blue sections. A third group of Journal sections was set up to carry the activities of the individual life, especially the relationships with other persons, and with work projects. These were brought together in the orange division of the workbook. Together with the *Period Log* and the *Daily Log* sections, these three groupings—the *life/time, depth* and *dialogue dimensions* of the *Intensive Journal* workbook, respectively—contained the sections that comprised the original *Intensive Journal* structure. They were modeled on the experiences of persons who were observed to have followed a sequence—spontaneously, as it seemed—that culminated in creative events. We were not trying to copy those events in order to repeat them. We were merely setting up a Journal framework that would carry the movement of experiences along paths parallel to the sequences of process that led to creative events in the individuals who had been observed.

This step, which seemed simple at the time and was intended mainly as a preliminary to extended work with creativity, proved to be effective in helping many people set their lives in order. As experience with the method continued and as it was used with an increasing number of persons, additional sections were added to the *Intensive Journal* structure, including the full set of sections for the deepening work of Process Meditation involving the experience of connection-to-life. The active exercises that had been modeled on the sequences of creativity were gradually extended into the Journal Feedback method. The net effect was that the *Intensive Journal* workbook, with its structure of sections and corresponding exercises, became the instrument for carrying out a sequence of experiences that paralleled what had been observed in creative persons. This was the beginning of the *Intensive Journal* program.

Subjective Process and Creativity

In reflecting on what was the turning point of my experience in making the *Intensive Journal* program, I am brought back to the crossroad of decision that also marked a major change in my relation to depth psychology. It was the point at which, instead of making interpretive statements about creativity—in which case creative persons would have become objects of my psychological study—I took the path of trying to structure a non-analytical workbook (the *Intensive Journal* workbook, as it turned out) that could serve as a vehicle for reconstructing the process of creativity as it takes place in an individual life. My thought at that time was that the structure of the workbook would provide the means of organizing further research in the study of lives, and that eventually it might serve a therapeutic purpose as well. As events turned out, the *Intensive Journal* workbook has served a more-than-therapeutic role. Its use has made it the core of a national program that provides a framework for *positioning* individuals between their past and their future, setting their lives in perspective, and enabling them to make their life-decisions in a self-reliant way. The continued growth of the program with its outreach into disadvantaged levels of society has tended to give second place to the original emphasis on research in the study of lives. That may change, however, now that the Life-Study component has been developed.

The hypothesis on which the *Intensive Journal* methods were originally based was a perception of process in the experience of creative persons. The effort was to observe as closely as possible the process that is spontaneously effective in the experience of creative persons, and then to find a means of replicating and adapting that process in the everyday events of individual lives. The thought was that this would make possible *creativity in everyday life*. It has in fact led to the *Intensive Journal* process.

At an early stage of study it became apparent that the process that is effective in the lives of creative persons is not the same type of process that we observe in the state of nature. It is not comparable to the regular, cyclical process that we observe in the tree that grows in summer, that sheds its leaves in fall, and remains dormant until it renews itself the following year. It is not that type of visible, repetitive process. Equally, it is not a process like the many hidden processes in the individual organs of the human body. Each of these processes moves through its necessary phases, expressing and responding to objective physical phenomena. In contrast, the process by which creative events come to pass in individual lives expresses changes in phenomena that are subjectively perceived. It is a subjective process that is at work there.

The distinction between these two types of process became increasingly important for developing the operational principles of the *Intensive Journal* method. On the one hand there are the physical processes which move through their phases of life in response to objective factors. On the other hand there are the subjective processes in the course of which individuals establish the goals and values, the sense of meaning and direction in their lives. Included in these are the purposes and plans of a life, the personal relationships and work activities, the cycles of experience through which a person passes, the striving, the frustration, the inspiration of new ideas, the achieving, the surrender, the anxiety during the empty period, and the renewal. All are part of the subjective processes of a human life. They comprise the qualitative content of a human existence.

In the human body, as in the physical world of nature, we can see the changes within the processes as they are tangibly taking place, and we can mark them off if we have the proper instruments. But the subjective processes of human existence are intangible. Since they are interior, we cannot see their movement and we cannot observe their cycles of development in the same way that we can see the changes that take place in the outer world of nature. We can identify the several subjective processes that occur in our individual lives only in very general terms. Since they are experiential, they are not objects that we can hold in our hands. When we seek to analyze subjective processes as though they were objects, they elude us. And they present the further difficulty that if we do analyze them, they will draw us into a self-conscious state that inhibits the next step in the unfoldment of our process.

Subjective process involves experiences and not things. By comparison with physical process, it is not only intangible but it can be misleading. When, for example, there are signs of disintegration in a physical process, the onset of a pathology is usually clear and the next developments are predictable. In the case of subjective process, however, depressed and chaotic behavior may not at all be preliminary to disintegration and pathology. In certain individuals these events may be the phase of behavior that occurs as part of a creative breakthrough in the movement of sub-jective process.

Since they are intangible and can be misleading when they are considered in terms of the usual physical categories, modes of in-tellectual perception that work very well elsewhere may not be valid where subjective process is concerned. Something else is needed, and it is at this point that the non-analytical approach of the *Intensive Journal* process was brought into use. In place of the accustomed analytical, intellectual approach to knowledge in which the subject of our study becomes an object to us, the *Inten-sive Journal* approach establishes a *relationship* with the contents of our subjective experience. On a practical level this is expressed in the various forms of dialogue exercises that are used in the *Inten-sive Journal* work. When we establish a relationship with the con-tents of subjective process in our lives, we do not react to them as objects, nor is it necessary for us to analyze and diagnose them. We can respond to them as subjects, approaching them as though they are persons too. In the course of using the *Intensive Journal* method, especially in the practice of the dialogue exercises, we discover that the contents of subjective process do indeed become persons to us.

When we have become accustomed to treating the small pro-cesses within our lives (the mini-processes) not as objects but as persons with whom we can have an unfolding relationship, the inhibiting aspect of self-conscious analysis tends to drop away. Being *in relationship* with the contents of the subjective processes within ourselves has the effect of loosening the flow of the inner material available for further experience. Because of this, one ad-vantage of using the mode of *relationship* rather than of analysis when we are in the low phase of a cycle is that we are able to nurture an unpromising factor and develop it instead of focusing on its difficulties and dismissing it. It gives us a protection against making premature judgments. Rather than judge a weak element in our subjective process and possibly negate its future develop-ment, we nurture it. We treat it as a person with potentials. One result of this can be that in time an act of creativity takes place where nothing constructive was expected before.

Working with subjective process in the *mode of relationship* rather than analysis opens many possibilities, but it has different requirements than the customary categories of intellectual thought. To work with it effectively we need a special kind of instrument capable of making the subjective processes of an individual life available to us in forms that are tangible. The contents of subjective processes cannot be held in our hands nor can they be measured, for they are not definite like the objective factors in physical processes. There is, however, another way that we can identify their continuity. When we observe a series of events, a series of states or conditions, we can, by linking one event to another in sequence, mark off the continuity of the process. Without limiting its content we establish its continuity, and thus we recognize the fact that a process is taking place. The process becomes tangible to us and identifiable because of the factor of continuity that we have marked off in it connecting its parts. Paradoxically, the content of the process is expressed and carried by the changes that take place within it. But that is inherent in the nature of process, for it is the changes that demonstrate the continuity and therefore the identity of a process.

Even though the individual segments of a subjective process are intangible, the continuity that we discern in its movement indicates that a process is present beneath the surface, connecting the changes. This is the reality of each specific process. Each small process (mini-process) is a unit of existence, and its varied, changing, intangible elements are the evidence of that. A primary criterion by which we can identify a process is by the fact that it expresses its underlying unity through a sequence of changed forms. The process is the elusive principle of unity that pervades and connects the continuity. But it is definite nonetheless.

Once we have identified this connective factor in a mini-process within a life, we can relate to its continuity in much the same way that we relate to the changing life of a human person. In both, the fact of change and continuity indicates the possibility of future development. That the conditions present at any given moment are transient and are subject to change is a sign that the individual parts express a larger process. Although the parts of the process are intangible, the process itself is definite and identifiable. We can relate to its continuity, and we can nurture its potentials.

These perceptions are the starting point for the *Intensive Journal* system, the structure of its workbook and the design of its various exercises. From the observations that we have made about subjective process, we can understand the fundamental reason why analytical approaches to human experience tend to be inadequate. It is because the analytical approach that treats knowledge as an object is generally valid for physical reality but is not appropriate for dealing with subjective process. It treats the subjective events of human experience with the same methods that have been used successfully for studying the objective physical aspects of life. But what works for one is misleading for the other.

The Instrument of the Workbook

When we have discerned the limitations of the analytical approach, we are brought face to face with the problem of providing an alternative. This need led to the design of the *Intensive Journal* workbook and the format of the Journal Workshop. These two together comprise an instrument for working with the contents of the subjective processes in our lives and for carrying their movement. They are designed to meet the need for an instrument that can be used in the midst of life-activity, while changes and developments are taking place.

From a functional point of view, the main task of the *Intensive Journal* workbook is to provide an instrument for establishing relationship with the contents of our subjective processes. The first step is to make these contents tangibly available to us, and the workbook does this in a physical manner. By means of its exercises it causes us to put our subjective experiences into writing. A basic aspect of the *Intensive Journal* work is that we express in written form our thoughts and feelings and other subjective perceptions regarding the contents of our life. The act of stating our experiences in writing within designated constructs gives tangible form to what is subjective. But this is only a small step toward the larger task of working tangibly with subjective process.

With the written word as its medium, the structure of the *Intensive Journal* workbook then goes to the heart of subjective process by setting up *channels of continuity* which contain (in written form) and carry the sequence of events taking place in each of the mini-processes in a person's life. The containers of these are the Journal sections within the workbook, and the mechanism for providing their contents is the variety of Journal exercises. Together the Journal sections and their accompanying exercises provide the equivalent of the process of spontaneous creativity that occurs in those individuals whom we are accustomed to call *creative persons*. In building a cumulative creative experience in each area of process in the person's life, the Journal sections are used not as categories or classifications but as channels of continuity. This is the consequence of following the non-analytical hypothesis of *holistic* depth psychology and providing a vehicle for future creativity rather than an interpretation of past creativity. As the Journal sections are filled in by the contents and circumstances of the person's life, the entries that are evoked by the exercises (which, as they build, feed into the Journal Feedback method) enlarge the situation within the workbook (corresponding to the contents of the life of the person) and they draw together the movement of the channels (the Journal sections) in groupings that make it possible for creative events (extras, emergents) to occur. In this way we are replicating the process of spontaneous creativity and enabling it to take place in terms of the possibilities and the needs of individual life. We specifically do not stop the action of creativity in order to analyze it. Rather we maintain the activity and nurture the energy that is generated by the Journal Feedback exercises in order that they can replicate the process of creativity in the context of every-day life. *

Journal Feedback is the method for interrelating the material that arises out of the various Journal exercises. It involves the active use of the Journal sections, working with the contents of a person's life in a way that parallels the creative process. Journal Feedback is a multiple procedure in the sense that it has available to it a number of techniques that can be combined in a variety of permutations depending on the spontaneity and intensity with which a person is using the method. At various points the Journal Feedback work often has the effect of drawing together the contents of more than one small process within the person, forming new constellations of awareness. These give new integrations of insight, new ideas, new perceptions of a person's life-situation. But they are unpredictable. The Journal Feedback exercises tend to give a person an influx of additional energy. This also, like the unpredictability of the new insights it brings, expresses the fact that Journal Feedback follows the model of the creative process.

In order to bring about its creative effects, the Journal Feedback method requires a sequence of two distinct steps. First the facts of the individual life need to be collected in a format that can be fed directly into the *Intensive Journal* process. When the method is used for one's own life, this is done in the Life Context workshop. After that, with the essential life-data available to us, the active procedures of Journal Feedback can be brought into play.

In Life-Study we follow the same sequence, first gathering the data of the life and then feeding the information into the Journal Feedback exercises. The structural procedure is the same. There are, however, significant differences in the kinds of life-data that are recorded in some of the workbook sections, and also in the way that the exercises using this material are carried out. These differences largely express the fact that in Life-Study we are not

* For a further discussion of these concepts, see Ira Progoff, *The Practice of Process Meditation*, Chapters 3 and 13.

doing the Journal work on behalf of our own life but the data we use are drawn from another person's experience. As a consequence the Life-Study exercises are carried out from a different vantage point than those in the personal use of the *Intensive Journal* work. This changes certain aspects of the *Intensive Journal* procedures to the extent that it has been necessary to alter the basic exercises at several points.

Incorporating the changes in procedure that are made necessary by the differences in subject matter, we are able to use as our instrument for Life-Study the same *Intensive Journal* workbook as in the personal component of the program. It has the same structure of Journal sections. In the Life-Study version of the workbook, however, three new sections have been added in order to meet the needs of serving as a Journal Trustee for another person's life. These three sections are: the *Journal Trustee Log;* the *Life-Study Research* section; and *Meetings.* They are included in the copy of the *Intensive Journal* workbook that is in the *Appendix* of this volume. The specific instructions for using each of these sections will be given as we come to the points in our Life-Study workshop where the exercises call for us to use them. In describing all the exercises that are presented in this volume I have tried as much as possible to bear in mind that some of the persons who are here working with Life-Study are using the *Intensive Journal* process for the first time. The fact is that, in both Life-Study and the personal use of the *Intensive Journal* process, it works best when we have become familiar enough with it to be able to move freely back and forth among the Journal sections. Our experience in recent years has shown that the easiest and best way to learn the *Intensive Journal* sections and their exercises is to use them. Soon enough we find that we are comfortable in working with them, and that we no longer need to remind ourselves consciously either of their contents or of the step-by-step procedures in using them. We reach a point where we seem to know directly and intuitively what each Journal section can do, and what we need to do in order to work with it. Many of us who carry out the details of the Life-Study exercises that are described in this book will find that in the course of doing the exercises we have become familiar and increasingly comfortable not only with the techniques but also with the underlying principles.

In Life-Study, when we have decided on the person for whom we wish to be a Journal Trustee, our first step is to set up an *Intensive Journal* workbook in the name of that person. This is their Life-Study Journal. Registered and numbered Life-Study Journals are issued at all Dialogue House Life-Study workshops, but if you are doing your Life-Study directly from the descriptions in this book, you can construct a Journal for your immediate use by following the model that is given in the *Appendix*.*

The Journal Workshop

The conception of subjective process is basic in the *Intensive Journal* framework of thought, as is the holistic principle of integration and creativity. These are extensions of theory from *holistic* depth psychology that led to the underlying *Intensive Journal* methodology with its numerous applications and special methods. On the basis of these it was possible to design the *Intensive Journal* workbook with its sectional divisions and their accompanying exercises. This workbook has served as the instrument that has enabled us to take the step from theory to practice, from *holistic* depth psychology to the National *Intensive Journal* Program.

An interesting discovery was made, however, when we first undertook to use the *Intensive Journal* workbook. We discovered that it is not like any ordinary notebook in which a person can write anywhere, at any time, and under any circumstances. At least in its first usage, it seemed that the *Intensive Journal* workbook requires a special situation with a particular atmosphere. The question arose as to whether that would limit its general usefulness.

* See p. 257 ff.

Closer examination of the Journal's contents led to the realization that there is a reason for the Journal's need of a special situation. It also led to the recognition that the same conditions might not always be required.

The first factor observed concerned the quality of the contents that are placed in an *Intensive Journal* workbook. The second factor concerned the sequence of steps in the *Intensive Journal* workbook. At the beginning it is necessary to gather together a diversity of data concerning the various aspects of a person's life; and this requires a concentration of effort and attention. After that, the *Intensive Journal* work has more of a piecemeal quality. It involves a continuity of entries made from time to time, from day to week to month, depending on the individual's intensity of concern and the immediacy of the issues in the life. In some situations many Journal entries are concentrated into a short span of time; this may be followed by a time when the Journal is hardly used at all, only to be followed by a period of very active use. The characteristic is *irregular continuity* in the use of the *Intensive Journal* workbook, and this quality, which is inherent in its concept, is taken into account in the procedures for using it.

The main factors in considering how to use the *Intensive Journal* workbook are:

1. The special quality of the material that is contained, and stimulated, in the *Intensive Journal* process.

2. The importance of collecting the basic life-data at the first sessions with the *Intensive Journal* workbook.

3. The characteristic of irregular continuity in the ongoing use of the *Intensive Journal* workbook.

These considerations led to the basic concept in which a *Journal workshop*, using the *Intensive Journal* workbook, has become the essential instrument of the *Intensive Journal* process. At a later stage it developed into the particular format of an *Intensive Journal* Life-Study workshop.

The fundamental purpose of the *Intensive Journal* workbook is to contain in a tangible and usable form the elusive data of subjective process. We do this first by stating our various life-experiences—feelings, thoughts, images, memories—in written form. Although these are subjective and intangible, they become tangible and available to our consciousness when we write them. We are, after all, doing more than merely writing them. As we write our Journal entries we are placing them as descriptions of the contents of our lives in the sections and sub-sections of our *Intensive Journal* workbooks. We are feeding them into the structure of the workbook whose Journal Feedback principles collect them in *clusters* that show us the movements taking place beneath the surface of our lives. As this aspect of our Journal work proceeds, it enables us to identify the several *mini-processes* that move within us at non-conscious levels. Further, as our Journal Feedback work expands, we establish a *relationship* with these mini-processes in which they show us the goals and direction of their development. This comes to expression when we are in a position to carry out the exercises of Journal Dialogue.

One main purpose of the *Intensive Journal* workbook is to give us a place—and, with the several Journal sections, places—in which we can record, make tangible and describe in definite terms the events and experiences of our individual lives. But, since they are subjective and by their nature intangible, the material that we need to record in our Journals is often difficult to identify. It is elusive to us, and it often gives us considerable trouble when we seek to pin it down and state specifically what it involves. It often eludes our memory just at the time when we feel that we are ready to describe it. We find that we cannot recall the details of events that we were certain we remembered.

Because of these aspects of subjective process, and especially the intangible, elusive quality of the life-data that are the primary content of the *Intensive Journal* process, it was concluded that a special situation is needed for using the *Intensive Journal* workbook. We require a place of quietness where a person can settle in concentration and feel comfortable in letting deep feelings be articulated amidst the protections of privacy. But these qualities involve more than a physical place; they constitute an atmosphere. The necessary condition for *Intensive Journal* work is an atmosphere of quiet that is conducive to depth and privacy in a person's experience. The quality of depth is necessary because of the fact that, when we seek to record subjective experiences, our memories and descriptive capacities often fail us. We therefore need a means of evoking our perceptions at subliminal, non-conscious levels; and further, we need to do this in an atmosphere that will support us in recording our inner experiences in full written form with no pressures of embarrassment or guilt to inhibit and censor what we write.

To meet these needs we undertake to have a situation of quietness wherever *Intensive Journal* work is being carried out. The means we use for meeting the requirement of a depth atmosphere is to begin each Journal workshop experience with an Entrance Meditation, using our readings as an inner doorway by which we can enter the twilight range of experience.* We have found that there is a particular benefit in using meditative procedures that have a neutral (i.e., non-doctrinal) symbolism in order to draw our consciousness into the twilight range. They have the effect of establishing a deep atmosphere with a universal quality that is conducive to our work in the *Intensive Journal* process.

In using the workbook there is an additional requirement that a sufficient amount of life-data be gathered at the beginning of the work in order to set the Journal process into motion. Our *Intensive Journal* work therefore needs more than quietness and a depth of atmosphere. It also requires a focused agenda by which we can carry out the exercises that will evoke experiences and information from the depth of us for use in our *Intensive Journal* workbooks.

Out of the composite of these requirements for the effective use of the *Intensive Journal* workbook there came the format of a *Journal Workshop*. As it has been developed over the years and been refined to serve specific purposes, a *Journal Workshop* is identified as a situation in which we have a definite time for directing our

---

* For readings of Entrance Meditations and references, see *Appendix* B, p. 288 ff., and also Chapter 4, *The Twilight Atmosphere of a Workshop*, p. 65 ff. See also *The Practice of Process Meditation*, Chapter 6; and Ira Progoff, *The Symbolic and the Real*, McGraw-Hill, New York, 1963.

attention to a *Journal Agenda* that calls for us to use the sections and exercises of the workbook in a disciplined way, in an atmosphere of depth with consideration for the privacy of our individual process.

Here we see the three main qualities of a Journal Workshop: an *atmosphere* of stillness and depth to support our interior work; a *Journal Agenda* that directs our attention to the inner process of our life by means of the sections in our workbook; and the *active privacy* that respects the rhythms and integrity of the individual life while providing the space in which each can establish its own tempo.

It must be observed that among the three essential characteristics of a Journal Workshop we have made no mention of a group of persons participating in the workshop. The reason is that a Journal Workshop does not depend on the number of persons who are taking part in it. It can be a Journal Workshop with hundreds of persons participating, *provided that* the active privacy of each individual is maintained in an atmosphere of depth while the Journal Agenda of exercises is followed with respect to the individual life. It can also be a Journal Workshop if no one else is present but yourself *provided also* that you maintain the three essential qualities of a Journal Workshop as you give yourself the focused experience.

There are several advantages in having the Journal Workshop experience alone, particularly at advanced levels of *Intensive Journal* work. The factor of privacy would seem to be obvious, but it does not in fact distinguish this from other *Intensive Journal* workshops. The principles of the *Intensive Journal* method make it possible to maintain privacy at a Journal Workshop no matter how large a number of persons are participating. From the point of view of privacy, therefore, it is not necessarily helpful to have your workshop experience by yourself. There is, however, a definite advantage with respect to the open-endedness of time and the greater possibility of spontaneous, unexpected experiences in the Journal Workshop that you give yourself. It is inherent in the logistics of life that any Journal Workshop in which many persons are participating must have a definite pre-set date and time stating when it begins and ends. In other words, it must be scheduled in advance in order that busy modern persons can fit it into their appointment books. But the inner process of human life does not necessarily accord with the scheduling on a calendar. If you have learned the techniques well enough to give yourself a Journal Workshop all alone, there is the substantial advantage that you will be free to use the *Intensive Journal* process at any time that the need arises in life with no need for prior scheduling. When you give yourself a Journal Workshop, however, it will be essential that you take the time to establish a depth of atmosphere before proceeding with the Journal exercises, and that you take the pains to maintain the discipline of working with the focused agenda and the appropriate Journal exercises.

Conducting a Journal Workshop for ourselves has its main advantages at the advanced levels of *Intensive Journal* work. At that point, when we are able to combine the techniques of Journal Feedback, it is good to be free to respond flexibly to the needs of our inner process with no limitation on the time that is available to us for extended experiences. Side by side with this, there are substantial advantages in having a Journal Workshop experience with a number of persons also participating. It often happens that the presence of many persons, each individually working in his or her own life, deepens the atmosphere in which all are working. This has frequently been experienced at Journal Workshops. Quite often, also, the participation of other persons adds a support that sustains us as we are working in our individual Journal Agenda, especially when we come to a knotty personal issue that we would rather avoid.

The overarching advantage, however, of being together with others when using the Journal Workshop format occurs when we are working at the basic level in each of the areas of the *Intensive Journal* program. We have seen this demonstrated time and again in the introductory workshops for each phase of the *Intensive Journal* program. In addition to the core of instructional material that has to be taught for the use of the method, when people are beginning to work with it, there is an area of subjective experience that must be evoked, often reawakened and described in the appropriate Journal sections. The essential raw material of the *Intensive Journal* process is the data of our inner experiences, and this requires a period of disciplined work that follows a definite Journal Agenda. There must be opportunity to gain an understanding of the Journal Process in action.

At the fundamental level the basic Journal Workshops provide a means of learning the *Intensive Journal* principles and techniques while building a foundation of life-data to which additions can be made in future Journal work. This is the material that we will progessively feed into the Journal Feedback process as our Journal experience continues. While the specific contents of the work are unique for each individual, the range of subject matter is the same for all within the *Intensive Journal* framework. At the basic Journal Workshops, whether they provide a basic experience of Life Context or the deepening of Process Meditation or the integrative effect of Journal Feedback, the core exercises are carried through in a way that makes it possible for the fundamental entries to be made.

The same principles that apply to the Journal Workshop format at the basic levels of *Intensive Journal* work hold true for Life-Study. In fact, it is even more important in Life-Study to follow the basic Journal Agenda since the first task of a Journal Trustee is to reconstruct the life in its main outlines, setting in perspective the key events and processes in the person's experience. The basic Life-Study workshop is the place where this is done. The sequence of exercises covers the essential Journal Agenda of Life-Study. The periods in the life, the Journal sections that carry the movement of the main mini-processes within the life, are each given focused attention in their turn in order to supply the Journal with its necessary information. Entry by entry the life-data is provided for its appropriate Journal sections, and suddenly we realize that our person's life has somehow been reconstructed. This is the function of the sequence of exercises that comprises the Journal Agenda of a basic Life-Study workshop. We carry out the exercises a step at a time until at some unexpected point it dawns on us that our person's life has been reconstructing itself under our hand and that now we are experiencing it from the inside. That is the point at which we can begin to use the Journal Feedback procedures in expanding our work as a Journal Trustee.

By carrying out the Journal exercises of a basic Life-Study workshop we bring about two conditions that are essential for our future work as a Journal Trustee. By making the entries that open a Journal section in each of the areas of the life to which the exercises lead us, we gradually establish a foundation for reconstructing the life of the person. As our Life-Study proceeds, the entries we have made in each section will serve as the foundation upon which we can build and to which we will add our next increments of information. In addition, while we are carrying out the exercises we find that the Journal acquires the qualities of the person whose life it contains. The entries seem to fit together in particular sections. They seem to know where to go, and in this way the exercises lead one to the other. Just as our basic Life-Study work has established a *foundation* on which we can build, it has also established a *framework* by which we can add to our experience of the life, especially when we are able to use the Journal Feedback procedures. In this sense, the basic Life-Study workshop may also be called a *Foundation and Framework* workshop. It provides the fundamentals of data and the organization of the individual Journal that make it possible for Life-Study to continue and to expand once this basic work has been done.

That a basic Life-Study workshop provides a foundation and framework with which a Journal Trustee can proceed indicates its function in the larger scheme of Life-Study. It provides the range of life-information that establishes the Journal as the embodiment of the person's life. Section by section, the Journal process has been set into motion. If further experiences are to be added, the foundation has been laid and the framework has been established with which to receive this new material and incorporate it into the Journal's process.

After a basic workshop there will be times when, as a Journal Trustee, we may wish to work deeply again in the life of our person. We will not need to follow the full sequence of exercises for reconstructing the life, since that has already been done. The foundation will already exist, and we will now need merely to fit our new material into the framework that we have established by our work in the Journal sections. For this purpose a Journal Workshop is the best format to follow. Seeking to deepen our experience of our person's life, we can carry out additional exercises at a workshop in which others are participating. Or, at a later stage in our Life-Study, when we are sufficiently familiar with Journal Feedback procedures, we can conduct the Journal Workshop for ourselves by ourselves, directing it to the exercises that we now find to be important in our person's life. We can extend our experience as a Journal Trustee by carrying out in our privacy a Journal workshop with a special focus. We must however remember to provide the three essentials of a Journal Workshop:

1. The *depth of atmosphere* that can be achieved by a time of quieting with the aid of an experience of Entrance Meditation.

2. The establishment of a specific *Journal Agenda,* a sequence of exercises that will enable us to work more deeply in the particular area of the life that is drawing our attention.

3. The experience of *active privacy* that recognizes the integrity of our own inner process and individual identity while honoring the equivalent identity in the person for whom we are Journal Trustee.

In the larger context, the two essentials for the practice of the *Intensive Journal* method are:

1. The workbook containing the *Intensive Journal* sections which enable it to serve as the instrument for a process that adjusts itself to each individual life.

2. The Journal Workshop that provides the situation for carrying out the Journal exercises in an atmosphere of depth and privacy.

Both the workbook and the workshop have been developed for use in the Personal Component of *Intensive Journal* work and they are here extended for use in the Life-Study Component. For the purposes of Life-Study, the Workbook has had three new sections added to it, and several of its existing sections are used with procedures that reflect the special nature of the Life-Study subject matter. In this version it is the Life-Study Journal. Correspondingly, while the Journal Workshop maintains its essential format, its agenda is changed to meet the needs of Life-Study. The basic Life-Study workshop is designed to establish a foundation and framework with which the work of a Journal Trustee can be continued, moving from the groundwork of reconstructing and re-experiencing a life—which is the main purpose of the exercises described in this volume—to the Journal Feedback procedures that extend the basic life-data in open-ended ways. We have a few more of the special aspects of Life-Study still to discuss, and then we will be ready to proceed into the basic Life-Study experience.

Chapter 3

Being a
Journal Trustee

The Persons We Choose

The backgrounds of the persons who may be appropriate subjects for our Life-Study are exceedingly varied. We may choose individuals from any period of history. They may have lived in recent times or many centuries ago in a culture that was distant from our own. They may be persons of a different sex than ours and of a different racial strain. They may have lived in an earlier era in a civilization that caused them to be guided by altogether different patterns of behavior. Regardless of the time and place of their existence and their special qualities as individuals, they are all distinguished by the fact that each is a person whose life we feel to be meaningful to our own. In addition, each is a person whose life has already been physically completed. Some are persons who have left behind the products of their creativity in the form of works that are of noted value. But all have left behind the events and experiences through which they lived, and these are the important content of our Life-Study.

One criterion that is essential for us to observe in choosing an individual who is to be a subject for our Life-Study is that it be a person whose life has already been physically completed. When a person has died, their full life span is placed before us. As an outsider to the life, we are then situated at a vantage point from which we can see the life as a whole with a view of all its cycles and all the variations through which it has passed . The full life context then gives us a perspective in which we can consider—and, for Life-Study purposes, re-experience—each of the individual events.

In a little while, after we have chosen our person and are ready to begin our Journal Workshop, we shall establish a point in time that will serve as our base-point in carrying out the exercises of Life-Study. That will be the point of reference from which we shall work, and we shall mark it off when we begin our actual workshop experience. For each of us that starting place will be a different date in chronological time, varying with the period of history from which we have chosen our person. In principle, however, it will be the same for all of us. It will be a point in time early in the period that follows the person's death. We will thus be able to include all the events of the life, not omitting the event and circumstances of the death, in our Life-Study of the person. Having established an operating base for our Life-Study during the period shortly after the death, we give ourselves an overview of the whole life history. We place ourselves in a position to see the life as a unit; and we are also positioned close enough to the actuality of events to distinguish the specific contents of the life, to describe the facts and incorporate them in the movement of the *Intensive Journal* process.

One result of our setting a point in time that shortly follows the death of the person is that it gives our reconstruction of the life an additional degree of objectivity. Working from a post-death position tends to have a quieting effect. It neutralizes any over-exuberant judgments that we might express about the person. Extending the range of time, it gives us room for an objective perspective in which we can set events in balance.

If, for example, the person for whom we are Journal Trustee was especially noted for having achieved a massive material success, or if the life was lived in the shadow of financial failure, the framework of time given by a whole life that includes the death makes it possible to set the extremes of a life in relation to each other. When all the facts are assembled and are placed in perspective, no single event need be over-emphasized. In the long-range view provided by the life as a whole, we can give consideration to all the factors. We can give equal weight to the times of dramatic excitement and to the periods of empty nothingness.

We give a moderated and factual attention to the events of the death itself. This is in keeping with the basic Life-Study approach of giving equal attention to each fact in a human existence. We include the death in the life, and we view all the experiences of the person in the context of the whole life span. Proceeding in this way tends to strengthen our awareness that time is ongoing and that it moves beyond individuals. It is a perspective in which it becomes self-evident that death is a marker, a kind of punctuation point, that separates the phases of human existence and indicates the transitions as individual lives merge into the units of a larger whole.

Considering that the more life-data we can feed into our Journal process the more our Life-Study can feed back to us in restructured forms, it is good if at least one of the persons whom we represent as Journal Trustee in the course of our Life-Study work has lived a long life. Persons who have lived at least the traditional "threescore years and ten" can spread out before us an ample history of life experiences with its cycles and changes. From their life-data we can form a perspective of the movement and variations of circumstances that can occur when the events of a life extend over many decades. We know that the events of our own life will not be the same as theirs, but the length of time they lived can enlarge our life-perspective. Together with other aspects of Life-Study, it can contribute an additional element to our wisdom of life.

While older people are a good source of Life-Study, we recognize also that the events of significance in a human life are not quantitative but qualitative. Short lives fully lived may contain more that is meaningful than the lengthy existence of persons who have lived many years but with little involvement. Persons like Wolfgang Mozart and John Keats, or Sylvia Plath and Franz Kafka, died at relatively young ages, but the intensity of their experience condensed a great deal into their lives. We should not overlook the fact that, while lives like theirs are of relatively short duration, they include much that may be of value to the Journal Trustees who are re-experiencing the events of those lives. We study the longer lives when we can, and we are glad also to study the shorter, more intense lives. The two together demonstrate to us the variety of forms in which human beings may experience their individual destinies.

Shorter lives and longer lives each mark off their own self-contained unity. Here we see one of the special values in our using the *Intensive Journal* process as our instrument for reconstructing an individual's existence. It enables us to perceive each life as a unit within its own terms. As the qualitative contents of each life are embodied in its own workbook, the life expresses its distinctive integrity.

The process aspect of *Intensive Journal* work is especially important in this regard. It reflects the movement within each life as the life follows its implicit sensing of wholeness as a possibility and seeks to establish its worthiness within its own framework of beliefs. One task that we have as Journal Trustee is to place ourselves deeply enough within the person's life to be able to feel the movement toward integrity that is trying to take place there. Sometimes, in the course of our Life-Study, we realize that the difficulties that were encountered at the time and the intensity of the depressed emotions that accumulated caused our persons to lose contact with the underlying movement toward integrity that had begun in them. But we should not lose contact with it as a Journal Trustee engaged in reconstructing the life by the light of its goals and its meaning. Neither should we overlook the fact that the loss of contact did take place. That would be to ignore an actuality of experience; to do that would be untrue to our work as a Journal Trustee. From our position as outsiders to the life who are nonetheless participating from the inside in the re-experiencing of it, we are able to see all the contradictories of the life. If we censor out any of them, we may falsify the process that was taking place.

Sometimes, because of the attitudes that we find to be arising within ourselves, it may be necessary for us deliberately to restrain our habits of thought. We do not wish to intervene in our person's life by becoming judgmental of what they did, nor by making analytical interpretations of why they did it. We may have a need to argue with what they believed during some particular phase or cycle of their life, but we must remember at those times that it is their life and not ours that is being reconstructed. Our responsibility is to give the life our *studied attention* with a total receptivity to the point of view from which it was lived. That is a necessity in Life-Study, for it is only when we come without prior judgments to the process that was working in our person's life that we are able to understand the life from the inside and learn the messages that it may have for us. Afterwards, when we have done the essential work of reconstructing the life and are ready for *Meetings* with our person, we shall have ample opportunity to state our opinions in relation to theirs. At that point, however, the ground rules of *Meetings* will be clear, and the interchange will clarify our Life-Study, not becloud it.

Since we set the base for our Life-Study in the period that follows the death of the person, we can experience each life for which we are Journal Trustee as a unit within its own terms. Shorter or longer, each is a statement of a human existence, and the quantitative number of the years is not the essence of the matter. We approach each life qualitatively in terms of its wholeness as we prepare to carry out the Life-Study exercises by which the life can express itself as a unity, as a work of art in its own terms. We find that we can serve equally well as Journal Trustee for a person who had a long life and for one whose life was cut short. Either one, and both, can be valid and valuable for us as a subject of Life-Study. But each is distinct.

In addition to the basic criteria that have been discussed, there are special factors to be considered when we choose the persons for whom we shall be Journal Trustee. In whatever form, there should be some printed information available to us regarding the person. A biography, an autobiography, any data that are more definite than what would be called "hearsay evidence," meet this requirement. The person we choose should have some type of objective material available regarding his or her life. This gives us a factual protection against the large element of subjectivity that is inherent in Life-Study. It gives us a balance, but this balancing material need be objective only in the external physical sense of being definite and tangible printed material. We make no judgment about its interior content, leaving that to be cited and explored in the course of the Life-Study exercises. We are merely using the printed material as a reference and as a base for considering the factuality of our data.

We should note that this requirement that some form of printed material be available is the only aspect of Life-Study in which the persons for whom we are Journal Trustee need have any degree of fame. They need be only notable enough to have left behind them some tangible information that can be drawn upon for the purpose of reconstructing their life.

The persons whom we choose as subjects for Life-Study are individuals to whom we feel drawn in a special way. They are not necessarily persons whom we take as models for our life, but they are attractive to us as individuals, and that is one reason why we wish to be Journal Trustees for them. We choose them because we sense the possibility that something in the content of their lives has a message that will contribute to the consciousness with which we can conduct our own life. While these individuals are attractive to us, the fact is that as persons they are usually not beautiful and not without flaws, as they might be expected to be if their lives were great works of art. On the contrary, we find that the lives that have the greatest power to evoke our emotions and to stimulate our deeper understanding have been lived in the midst of many pressures and difficulties. Rather than be perfect works of art, these persons seem to have many imperfections, especially at the points where the troubles of their lives left indelible marks. But it is just these imperfections, which are the residues of their difficulties, that speak to us. We may see them at first only as accidental breaks in the harmonious surface of the person's life, but soon we realize that these are openings that enable us to see what is taking place within. By means of these imperfections we build an under standing of our person's life, not intellectually but with empathy.

These flaws can be our best teachers, as the problems of their lives enlarge our perspective of human experience and our perceptions within it.

When we are considering the persons for whom we shall be Journal Trustee, it is important that we choose individuals whose weaknesses are accessible to us. If we idolize them with absolute devotion, that will not do. We will then not be free to see the flaws in their nature. When we serve as Journal Trustee we must be able to look with objectivity at the limitations and the problems of the life. It is important that we be able to describe failings without making personal judgments of them, and also without having emotional reactions to them.

This is a main reason for the rule in Life-Study that we not be Journal Trustee for an individual with whom we have been directly involved in any personal aspect of our life. If we have had a close personal relationship with them in any specific context—as their child, or as their lover, or as a close friend—there is bound to be a residue of emotion that will carry over. We need protection against this. In a sense we need the neutralizing effect of an emotional buffer zone. Our work in Life-Study requires a distance between ourselves and the person to whom we are giving our *studied attention*. There needs to be an area of separation large enough to assure the fact that our personal emotions will not intrude into our Life-Study. Then we can experience the broadening of consciousness that comes from emotions and awarenesses that are stimulated at a deeper-than-personal level.

This rule of distance applies even if we feel that the life-content of an individual with whom we have been personally involved is objectively important to us and is essential to our Journal work. There are other means within the *Intensive Journal* process by which we can explore the various factors that link that life with ours. We can do it better in the personal component of *Intensive Journal* work than in the Life-Study component. For example, to speak of publicly known persons, there are many who might appropriately choose to be Journal Trustee for Henry Fonda. It would not, however, be appropriate for his daughter, Jane Fonda, to choose her father as a subject for Life-Study even though, as an actress, she might have non-personal reasons for wanting to explore her relation to her father's approach to the theatre. His conception of acting as an artform would involve an objective content of Henry Fonda's life, and this would be distinct from their personal relationship. If she would care to do so, the relevant place for his daughter to work with this material would be in her own *Intensive Journal* workbook in the section for *Dialogue with Works*.

Equally, to cite an example drawn from the illustrative material used elsewhere in this volume, it would not be appropriate for Martita Casals, the widow of Pablo, to be a Journal Trustee for Casals himself. On the other hand, it might be very important for her to work in an objective context with Casals' approach to music, his social philosophy, or perhaps his response to the musical work that she has done since his death. These Journal experiences, however, would be carried out not in a Life-Study Journal for Pablo Casals but in her own *Intensive Journal* workbook, using such sections as *Dialogue with Works, Dialogue with Society, Inner Wisdom Dialogue,* and *Peaks, Depths and Explorations,* among others. At that point the exercises will have moved actively into the Journal Feedback phase of *Intensive Journal* work.

This requirement of separateness in the choice of persons for whom we can be a Journal Trustee leads to an interesting question. On the one hand the reason for making this qualification is obvious: we want to avoid the intrusion of purely personal emotions into our Life-Study. Nonetheless, persons who have used the Life-Study methods have found that it gives them a deep and empathic understanding of a person. Why then, they ask, can they not use the Life-Study procedures—working as a Journal Trustee, setting up a Life-Study Journal, and following the Life-Study agenda of exercises in reconstructing a life—for a person who has an inner importance of major proportions to them, for example, a father or a mother who has died and with whom they are now seeking to establish a deeper relationship by means of the *Intensive Journal* process?

In considering this question, it seems to me that we should be able to take advantage of the benefits of our Life-Study method while avoiding the pitfalls that can be part of its use in personal

Journal work. The first step for us to take remains the basic one of serving as Journal Trustee for a person in whose life we have never been personally involved. In doing that we have a learning experience for ourselves that is essential before we can proceed to use the Life-Study method in reconstructing the life of an individual who belongs to our own personal life. Without the practice of that work as a Journal Trustee, and without the balance of having worked with a subject matter that is (at least in some sense) neutral to us, we would be vulnerable to making errors in our Journal work that would have a personal emotional root. These could be substantial, and could have confusing consequences in other aspects of our Journal work. With the prior practice, however, of having served as a Journal Trustee for a person with whom we have had no direct relationship, it is altogether possible that the Life-Study procedures can provide a valuable aid in the Journal work that we do with regard to those persons who have played a significant role in our lives. For those who have acquired the necessary experience, an additional registered Life-Study Journal can be available from Dialogue House for this purpose.

A Human Resource

As we approach the experience of a Life-Study workshop we may be asking ourselves: Who is the person for whom I can most fruitfully serve as a Journal Trustee? It is not necessary, however, for us to pose that question in strict and absolute terms. We cannot truly know in advance which person will eventually prove to be the *most* fruitful for us in Life-Study. It is best, in fact, for us to be open to some surprises. Since we cannot know in advance who will prove to be the most fruitful, it is sufficient for us to choose a person whose life we feel, intuitively and emotionally, is relevant to our own concerns. Especially if this is the first person for whom we will serve as a Journal Trustee, we can be flexible in making our choice.

As we now choose a person for whom we shall be a Journal

Trustee, we should bear in mind that the choice we make does not eliminate anyone from future consideration. We are not making a permanent or exclusive choice that will prevent us from becoming a Journal Trustee for someone else at a later time. When we make the decision to become a Journal Trustee for a particular individual, we are not giving that person an exclusive claim upon our attention. Correspondingly, the person whom we choose does not become exclusively ours to study. Each of the individuals for whom we are Journal Trustee may also have several other persons who are Journal Trustees for them. There is no conflict in either direction since a principle of Life-Study is that, while we choose one at a time the individuals for whom we shall be a Journal Trustee, we are committed to work actively in the life only for as long or as short a time as feels personally valid and meaningful to us. We can change or add new persons at any time—but with one important condition. When we choose to be a Journal Trustee for a person we are committing ourselves to do two things on that person's behalf, and these we are obliged to carry out. We are committing ourselves to set up a Life-Study Journal in their name; and we are committing ourselves to make the entries in that person's Journal that will serve to reconstruct that person's life from birth to death. The first part of our commitment is superficially fulfilled in a moment as we establish a Life-Study Journal in their name; but it is not truly fulfilled until we have made the entries that express the content and movement in the person's life.

In order to carry out the second part of our commitment, we take the further step of carrying out the sequence of exercises of a basic Life-Study workshop. As these exercises lead from one to the other, the Journal entries they evoke provide the essential data for reconstructing the life. Now we have a foundation, a base of information, to which we can add whatever further experiences come to us from time to time with respect to this person's life. We can build upon this foundation. More than that, the composite of exercises in the basic Life-Study workshop establishes a framework within the Journal sections that reflects the specific circumstances and contents of the person's life. Since the framework is already established, when we come at a later time to move further and deeper into the person's life, the way is prepared for us. This is particularly valuable when we have let the person's Journal lie fallow for a period of time and are spontaneously moved to take a further step in Life-Study. Having the Journal available with its foundation and framework of material facilitates the work that we can do. Without difficulty we can pick up where we left off, moving further and deeper than would be possible if we had not carried through the exercises of a basic Life-Study workshop.

Once we have fulfilled our commitment and have carried out the foundation and framework exercises in the person's Life-Study Journal, we are free to make whatever further choices we wish as a Journal Trustee. We may find that ideas and feelings stirring within us impel us to pursue the life-questions that were called to our attention when we were engaged in our basic Life-Study work as that person's Journal Trustee. In that case we continue with the Feedback Leads that emerged in our experience of the basic exercises and we extend our Journal Feedback work, following where it leads us. But if, at any point, the intensity of interest in this aspect of our Life-Study slackens, we can let go of it and the work we have done will remain intact. We can let it rest and it will be there when we come back to it at a later time, whenever the interest stirs in us again. Since we now have the Journal with its basic Life-Study material assembled within it—containing the foundation of essential data and the framework for extending the exercises—we can be assured that even a long pause in the work will not disrupt the process. The Journal containing the material of the life will be there to continue the Life-Study process when we feel drawn to return to it. Whenever, to whatever degree and in whatever aspect, we are stimulated at a later time to become involved again in that person's life, the data will be ready at hand and the framework for extending our work will be available for us to use. As long as we preserve their Life-Study Journal we remain a Journal Trustee for that person. Even though dust may accumulate on the workbook as it rests on a shelf for a long period of time, we can always return to it. And if we work in it for a while, leave it, and return to it again and again, the nature of Life-Study can absorb that and sustain the value of the work that we do. The fact is that if we work in a person's life, leave it, and then return to it again and again, we are actually building a special kind of Journal Relationship between ourselves and that person. It can build in significance for us and eventually become a valuable point of contact for our inner life.

There are several forms in which a Journal Relationship can develop between ourselves and the person for whom we are a Journal Trustee. Whatever the form, it will have our personal stamp showing on it since each Journal Relationship, like an intimate friendship, increases in specialness, even in uniqueness, as it grows. In the context of *Intensive Journal* work the deepening of a Journal Relationship is bound to involve the extension of Journal Feedback exercises as we pursue further leads into the depth and range of our person's experiences. Following progressive leads in our Journal Feedback work, the exercises will gradually extend through all the sections of the Journal as they come to questions of meaning and goals in the activities of the life. As the work proceeds it will tend to move increasingly toward the Process Meditation area of the Journal as the ultimate concerns of the life come to the fore. The personal and transpersonal issues that open here may take us into unsuspected areas in the life of our person, as well as in our own life.

Here we should take note of a distinction that is not significant at an early point in Life-Study but can eventually have very large consequences for some of us. It is worth bearing in mind at the outset, especially because of its eventual use in the larger development of the *Intensive Journal* program. It is the distinction between Journal Feedback and Journal Interplay.

At numerous points in the discussions of the Life-Study exercises we find ourselves referring to Journal Feedback both for its underlying principles and its specific techniques. This is because, within the *Intensive Journal* process, Journal Feedback is the main active method of working with life-material. It is often capable of activating in a person's life factors that have long been dormant or have been inaccessible for further development. A particular value of Journal Feedback is that it seems to generate new energies where none had been visible before. It is, in fact, not creating new energies but is awakening and bringing back to life factors in the depth of a person that had been in a state of heavy slumber. Once these are awakened, their energies are added to the life-experience where they are strengthened as they are fed into the context and movement of the life as a whole.

This capacity to generate energies is especially apparent when Journal Feedback is used in the Personal Component of *Intensive Journal* work. But it can have this effect in the Life-Study Component as well, although in special ways. Indirectly it can have the effect of generating new energies in the person who is serving as Journal Trustee. It does this by Journal Interplay.

A primary means by which Journal Feedback reaches and awakens the dormant factors in a person's life is by its procedures for following the Journal Feedback Leads as they take us from section to section within the *Intensive Journal* structure. Corresponding to this, they are moving from area to area within the person's life. As the Journal Feedback Leads move from section to section within the Journal, they have a parallel effect on the outer level. They expand the range of experience in the life.

With this, a further possibility opens for us by means of Life-Study. As the principles and techniques of Journal feedback operate within the *Intensive Journal* process of each individual life, we see the effects most visibly in personal Journal experience. But where a Journal Trustee is working in his or her own *Intensive Journal* workbook and is also maintaining a Life-Study Journal for another person, the contents and issues of *two lives* are involved. One may have something significant to say to the other, and the means of this active relationship will be a movement from Journal to Journal back and forth. When we find in the Life-Study Journal of the person for whom we are a Journal Trustee an event or a belief that speaks to our own concerns and that stimulates us to consider it further in the context of our own life, we go from Journal to Journal, from theirs to ours. Working in our own Journal in the appropriate sections we can draw upon our several Journal techniques to explore the subject until the experiences that have taken place in another person's life yield fruit for our own life in the form of new understandings and new ideas for our life activities.

Whereas one life is involved in Journal Feedback, the lives of two persons are involved in Journal Interplay. It opens a number of possibilities for expanding our contact with sources of wisdom in our life. By means of Journal Interplay we can draw on the experiences of human beings who have lived before us, to learn from their errors and also from their insights. We use Journal Feedback as the means of finding and developing the leads within a life, our own life and the life of the person for whom we are Journal Trustee; and we use Journal Interplay as the means of moving from the Journal of the person whose life we are studying into our own Journal, and back again.

Journal Interplay opens a great resource to us. The experiences of human beings who lived in history can become teachers to us, can give us perspective and perhaps even an element of wisdom for the conduct of our lives .But there are two prerequisites: that we work personally in our own *Intensive Journal* process; and that we be a Journal Trustee for a person with whom we will eventually share in an Interplay of lives and of Journals. If we are a Journal Trustee for one person, we can eventually meet in an Interplay of Journals with that one individual. But if we are Journal Trustee for three or four or more persons, we have the possibility of Journal Interplay with each of them. Then indeed we have personally available to us a significant human resource: the lives and experiences of several significant human beings. By means of Life-Study using the *Intensive Journal* process we can each build a personal human resource that gives us contact with several lives of the past as we make our decisions for the future.

Collecting Information: Life-Study Research

Since Life-Study deals with lives other than our own, some factual research is necessary to give us a base of detailed information about the person. Many of us will already have at the beginning of Life-Study a general knowledge, if not more, of the experiences of the individual for whom we choose to be a Journal

Trustee. This knowledge was very likely one of the factors in our choice in the first place. Sometimes the person we choose for Life-Study is one with whose life we are already familiar and about whose experiences we know many details. At other times our knowledge of the person we choose is minimal, only enough to indicate to us that there is reason for us to have a deeper interest in that person. In those circumstances our factual knowledge may be just sufficient to set our intuitions into motion. When we are engaged in Life-Study we should bear in mind that, while it is essential for us to be familiar with the data that comprise the external facts of our person's life, it is our re-experiencing of the life from the inside that has the greatest importance in the Life-Study process. The factual information that we gather about the person's life provides us with raw material and gives us a point of departure.

We often find that the knowledge we have about a person, the first information that originally stimulated us to inquire further into their life, was gained inadvertently. It may have come about while we were engaged in some other area of work or study. Perhaps it was a chance event that resonated in the depth of us and started a sequence of thoughts which we now have an opportunity to explore further as a Journal Trustee. We begin our Life-Study with some knowledge, but not with a great deal. Just a little is sufficient, *provided that* we add to it a *recent* reading of a biographical or an autobiographical book in order to refresh our memory and to help place us in the atmosphere of the life. We may bring a biography or other reference aid to the workshop, mainly because having it present as a support may give us more self-confidence in what we are doing. The chances are, however, that we will hardly use our reference aid at the workshop. At the workshop itself— that is to say, at the time when we are actively engaged in making the entries in our person's Journal—our most valuable material will be the notes that we ourselves have made, the data that we have described and collected as part of our preparation for being a Journal Trustee. For many of us an important aspect of this will be the notes that we have made in the course of our various readings and other researches, copying for our personal use the information that we feel to be relevant, inserting our comments, observations and individual responses in our notes as we proceed.

For the purposes of Life-Study a section has been added to the *Intensive Journal* workbook specifically to contain our personal record of the varied aspects of research that accompany our work as a Journal Trustee. This is the *Life-Study Research* section. It is one of the Journal sections in which the entries are not made on behalf of the person we are studying but are made in our own name. In the Life-Study Journal it is the place where we record all our efforts at gathering information regarding our person's life. Here we keep a record of all the research and investigations of every kind in which we may become engaged. We build our bibliography here, listing the books that we have read and those that we intend to read some day. We collect our notes here on our reading, and on more than our readings. We may have attended a play or a film or seen a television broadcast in which our person was represented. We may have followed a piece of gossip regarding someone who knew our person, or who knew someone who knew someone who knew someone, and so on. Whatever we do, whatever we discover or fail to discover, we record here in the Journal section for Life-Study Research.

We may have found ourselves in the midst of a stream of thoughts, or of dreams, that we feel may be telling us something about our person's life. We consider all the possibilities and record them. Here in the Life-Study Research section we make note of whatever thoughts or observations or considerations of any kind come into our minds or into our emotions. We record whatever presents itself to us, whether it be an intellectual insight or a perception that can only be called a "hunch." We draw together all the forms of information that may come to us about the person: newspaper reports, magazine articles, discussions that were ancillary to other subjects but relevant to this person's life, sections of books in which aspects of the life were dealt with as part of a larger subject matter, and entire books devoted to the single subject of that life. We use the section for Life-Study Research at the start of our Life-Study, and we use it as a working section that supplies us with data as we continue our Life-Study work. We gather our material here as we do additional readings, and as we conduct our investiagations in quest of further information. The Life-Study Research section serves as the repository in which we accumulate a resource of life-data regarding all of our person's background and experiences. We draw upon conscious and unconscious sources, collecting all the information that comes to us regardless of its type or validity. As we gather our data we make no judgments but we make voluminous notes as we record our comments here where we can refer to them as we proceed in our work as a Journal Trustee.

It is important for us to bear in mind as we work with the Life-Study Research section that it serves a neutral role. It is not a place for interpretation, nor for selecting one line of data in preference to another. It is simply a source of supply for our Journal work to be maintained and enlarged as we continue. The Life-Study Research section is a place for information collecting. Some of it comes in the form of external data; and some of it comes in the form of intuitive perceptions. We record it all, considering the possibility that something may unexpectedly turn out to be of help. In any case, we know that as we follow the *Intensive Journal* methodology any erroneous data that do not apply will simply drop away as being irrelevant. On the other hand, the data that accord with the context of the life as a whole will become established as part of the larger framework of experience.

Primarily the Life-Study Research section is a place for fact-collecting, but sometimes it may also become a place for opinion-collecting. When that happens it is inadvertent, for we gather data of all kinds in it. We record data in the Life-Study Research section whether they are verified or not. Sometimes, because of its personal nature, the material that we collect in this Journal section is inherently non-verifiable. Nonetheless, we draw together everything that we can. We record it all here, making no judgment. We favor no special theory, simply recording the data and not emphasizing any set of factors in the life at the expense of others. Whatever observations we record regarding the reliability of the data are objective comments. We may point out the nature of the source and its background, the circumstances in which the statements were made, how the events came to be recorded, and by whom. Insofar as these are evaluations, they reflect our concern with objectivity. They express the judgments that we make with regard to the external quality of the data that we are collecting. We make no judgments with regard to the quality of their interior, subjective content.

Considering the way we use the data of the Life-Study Research section gives us a preliminary perspective of how the *Intensive Journal* process actually works as it moves through the steps of Life-Study. It is indicative of a fundamental operational principle in the *Intensive Journal* methodology that we make no judgments or interpretations whatsoever in dealing with the data that we collect in this section. In the *Intensive Journal* process, whatever interpretations are necessary are provided by the body of life-data itself as it comes together in each person's life. In this sense the information gathered in the Life-Study Research section serves as raw material. When we become engaged in actively carrying out the Life-Study exercises, we draw upon this raw data to provide the contents of the exercises. We do the exercises one by one in their specified sequence, but their overall effect is to set an integrative process into motion. Not by one exercise alone, but by the cumulative movement of the sequence of exercises, new unities gradually emerge in which the raw material from one aspect of the life fits together with pieces from other areas of the life. Not by our theories or interpretations but by the Life-Study exercises as we progressively do them, the life-data are sorted and grouped in ways that express the small processes moving within the person's life. In the course of the exercises these come together to form new integrations that embody the goals and directions implicit in the life. These integrations, which draw together the contents of our Journal work, show us where the life was seeking to go and what the person was seeking to become. They also establish a point of deepening contact between another person's life and our own.

Now we can each experience this for ourselves step by step at a Life-Study workshop as we each work in the Journal that carries the life of the person for whom we are a Journal Trustee.

Chapter 4

The Twilight Atmosphere
of a Workshop

While the content of a Life-Study workshop is different from that of other *Intensive Journal* workshops, the way we set the process of the workshop into motion is the same whether we are working in a group or by ourselves alone. We set the tone for our Journal work by establishing an atmosphere of stillness.

This means more than becoming quiet as the workshop starts. At a Journal Workshop stillness is not merely the absence of noise. It is an active factor that expresses the principle of *progressive deepening* which plays an important role in the *Intensive Journal* process.

One consideration in determining the sequence of exercises at a workshop is that we seek to bring about in a gradual and continuing way an atmosphere of deepening stillness. More than quietness, the stillness carries with it a serious commitment to the work at hand. We are not working only with our minds but with our interior attention. Over the years our experience at Journal Workshops has demonstrated how important this can be. The more we focus our attention at a level of depth within the workshop, the larger the range of memory and perception to which we have access. The movement of recollection is free then, and the fluidity of our intuitions is greater. We find also that perceptions of a subliminal kind are drawn more easily to the surface of consciousness. The observation of this effect, which became clear quite early in the *Intensive Journal* work, emphasized the importance of the depth factor in personal work, especially where experiences of creativity or the redirection of a life may be involved. Within the *Intensive Journal* process it has led to several procedures that draw a person's experiences toward an inward depth. The methods of working actively in the twilight atmosphere are particularly valuable in Life-Study because they help Journal Trustees establish an empathic connection with the lives of the persons they represent. That is one important reason why we begin all Journal Workshops by establishing an atmosphere of stillness and by seeking to set the process of progressive deepening into motion.

The term, *twilight,* is the key to *progressive deepening.* The *twilight range* is an interim realm in human consciousness. It is the range between sleeping and waking. In the sleep state our dreams come to us fully formed and give us in symbolic forms the results of thoughts that we were not aware of thinking. In the waking state the opposite is true, for there our thoughts move forward only as we direct them and as we point them toward a goal. In the waking state we do *directed thinking.* But in the sleep state whatever perceptions come to us are at an unconscious level, and these are not directed at all. They come as though of themselves.

In between these two, the states of sleep and of waking, is the twilight range of consciousness. It contains something of the qualities of both sides. On the one hand, as in the waking state, we can be aware of what comes to us in twilight experiences. We can remember their content and record them. On the other hand, as in the sleep state, we cannot control the perceptions that come to us in the twilight range. In fact, when we try to control its movement, the spontaneous flow and creativity of the twilight range seems to dry up within us and become inaccessible to us. At that point it loses its quality of creativity and becomes no more than directed thinking. It becomes, that is to say, the equivalent of thinking that is directed by the knowledge and the attitudes that we already possessed before we entered the twilight range.

We have two purposes in working with the process of *progressive deepening*. The first is to establish an atmosphere of interior quiet where we can carry out our Journal exercises free from the pressures and anxieties of our daily life. All too often when we begin a Journal Workshop experience, whether in our privacy or in a group, we are still spinning internally from the conflicts both of our emotions and the analytical ideas that are moving within our minds. We need to quiet this spinning effect before we do our Journal work. The main method we have for doing this is to move away from the surface of our mental consciousness into the depths of the twilight range. Once we are there, the process of progressive deepening can begin. As it takes us deeper into the twilight range new understandings come to us in the form of images. Increasingly we perceive the situations of our life in symbolic rather than in literal terms. We find that we are responding to reality more by means of our intuition than our intellect.

Working within the framework of the *Intensive Journal* process, the practice of Entrance Meditation gives us a convenient means of achieving our two goals: first of internal quieting, and then of increasing intuitive perceptions by means of symbols. In using the way of Entrance Meditation we begin by letting our breathing become slower and slower as we move inward.

> Letting the Self become still,
> Letting the breath become slow,
> Letting the thoughts come to rest.

In the quiet atmosphere that gradually establishes itself we perceive images and symbols, body feelings, emotions and intuitions, inward words and sounds that we hear, elusive aromas that we smell. Whatever their sensory form, we perceive them inwardly with our eyes closed in the twilight range of perception. And we record them in our workbook.

At an *Intensive Journal* workshop when we are working in our own life, we may record these perceptions in the *Twilight Imagery Log* as they come to us. Now, at a Life-Study workshop, we have another purpose for that section. The Twilight Imagery Log is where we record the twilight experiences of the person for whom we are serving as Journal Trustee. The twilight perceptions that we ourselves experience must therefore be recorded elsewhere, and we place them in the Journal Trustee Log, the section of our Life-Study workbook that is reserved for our own experience as a Journal Trustee.

Our purpose now is to enter the twilight range and to establish a deep and quiet atmosphere in which we can carry out our Journal work. To do this, we sit in quietness, eyes closed, our Journal workbook open and our pen handy. Whatever experiences or perceptions come to us in the twilight range we record in our Journal Trustee Log. And then we return to the quiet of the twilight range to continue moving inward. Sometimes we use readings of Entrance Meditations to help establish the quiet atmosphere and take us into the twilight range. In the *Appendix* ★ we have included excerpts from *The Well and the Cathedral, The Star/Cross,* and *The White Robed Monk,* which we may use at one time or another to help us move into a twilight atmosphere. These excerpts were chosen because of their appropriateness for particular exercises that we may wish to carry out at various points in our Life-Study work. We can work with them later on. For now, however, we merely wish to let the depth and quiet of a twilight atmosphere establish itself around us.

We sit in stillness, our eyes closed. We do not think any thoughts in particular, but we let ourselves feel the presence and the quality of being of the person for whom we are serving as Journal Trustee. It may be that images will come to us, images that we see, or that we hear. It may be that bodily feelings, emotions, or other sensations come to us at the twilight level. We record them as they come to us, describing them as we perceive them, as they are in themselves without our adding any comment or reactions or interpretation. We sit in silence, letting the stillness

★ See p. 288 ff.

form itself around us. Presently, not all at once but soon, we begin to feel this stillness forming not only around us but within us as well. Nothing we do brings it about. It comes of itself as we wait, not thinking, but with our minds open and receptive. Soon we perceive that the stillness is larger than we are. It is not only a stillness within us; it is also a stillness around us. It has become a twilight atmosphere that supports and carries our inner work. It is within us, and we are within it. We establish this atmosphere by sitting and by turning our attention inward. We do it whenever we undertake a portion of Life-Study or any Journal work.

We begin by sitting in stillness, our eyes closed now as we enter the twilight atmosphere.

Chapter 5

The Steppingstones of a Life

When we have placed ourselves in an atmosphere of stillness in the twilight range of experience, we can proceed to the larger task of reconstructing the context and continuity of the whole life of the person for whom we are Journal Trustee.

Our first step is to draw together an overview of the life to give ourselves a perspective of its continuity and a feeling for the rhythm of its changes. For this purpose we adapt the Steppingstones procedures of the *Intensive Journal* process. They enable us to establish a framework and place us in a position to fill in the details of the several life/time units in the person's life.

Over the years the particular use of the Steppingstones exercises has been to help individuals position themselves in the movement of their lives. In various applications it has had a great practical value, especially for persons who find themselves in a time of transition. Working with the Steppingstones concept provides an effective and concise means—particularly economical with respect to the time that it requires—for placing the developments and changes of a life in perspective. In this regard it has played an important role in the personal use of the *Intensive Journal* method, and it performs an equivalent function in Life-Study. Here, however, we have to adjust the concept of Steppingstones and alter its techniques in order to meet the needs of Life-Study where we are engaged in reconstructing and re-experiencing a life other than our own.

The core definition of Steppingstones that has evolved out of its use in the *Intensive Journal* program is that *Steppingstones are the meaningful events that mark off the movement of a person's life from that person's own point of view.* Stated in this way, Steppingstones may not be objectively important—that is, not from the point of view of an outsider—but they are always personally important. They are the events of a life that are perceived as being important through the eyes and through the experience of the person who is living the life. Inherently, therefore, the Steppingstones are subjective.

What are regarded as the *facts* of a person's life may be colored by that person's point of view. And the memory of the facts may alter with time. They may be enlarged by elaborations that are inadvertently imaginative, and allowance must be made for that. Sometimes the relative importance of individual events may change with the passage of the years, not only because a person may falsify events without intending to, but because an event that was thought to be of crucial importance at the time it happened may be seen to be of only passing significance in the light of subsequent occurrences. Sometimes in retrospect an event can be seen to have a much greater importance than it was thought to have when it happened. Further, when our view of the significance of an event changes, our remembrance of what was contained in it may also change. If it becomes more important to us, we remember more, and we fill in more of the details. If it becomes less important to us, we overlook more. And so it goes.

The way we work with Steppingstones in the *Intensive Journal* process reflects the fact that each person perceives his or her life as seen from the inside of it while it is in process of unfolding. This is a subjective factor that lies at the heart of everyone's life. We can understand a great deal of the *Intensive Journal* process—the structure of the sections in the workbook, the format of the exercises, their sequence and combinations, the special procedures of the method as a whole—as a reflection of this subjective factor and especially as an attempt to provide an operational and continuous means of working with the subjective contents of a life. To do this effectively, we have to make the subjective contents available to us in a tangible form. Since they are inherently subjective, we cannot make them objective, but we can give them some of the protections of objectivity. One way that we do this is by providing carriers in the form of the Journal sections to protect the delicate personal material of subjective experience, and to maintain it in a form that can be explored and developed further. The *Intensive Journal* structure gives us an instrument for doing this. The process that results from our using this structure represents in each case the unique form in which an individual is brought into existence as a person by the continuity of events that comprise the life.

The *Intensive Journal* structure absorbs the subjectivity of events and gives each life an objective form that can be worked with in personal terms. This is a principle that underlies the *Intensive Journal* process. The fact that the Steppingstones exercises play an essential role in this is the main reason why they come early in the workshop sequence of *Intensive Journal* exercises for working with our personal life. When we are serving as the Journal Trustee for a person the principle is the same, but adjustments must be made for the fact that we are working in another person's life. Since we begin by being outsiders to the life of the person we are studying, it is necessary to use special techniques that draw us into the person's life. Working with Steppingstones is one of the techniques that enables us to build an intimacy of feeling that places us inside the person's life. But we must do it in a way that fits the particular needs of Life-Study.

When we list the Steppingstones in the life of the person for whom we are Journal Trustee, we do so in the first person. We list the Steppingstones of their life on their behalf. In order to do this, it is necessary for us to enter their life at a feeling level and to be subjectively within them. To do this we adopt a viewpoint that enables us to perceive their experiences as they themselves perceived them while the events were unfolding. Special efforts and discipline on our part are required at first in order to make the psychological transfer, but once we have done it we are in a position truly to speak in the first person for them. At that point our listing of the Steppingstones in the first person as a Journal Trustee becomes an act that places us psychologically within another person's life. Being within their life, we can speak on their behalf with respect to the issues of their life.

Another adaptation of the Steppingstones concept in Life-Study involves the point in time at which a particular listing of Steppingstones is made. When we are working on our own behalf in the Personal Component of the *Intensive Journal* process, we list our Steppingstones from the midst of the movement of our life. Each time that we come to a workshop or on any other occasions or for any other reasons—as when we are in a time of transition or at a crisis of decision—when we do the Journal exercise of listing the Steppingstones of our life, we take the present moment as our base point. Whatever the present time is, that is the point of reference for the listing of our Steppingstones. From there we go back over our life from the time of birth, recapitulating the main events from the vantage point of the present.

That is the stretch of time that our listing of Steppingstones covers: from birth to our current circumstance. Our first Steppingstone is, "I was born . . ." And from that point onward we list a dozen or so Steppingstones—give or take one or two is our rule of thumb—with just a phrase, or at most a sentence, to mark off and describe each one. The basic exercise is for us to list about a dozen meaningful events in the movement of our life up to the present point in time. We do that for ourselves, and it gives us a perspective of our life as a whole from the time of our birth to our situation at the time when we are listing our Steppingstones. The listing of the Steppingstones of our life is the basic step in positioning ourselves between our past and our future. It is a fundamental technique in the *Intensive Journal* process, and we use it in Life-Study as well.

Because of the difference in the nature of the subject matter in the Life-Study, however, it is necessary for us to alter the Steppingstones procedures in two important ways when we use them here. The first change concerns the point in time that serves as our base point for listing the Steppingstones. In Life-Study we take as our vantage point a time shortly after the death of the person. It need not be a specific time that we can identify by the occurrence of a particular event. It is sufficient if we set our position for the Steppingstones in a general way, taking any point in time that comes early in the period following the person's death. Our purpose in this is to give ourselves an overview that includes the whole of the life from birth to death.

The second important adaptation that we make in our use of the Steppingstones is that for the purpose of Life-Study we distinguish two types of Steppingstones. We record them in two separate listings, identifying them in two distinct Journal exercises. In Life-Study we mark off first the Primary Steppingstones and then the Extended Steppingstones. When we have made each listing within its own terms, we place the two sets of Steppingstones in relation to each other. From that relationship we draw the basis for the next major phase in our Life-Study. But first the Steppingstones of the life.

Chapter 6

The Primary Steppingstones

Feeling the Flow of the Life

The listing of Primary Steppingstones, which is basic in our work as Journal Trustees, can be compared to our moving along the road of a person's life taking long strides as we tread lightly on each of the Steppingstones from birth to death. We do this listing of the Steppingstones as a spontaneous recapitulation of the outline of the life. It is basic for Life-Study that we place ourselves at a point in time shortly after the person's death. We do this in order that, looking through their eyes from that vantage point, we can list what appear to them to be the events of major significance as they view their life as a whole. Among these, as we begin with the event of their birth, we end with the event of their death.

Altogether we include in this basic listing approximately a dozen Steppingstones—sometimes as few as ten or as many as fifteen. Each is stated briefly. For each Steppingstone we write only a few words, a phrase or two, perhaps a sentence at the most. And then we write no more than another sentence to indicate its most important features. These Steppingstones are the markings that come to our mind out of the range of background knowledge that we have acquired regarding the life of the person.

To make our listing of the Primary Steppingstones, we begin by sitting in stillness. Just sitting. We do not think about the contents of the life of the person whom we are studying. We do not think now of the material that we have read, nor of the data that we have collected in the workbook. We do not judge the Journal entries. We do not interpret them. We are just sitting, sitting in silence, letting our thoughts come to rest. It is a time of quieting.

Whatever muddiness there may be in the waters of our own life we let drop to the bottom in the stillness. The questions of our own life are not the issue now. For the present our attention is directed to another person's life. Therefore, as we sit in silence we let ourselves feel the presence of the person for whom we are serving as Journal Trustee. We may even—if it comes to us that way—envision the presence of that person and see them inwardly as being present with us. Visualizing them, we may also feel the movement of their life.

Sitting in stillness and feeling the presence of the person, now we are *feeling the flow of the life.** Feeling the flow of the life.* We are within their life now, participating in it. Emotions that arose in the course of that person's life now arise in us. We experience them as though they were our own. We share their feelings, we share their emotions, in empathy. We are *feeling the flow of their life,* feeling it from within its problems as well as its achievements. We are becoming one with the inner continuity of that life. We experience an empathy, a connection with that life, knowing it from within. We are entering that life at a twilight level of our perception.

* This is a seven-syllable Mantra/Crystal. Some of us who are now working in Life-Study may be familiar with practicing the kind of neutral, quieting meditation that uses a mantra/crystal phrase. The preparation for listing the Steppingstones of a life is an appropriate time to use that approach since it gives us a means of establishing an atmosphere of stillness within ourselves that is both neutral and related to the subject in which we are involved. You may, however, wish to adjust this mantra/crystal phrase to fit your own experience. Or perhaps you may wish to use a mantra/crystal phrase that is drawn directly from the context of the work you are doing. See *The Practice of Process Meditation,* Part IV, Mantra/Crystals, pp. 186-270, for a description of this form of meditative practice and the ways of composing your own mantra/crystals.

In this atmosphere we place ourselves at a point in time just after the person's death. Now, *feeling the flow of the life,* the whole of it recapitulates itself event by event, circumstance by circumstance. The continuity of the movement of the life presents itself to us, the significant events becoming markers of the unfoldment of the life. These are the Steppingstones of the life of the person for whom we are Journal Trustee. As they come to us we record them in the Steppingstones section. We write them in the first person on behalf of the person we represent.

"I was born," we write for them; and then we add the details of when and where. And then . . . for another Steppingstone. And then . . . for another. Until the closing Steppingstone, "I died." And we add the details of when, where, how.

About a dozen Steppingstones we write on their behalf in this way. Perhaps a few more than a dozen if we feel that the extra Steppingstones are required. Perhaps as many as fifteen or sixteen, if need be. Each Steppingstone as we write it is just a sentence or two. Just enough to be indicative.

Now we are in the silence of the twilight atmosphere, *feeling the flow of the life.* As they come to us from birth to the event of death, we record the Steppingstones of the life of the person for whom we are Journal Trustee.

We do this each in our own silence.

The Readback Experience

Having gone inward in order to make the primary listing of the Steppingstones of the life, we now come back to the surface of our consciousness. Our listing of Steppingstones is before us. We have the opportunity now to check it with ourselves by reading it back to ourselves to see how it speaks to us. What responses does it stir in us? Are there significant changes that we feel we need to make, an event to add, a group of entries to consolidate, to modify, to correct, or perhaps to delete? We should record any thoughts and feelings that arise in us in this regard, considering them as being additional to our listing of Primary Steppingstones. We want to encourage ourselves to record in writing any observations and comments that come to us at this time, but it is best for us to keep these distinct from the listing of Steppingstones that we have made. Therefore we make them as a separate entry. We take a fresh page following the listing of Primary Steppingstones, making sure to note the date at the head of the page, and then we record whatever additional thoughts, feelings, perceptions come to us as a response to our reading the Steppingstones back to ourselves.

It is important that, after we have made our primary listing of Steppingstones, we allow ourselves a sufficient period of silence. This silence is a time when we can read back to ourselves what we have written spontaneously, feeling the continuity of the life, responding to it, and considering the implications of the various changes and rhythms within the life. This silence is also a time when we can have a further experience and inner perception of the issues that may be involved in the life.

In addition to reading the Steppingstones back to ourselves in silence we can also read this primary listing of Steppingstones aloud. We have found that when individuals participate in an *Intensive Journal* workshop with respect to the contents of their own life, it is helpful for them to read their Steppingstones aloud to the group. The same applies when we are serving as Journal Trustee and have listed the Steppingstones of another person's life. We should not say, however, that at a workshop we are reading the Steppingstones to the group, for we are not. It is rather that we are reading the Steppingstones *in the presence of the group*. The fact is that each of the persons present at the workshop is concerned with the listing of Steppingstones that they themselves have just collected. That is where their interest lies. Therefore, when you read the list that you have written, you should not feel that you are reading it in order to tell your life to anyone else nor the life of the person for whom you are Journal Trustee. You are not reading your Steppingstones in order to communicate your life story but rather so that you yourself can *hear* the entirety of your life history expressed as a whole in its flow. This gives you an opportunity to respond to it within yourself at a deeper-than-conscious level. The consequences of doing that can be very valuable.

The principle that we follow at Life-Study workshops is the same as at personal *Intensive Journal* workshops where participants read aloud from their workbook entries. At the workshops where we are working with the contents of our own lives, since we are not reading aloud in order to communicate to others, we listen only slightly to what other persons are reading. You might say that we listen with only one ear, or perhaps with only half an ear, just in case something is read that is relevant to our own deepening experience. We are each working in our individual process. The attention of each person is focused on the task of going down his or her own well. Paradoxically, it is by means of this focused quality of individual attention that a supportive atmosphere is built in the workshop as a whole and that the individual person can be sustained through whatever difficulties may be encountered.

In the atmosphere of a workshop when we choose to read aloud it is in order to stimulate and deepen our own awareness of the issues that are involved in the particular life whose Steppingstones we have assembled. Many people report that reading their Steppingstones back to themselves, even in silence but especially aloud, is a very helpful exercise. The experience of *readback* can lead to responses within yourself and can stimulate further entries that may significantly expand the scope of your Journal work.

Sometimes when we are listing the Steppingstones of our own life at a workshop we may feel that the needs of privacy prevent us from reading aloud. That is in accord with the principle of privacy that is fundamental in *Intensive Journal* work, and we should certainly honor such a feeling when it comes to us. In this regard one practice that has become quite common in *Intensive Journal* work enables us both to protect our privacy and to have the experience of hearing ourselves read aloud the Steppingstones that express the movement of our life. We read aloud from our Journal, but not at a workshop. We read in our own privacy with a cassette recorder present. Then we can play it back to ourselves as often as we feel is useful, and each time we may add another response if it comes to us.

In the case of our Life-Study work we usually have little need to make this reservation regarding privacy. Most of the material with which we are dealing is already publicly available. In most cases it has already been published and that is how we have access to it. We can usually feel free therefore to read from the workshop floor the listing of Steppingstones that we make as a Journal Trustee.

It is good to read aloud, but it is not good to become judgmental of ourselves. When you read back the Steppingstones listing you must bear in mind that the listing you made was not intended to be complete, and that there was no thought of being perfect or final. Remember that it was written in a twilight atmosphere, more or less spontaneously, drawing on your general familiarity, your knowledge and feelings of the person you are studying. Now you are feeding it back to yourself in a readback exercise to see what additional experiences and perceptions it stirs in you. The attitude with which you hear your readback of the Steppingstones is therefore not intellectually critical and judgmental but is open and exploratory. Proceeding in that spirit and with that understanding, the *readback* experience of reading the Steppingstones aloud from the workshop floor or privately into your cassette recorder can be a valuable catalyst for your Life-Study work.

In the following pages, I have brought together a number of the listings of the Primary Steppingstones of lives that have been reconstructed at Life-Study workshops. They are illustrative, but do not regard them as models of correctness for you to follow. In fact, none of the examples given in any part of this volume should be regarded as being definitive reconstructions of the life. They are intended to be merely *indications* of an open-ended approach that leads to many possibilities. The work we do in Life-Study, as in our personal use of the *Intensive Journal* method, proceeds and builds its cumulative effect by means of spontaneous entries that record perceptions and inner experiences as they come to us. All are intended as partial contributions to the total work, subject to change and to the addition of the further awareness that may arise in us in the future. No Journal entry is to be regarded as a finality. Neither can any Journal entry be taken as a model for any other Journal entry. This is for the elemental reason that each life is unique and the individual contents of a life reflect its uniqueness. The Journal entries that express these contents must do the same. The sets of Steppingstones that are given below are therefore to be understood as being merely illustrations. By no means are they models, neither from the point of view of showing how a Journal Trustee should draw together the Steppingstones of a life, nor as a definitive statement of what that particular life contains.

It may very well be that you yourself are working with one of the lives that is quoted here as an example, and that your reconstruction of the Steppingstones of that life has quite a different emphasis. So be it. Stick to your guns. The listings of Steppingstones that are given here are not necessarily correct, especially since there is no single correct way to perceive the Steppingstones of any human being's life. But the listing of Steppingstones gives us a starting point, and it serves as a doorway by which we can enter the inner precincts of the life. Most important, when we work with the Extended Steppingstones in addition to the Primary Steppingstones that we have just listed, the combination gives us both a perspective and a supply of raw data with which to proceed in our Life-Study. We shall take that further step shortly. But first we have the experience of reading back the Steppingstones of the life for which we are Journal Trustee, and listening— with half an ear, or as much of an ear as suits us—to the reading of the Primary Steppingstones of various lives by their Journal Trustees from the workshop floor.

From the Life-Study Journals

I AM PABLO CASALS

I was born in 1867 in Catalonia of poor people.

My mother and father loved both me and my music very much. But that caused great tension between them and also within me.

At age seventeen I was depressed and desired suicide.

My life was restored by my studies with Count de Morphy in Madrid and by the most helpful support of the Royal Family.

I came to know the monks at the monastery of Montserrat.

I received increasing musical recognition, traveling the world with Paris as my base. I came to know many great musicians and other famous persons.

I had premonitions of their death when my father died and later when my mother died.

World War I filled me with despair for mankind. Only my music sustained me and kept me sane.

After World War I, I was active with the Catalonian people, forming an orchestra and the workingmen's concerts. I was active in the Republican government.

I suffered exile during the years of Franco and the Nazis, and I saw my people betrayed even after World War II.

I married Martita and moved to Puerto Rico.

I had many honors, festivals, and musical joys in the sunset period of my life. But composing and performing *El Pesebre (The Manger)* is my message of peace among mankind.

I died in 1963 with personal happiness, but feeling sadness for humanity and for my people.

I AM ELEANOR ROOSEVELT

I was born in 1884 into the high society of New York City. My father was Theodore Roosevelt's brother.

I had a very difficult childhood with an alcoholic although beloved father and a very negative and beautiful mother. Both of them died before I was ten years old.

The Allenswood School in England opened my eyes to the world.

I married Franklin and could hardly believe it.

The years of childbearing and raising a family. I bore six children, five of whom are living.

I learned about Franklin's affair with Lucy Mercer.

Franklin contracted polio.

I began political activity.

I was a governor's wife.

I became First Lady of the United States.

I was a target of political ridicule.

Franklin died in office.

I was a United Nations Representative.

I traveled the world.

It was my time to die.

I AM ABRAHAM LINCOLN

I was born in 1809 in Kentucky of poor people.

While I was still a small boy we moved further out on the frontier where we were isolated and everything was very simple.

In my late teens some cargo trips down the Mississippi River gave me my first view of the larger world.

I got a taste of politics at a local level, liked it, and went to the state level.

I applied for and received a license to practice law. That gave me a means of earning a livelihood.

After an uncertain love life, I married Mary.

My children began to be born over the years, and some died.

I had a single term in Congress and was then returned to private life where I tried to concentrate on restoring my finances and writing poetry again.

The controversy over the Kansas-Nebraska Bill drew me back into politics.

The Douglas debates led me to realize that my flair for speechmaking had reached a good point of development. This was something I could really do well, especially now that there were issues I deeply cared about.

I saw that I had a chance to win the Presidency, and I resolved to attain it.

I won the Presidency, and I paid the price for it.

I AM JAN CHRISTIAN SMUTS

I was born on a farm in South Africa in 1870.

I grew up as a serious intellectual-type boy in a very difficult and dangerous environment close to nature and primitive life.

Some time before I was twenty years old, I had an experience of wholeness and of Walt Whitman. It was during my college education in South Africa.

I went to Cambridge to study law and I also wrote my study of Walt Whitman's life.

After graduating from Cambridge I decided to go back to South Africa, where I married and raised a family.

I obtained the government post of Minister of the Interior and in that role I had my encounter with Mohandas Gandhi.

I served as a general in the Boer War and negotiated the peace settlement with England.

I became Prime Minister of South Africa and I stayed continuously in office.

I helped England in World War I and was rewarded with honors in the postwar years.

I was startled by being upset in the elections of 1924 and being thrown out of office.

In semi-retirement and shock I returned to my earlier philosophy and wrote *Holism and Evolution*.

The acceptance of the book led to a restless period of intellectual honors, Chancellor of Cambridge University, etc.

I helped the Allies in World War II and had an early role in the United Nations.

I died in 1950 pondering my life. My early vision of wholeness led to many achievements, but there are also many ironies in my life.

I AM VINCENT VAN GOGH

I was born in Holland in 1853.

My father was a Dutch Reformed minister. He was strict in religion and in the way he ruled the family.

My family life was pleasant. I had a brother and three sisters and several well-to-do and successful relatives who liked me. I know that my brothers and sisters liked me, but I think that some of the adults considered me to be strange.

I was sent to boarding school at age twelve where I missed my family and developed a love for books and ideas.

At sixteen I left school and went to work for an international art firm in which my uncle was a partner. It went well at first.

In England I fell in love with the daughter of my landlady, but she rejected me. I was devastated.

I tried to be trained to be a minister, but the Greek and Latin studies seemed irrelevant to me, so I gave it up.

I did become a lay missionary in the coal mining district, but I was dismissed because of my "excessive zeal" in helping poor people.

I remained in the mining district for about a year subsisting on almost nothing and going through a time of absolute blackness. But it passed. This was the time when I made the decision to become an artist with all my being.

I wrote and told my troubles to my brother, Theo. He was the only person who understood me and tried to befriend me.

The first years as artist were very difficult. I had to give up living in The Hague and in Brussels.

In 1885 my father died. Later in 1885 I painted *The Potato Eaters,* but nobody noticed it.

In 1886 I went to Paris and lived with Theo and his wife. I also began to mingle there with other artists.

I had a friendship with Paul Gauguin but I broke it. I was just too difficult a person.

In despair and loneliness I cut off a piece of my ear.

I committed myself to an asylum.

I continued to paint at a feverish pace. I felt that I knew what I was doing.

In early 1890 I received my first favorable review.

In the summer of 1890 I took a shotgun into the fields and I shot myself.

I AM THOMAS JEFFERSON

I was born and grew up in the hill country of Virginia with a good and pleasant family background.

I had a classical education at William and Mary College, but I also learned about the new philosophies of society and human rights.

I was apprenticed to a lawyer and eventually became a practicing attorney myself. But I continued to be interested in the larger issues of society and government.

When I was selected for the House of Burgesses in Virginia I had the opportunity to write the statement on the Religious Freedom of Virginia. I not only enjoyed doing this but I had a strong sense that something important in history was taking place.

This feeling built in me when I was elected to the Congress and when I had the opportunity to write the Declaration of Independence. All my studies and thoughts could now be put to use.

While the Revolution of the states was taking place I served as Governor of the State of Virginia.

I had a period of private life during which I built Monticello and developed my interests in art and architecture as well as some of my personal relationships.

After my wife died I returned to public life. I became Secretary of State and then served as Minister to France.

Eventually I became President of the United States and served for eight years during which we were able to take some large steps for future development.

After the Presidency there was nothing to do but to retire and enjoy the recognition of being "The Sage of Monticello."

Nonetheless I continued to be restless in my mind and actions and I overstretched myself financially. There were difficulties in my later years that I probably could have avoided.

When I died I was advanced in years but I was still involved in trying new things.

I AM QUEEN VICTORIA OF ENGLAND

I was born in England in 1819, an only child and in the line of succession to the throne.

My upbringing and education were based on the traditions of British royalty, for I was expected to become Queen one day.

I did become Queen when I was only eighteen years old. I did not feel unprepared for I had been taught that this was what my life was for. I felt that I had a responsibility both to restore respect for the throne and to prove what a woman is capable of doing.

I married my cousin Albert both because I loved him and because he was a person who was capable of sharing the throne with me. He understood that we had been born to a great responsibility, and he shared it with me. We had a close and loving marriage.

I built a family with Albert. My first child was a daughter. I had nine children altogether.

Once I was established as Queen, I made a strong point of insisting on strict standards for myself, for my family, and for the people of my country.

When Albert died I was overcome by grief. I retired in mourning to express my personal feelings but I maintained my responsibilities as Queen. I made it a point to keep in touch with the affairs of the government.

After Albert's death, Benjamin Disraeli became my confidant and my advisor. His talents and great abilities were of great assistance to me in enabling me to govern.

I knew that for the good of the country I had to live a model life, and I fulfilled my responsibility. I felt that I had no choice. The years after Albert's death were therefore very lonely.

I was eighty-two years old when I died after reigning for sixty-three years as Queen. I did what I had to do.

Chapter 7

The Extended
Steppingstones

The Continuity and the Content

Each list of Primary Steppingstones gives us a view of the life as a whole. It expresses in a brief form the movement of the life through its phases and cycles, and thus it enables us to recognize the rhythms of change in the life. It also indicates to us the person's main concerns and interests. But it only points to them as it outlines in general terms the movement and contents of the life. The Primary Steppingstones do not give the details, and yet we need to know what was taking place in the life if we are to understand how it developed, and especially if we are to appreciate the goals toward which the person was striving and the problems that were encountered along the way.

In order to experience another person's life with empathy we require two complementary kinds of knowledge. One is a knowledge of the movement of events as they form the outlines of the life. The other is a knowledge of the specific contents of those events, the persons and the issues that they involved. The two essential factors are the continuity and the contents of the life. We established our base perception of the continuity of the life when we listed the Primary Steppingstones. Now we need to maintain that sense of movement and to fill it in with the main details of events that were only indicated in outline before. For this purpose we make a second listing of Steppingstones, the Extended Steppingstones in which we can include much more of the information that we have about the life.

In listing the Extended Steppingstones we follow the same chronological sequence as we did before in marking off the Primary Steppingstones. Since we are recapitulating the sequential development of the life, we begin with the same simple entry, "I was born . . ." This time, however, our entry is longer and fuller in its contents. We may say more about the background of the birth, the circumstances surrounding it and other aspects of the early life of the person. The first entry is the same, but now there is much more to it.

In listing the Extended Steppingstones, we use the same Journal Section as before. We use the Steppingstones section in the red part of the workbook where we make the entries for the experiences of life/time. We listed the Primary Steppingstones there. Now we take a fresh page in order to begin a new sub-section for the Extended Steppingstones. We write the heading and the date.

Our first entry starts with the lead-in phrase, "I was born . . ." Where we added only a phrase or two with the essential information in listing the Primary Steppingstones, we now may write a sentence or two or three. In listing our Extended Steppingstones we can write as much as is necessary in order to make a clear statement about that event in the life. We wish to record the essential information, including the necessary details while keeping the entry as concise as we can. Having made the first entry, we can help ourselves build the continuity of the life by using the same linkage phrase that we used for the Primary Steppingstones. After completing the entry that begins with "I was born," we say, "And then . . . ." "And then . . . ." And thus we continue filling in the Extended Steppingstones of the life, filling in as many of the details as we require in order to give a clear perspective both of the continuity and the contents of the life.

There is a simple criterion that can guide us in writing the

Extended Steppingstones and in differentiating them from the kind of entries that we make in our listing of the Primary Steppingstones. When we made the brief entries of a phrase or two to establish the *thread of continuity* within the life with the Primary Steppingstones, we were following the same principle as when we list our own Life-Steppingstones in our personal use of the *Intensive Journal* process. There our main concern is to establish our sense of meaningful movement within the life, and we do not include the details of the life in our listing of the Steppingstones. It is sufficient to make brief entries there that are merely indicative of the events, since it is our own life that we are working with and we are familiar with the details to which our general entries are referring. Making the Steppingstones entries with this brief form in our personal work enables us to have a strong perception of the thread of continuity in our life and also the rhythm of our inner process. In addition, if we choose to read our Steppingstones aloud in the atmosphere of a workshop, we can do so with an essential privacy since we have written our Life-Steppingstones only with indication phrases and have not included the details.

This personal listing of Life-Steppingstones is comparable to the listing of Primary Steppingstones that we make as a Journal Trustee. Here we are not actually representing our own life, but we write the Primary Steppingstones with only brief, indicative entries nonetheless. We write as though they were expressing our own life and we knew them so intimately from within that we did not need to write the details. In principle that is true, or will eventually be true, when we are working as a Journal Trustee. When we write the Extended Steppingstones, however, we have a purpose that is additional to perceiving the thread of continuity in the movement of the life. Now we are beginning the process of drawing together the contents of the life in order to reconstruct it as a whole and to use the active procedures of Journal Feedback in it. The details of the life are necessary for this, and thus the brief entries are not sufficient. The criterion that can guide us in describing the Extended Steppingstones is that these entries should contain sufficient data to enable an outsider who did not know the person to gain from reading the list at least a cursory overview of the direction and main interests of the person's life.

In listing the Extended Steppingstones we follow the basic chronological sequence of the life, beginning with "I was born . . ." and adding the data for the subsequent Steppingstones, "And then . . . , And then. . . ." We continue listing the Steppingstones with whatever extended details they require until we come to the event of the death. This also is included in the life with an indication of the circumstances. As a Journal Trustee we are working from a position in time just after the death of the person, and thus the Steppingstones cover the full life-span from the birth through the death.

Since our listing of Extended Steppingstones draws on information we have been gathering regarding the specific facts of the life, it is good to have our research materials available to us. We may now make use of the books of biography or autobiography that we are using as our sources. Much of the data that we need may already be contained in the notes that we have been collecting in the Life-Study Research section of our workbook. Now we call upon all the data that we have gathered up to this point in our work. The listing of Primary Steppingstones that we made in the twilight atmosphere can serve us now as a general framework giving us starting points for describing the specific events in the life. At many points our listing of Extended Steppingstones becomes an enlargement of the Primary Steppingstones. We now have the opportunity, however, to insert Steppingstones that were not mentioned at all in the Primary listing. As we work with the Extended Steppingstones, therefore, we can approach the life afresh as though this were the first time we were reconstructing it from the point of view of its Steppingstones. Additional events may come to our mind now as being meaningful in the life and we can give these their place as we are building the continuity and describing the contents of the life.

In making this extended listing there is no restriction on the number of Steppingstones that can be included. We begin with the same base point as in the listing of Primary Steppingstones, starting with the point in time just after the transition from physical life. That is our vantage point and we move onwards from the point of physical birth to mark off as many events as are significant to us. We choose those that establish the atmosphere of the life and especially those that convey the tone and quality of the main events in the life as they reflect the tempo of change.

We list as many Steppingstones as we feel to be necessary in order to traverse the full span of the life and describe its range of activities. The Extended Steppingstones can be whatever number we require in order to cover the journey from birth to death. We follow the conception of Steppingstones as the events that mark off the meaningful movement within a life, including both the inner and the outer experiences. We retain the principle of brevity in Steppingstones as much as we can, since we recognize that when the Steppingstones in a list are briefly stated it helps us experience the *thread of continuity* that is the connecting factor in the life. Since we have an additional purpose in working with the Extended Steppingstones, however, we have to include much more material.

The rule of thumb that we follow in writing the Extended Steppingstones is that our descriptions should be as full as is necessary and as brief as will suffice to establish a perspective of the person's life while giving an understanding of the content of the cycles and changes through which that life has passed. As we work in Life-Study, the experience we gain with practice will enable us to determine the number and length of the Extended Steppingstones. We need to allow ourselves sufficient leeway to include whatever points may come to our mind as possibly being relevant, just on the chance that some of these will prove to be valuable when all the data and exercises have been brought together. Keeping that possibility open is a prime consideration as our Life-Study proceeds. We want to have room for whatever information can eventually prove to be meaningful and helpful. Nonetheless, for reasons of time and the limitations of space in our workbooks, we try to limit our descriptions of each Steppingstone to keep our listing of the Extended Steppingstones within manageable boundaries. We want to mention here whatever data may prove to be relevant for our further Journal work when we draw upon the material mentioned in Steppingstones for the Journal Feedback exercises that we use at a later stage of our Life-Study.

We did our listing of Primary Steppingstones in the quiet and depth of the twilight range of consciousness. We do our work with the Extended Steppingstones, however, at the level of mental consciousness. We are making use here of whatever data we have been able to gather by means of our reading and general research. We do, however, try to remain in contact with the twilight range of our perceptions. It is important that we keep and build our empathic connections with the person for whom we are Journal Trustee in order that the work we do in Steppingstones will reflect the unfoldment of their life as they would perceive it.

Now we become quiet and let ourselves feel the context and continuity in the life of our person. Our listing of Primary Steppingstones gives us the basis for that. We take a fresh page in the Steppingstones section of the workbook, write the heading, *Extended Steppingstones,* and the date. Now, step by step, we reconstruct the movement of that life, providing whatever details come to our mind as being relevant to the life.

Since we have considerable flexibility in the number of Steppingstones that we can include here and the extent of the descriptions we provide for each of them, the way we do the Extended Steppingstones will reflect the degree of knowledge that we now possess regarding the life of the person we are representing. Do it as well as you can at this point, not too long and not too short, with the knowledge available to you. Bear in mind that, if at a later time you feel you can do it more meaningfully, you can always do another listing of Extended Steppingstones, and you can add to the present list. Therefore it is not necessary for you to make this listing complete and perfect. The material you draw together now in this listing of the Extended Steppingstones will be data that you use for taking your next step in Life-Study.

The following are some illustrative listings of Extended Steppingstones taken from Life-Study Journals.

From the Life-Study Journals

I AM PABLO CASALS

I was born in Catalonia on December 29, 1867.

My first years were very different from the rest of my life. They were spent in poor and simple surroundings on the coast of Spain. That is where I began.

The first Steppingstone of my life is my memory of my father teaching me music in my very early years. For my father music was a part of life. He did not regard it as a means of earning a livelihood. He saw it as a joy but not as a career.

My second Steppingstone is my realization of how much my mother loved me, that she was committed to me and to my having a career in music. I soon recognized that she was stronger than my father in the power of her will, and also, I think, in the power of her mind. I was glad of that because she believed that I could make a good living as a musician, and she overruled my father who did not think so.

The next key event in my life came from this. It happened so gradually that I hardly noticed it, but it was a definite event. It was possibly the most basic event in my life because, without it, everything would have been different. Perhaps nothing would have happened as it did. I might have become a poor carpenter in a Spanish town and only played the organ in church on Sundays. This key Steppingstone in my life is that, while my father started me in music, my mother took over and managed my musical education and the development of my career.

One day when I was thirteen years old and was performing in a café in Barcelona I was browsing in a music store with my father when I came across an old manuscript by Bach, his *Six Suites for Violincello Solo*. That was a chance event that had a tremendous effect on the development of my music.

Around the age of seventeen I went into a terrible depression. I wanted to die and I almost committed suicide. That was a low point but I was fortunate to pass through it, and I lived eighty years after that. I still find it hard to believe, but after that I did not ever really want to die. After that I loved life even when it was very unpleasant.

My education was taken over by Count de Morphy, the marvelous Irishman, in Madrid. He taught me philosophy as well as music. He was responsible for my close relationship with the Royal Family and the support they gave me to launch my career.

The establishment of my career in Paris after a very difficult time of traveling around Europe with my mother in much poverty.

My connection with the monks at the Monastery of Montserrat started early, built gradually, and eventually became a most important part of my life. I composed a great deal for the monks. There were several years, especially during the time of exile, when the one thing that truly comforted me was the knowledge that those monks were chanting my compositions every day.

The time of success in Paris was very satisfying, even exhilarating. I was friends with many wonderful people, Henri Bergson, Romain Rolland, many musicians. I even knew the people who worked for freedom in the Dreyfus affair.

In 1901 I broke my hand in an accident on Mount Tamalpais near San Francisco. I was glad because I thought, "Now I won't be able to play the cello any more so I can become a conductor." But my hand healed as though by a miracle. So I suppose it was my destiny to play the cello.

In 1906 I was on a concert tour in Switzerland when I knew telepathically that my father was dying. I canceled my tour, went to him, and he did die then. Later on, the same thing happened when my mother died. I was also in Switzerland on tour at the time.

When World War I came, I thought the world had gone crazy and there was nothing to hope for. I thank God for my music and for the fact that the war ended as soon as it did.

After World War I, I spent a great deal of time and energy in Catalonia. I formed my own orchestra, the Pau Casals Orchestra, and I managed to keep it going at great personal expense and with great difficulty.

I formed the Workingmen's Concert Association. I believe this proved the correctness of my idea that music is for the common people. The two go together.

I played an active role in the Spanish Republican government. I was named President of the Council on Music. Everybody accepted the fact that I was both a close friend of the Royal Family and a strong Republican.

I was in despair for my country and my people when Hitler helped Franco while the western democracies did nothing for Spain. That was a terrible pain to me. I could bear leaving Spain and going into exile, but I could not bear the betrayal of Spain by the other democratic countries that I believed in and trusted. It was no satisfaction for me to know that all of western civilization suffered terribly because Spain had been betrayed and Hitler had not been stopped from helping Franco.

After World War II, I felt that the betrayal of my people continued, and I refused to play my cello in public as a protest. Well, I hope it was not a futile gesture.

In 1950 my friends, especially Alexander Schneider, brought the world to me with the Prades Festival. That was a marvelous event in my life, and in the life-history of music too.

The Prades Festival brought Martita to me. Later, when I asked her to marry me, she accepted despite my age and her youth. That was the ultimate blessing of my life.

After the first Festival Casals in Puerto Rico, we moved there. Catalonia was my home, but somehow Puerto Rico was also my home. In 1957 my thoughts were only of life even though I was already ninety years old. But I felt that if I died in Puerto Rico I would be at home.

My last years were a pleasure, blessed by Martita and many honors, wonderful visitors and friends. But I worry about the human race. I am afraid that it will destroy itself and everything will have been for naught.

My small gesture was to compose the oratorio, *El Pesebre (The Manger)* and to contribute it to peace for mankind.

Well, finally I died in my ninety-seventh year in 1963. It concerns me that if mankind destroys itself there will be no more music in the world.

I AM ABRAHAM LINCOLN

I was born in 1809 to a family of poor farmers in Kentucky. It was a hand-to-mouth existence. The people around me were generally illiterate.

When I was three years old the family moved further west into the frontier of Indiana. This was a very difficult life in addition to the conditions of poverty. I have a memory of helping my father sow the seeds when he first broke ground, and then watching with him as torrents of rain washed all the seeds away. I wondered if that was how my life would be.

The winters were cold and hard and many people became ill. My mother took sick and died. My father went back to Kentucky and returned with a new wife who also had her own children. We grew to love each other, and she became a wonderful mother to me.

I grew to be tall and strong and developed a talent for wrestling and chopping wood. Once I pulled the trigger and killed a wild turkey, but I never did that again. I seemed to have a talent also for telling tall stories. Making people laugh was the pleasure I enjoyed most.

When I was in my late teens I got a job taking a cargo down the Mississippi River. That gave me a chance to see New Orleans with its different kinds of people and its activities, especially the slave market. It made me realize that there was a lot more in the world than a poor country boy knew about.

In 1832 the Black Hawks attacked and I enlisted in the army. My regiment elected me captain, but we were out again in a few months and saw no combat. That experience made me realize that it would be easy for me to win elections. So I thought more about politics after that.

I was defeated on my first try, but I was elected to the State Legislature in Illinois in 1834.

I thought I had found a girl for me in Anne Rutledge, but she died. This was a very troublesome event in my life. I thought about it for a long time.

I was re-elected to the Illinois Legislature in 1836 and I began to think that I could establish myself as a person with a family. I took steps to get a profession as a lawyer, and I started to look for a woman who would make a compatible wife.

Becoming a lawyer was easy. I had my license within a year. Immediately I went into partnership with John Stuart. This was the first of several law partnerships.

Finding a wife was more difficult and took longer. I am sure that has to do with my being a person who has difficult traits. I was with Mary Owens but that did not work. Then I was with Mary Todd and I almost married her, but I broke it off. Finally I did marry her in late 1842. I wanted a family, but it had taken me a long time to get one started.

A son, Robert, was born in 1843 and another, Edward, three years later.

I was establishing a family and I was supporting it with the profession of being a lawyer. I became very earnest about writing poetry, but I kept it private except to show to a few friends.

I was elected to Congress, but when the Mexican War was declared I submitted my "Spot Resolution" which very nearly put me out of politics forever. I was not re-elected.

Within a month at the turn of 1850-1851 a third son, William, was born and my father died.

In 1853 Tad, my fourth son, was born.

After my term in Congress I stepped back from politics. I turned my attention to building my practice as a lawyer, and I wrote more poetry. I was very devoted to my family, but my family life gave me some very difficult problems.

When the fight over the Kansas-Nebraska Bill became intense in the summer of 1854, I felt drawn to become active in politics again.

I began a series of many debates with Douglas which lasted through 1859. Twice the Illinois Legislature voted to send him to the Senate rather than me. In 1856 the Republican Convention turned me down for Vice-President. It was not a time of victory. But the Republicans sent me all over the country in 1856 and again from 1858 on. I gave a great many speeches, and I was glad to do so.

In early 1860 I gave several speeches on a tour of New England. And I gave my Cooper Union address in New York City. This was the time when I decided to try to become President.

After I was nominated in the summer of 1860 I stayed at home while other people campaigned for me. In those days it was not considered good manners to go out and promote yourself for office.

I was elected in November, 1860, but seven states had seceded by the time I was inaugurated in March. We had the trouble at Fort Sumter. Then Virginia seceded. Suddenly it looked very dark.

All of 1861 was a difficult year. Things became worse as they went along. Finally in early 1862 the worst thing of all happened. My little boy, Willie, became ill and died in the White House while I was struggling with the troubles of the country.

It was very difficult for me to absorb this death. I felt powerless in the face of a force in life that I did not understand. That was a time when all of my energies were very weak. I did not have mind enough to understand what had happened to Willie; yet I had to solve the question of slavery, hold the union together, and maintain a strategy that would win the war. For months after Willie died, I felt that the difficulties were more than I could handle. I could barely manage to show myself to the public. But somehow in that dark period answers were taking shape.

Eventually I came to the place where I could issue the Emancipation Proclamation in September 1862. I had been fearful of how the Southern States would react to this, and whether it would extend the war interminably. I had no question about slavery being wrong, but I had serious concerns about what a blanket emancipation would do. After struggling with the question in my dark time, it was finally resolved for me as a matter of military necessity.

The Emancipation Proclamation did not ease our troubles. A very difficult year followed. Finally by late 1863, we had the victory at Gettysburg and I could feel that the tide was turning; but we were still far from victory.

I was re-elected in 1864, but it was a very dangerous election. I had great fears that the Union would not survive it.

I was inaugurated for my second term and about a month later Lee surrendered. We were finally in a position to consider what to do about reconstruction when, a week after Lee's surrender, I was shot.

I AM ELEANOR ROOSEVELT

I was born in 1884 in New York City into a socially prominent family. My father was the brother of President Theodore Roosevelt. He had many personal troubles but I loved him and felt very close to him.

My mother was considered to be one of the great beauties of New York society. She nicknamed me "Granny" and caused me to feel as a child that I was ugly.

When I was seven years old my parents separated. When I was eight my mother died. When I was ten my father died. I was brought up by my grandmother Hall, my mother's mother.

After the separation my father wrote me letters that gave me hope we would have a future together. When he died he returned in my dreams and that continued for many years.

When I was fifteen I was sent to Allenswood, a private girls' school in England. Mlle. Souvestre, the headmistress, became a very important influence in my life. She gave me a sense of my intellectual capacity. Those three years were the happiest of my young life. When I was eighteen I returned to the United States and made my debut in New York society. It was an agony for me.

At nineteen I became engaged to my cousin, Franklin Roosevelt. After a year, in 1904, we married. Then he finished law school and took a job in a law firm in New York City.

I bore six children to Franklin in a period of ten years (1906-16). One of the children died of an infant disease.

During the early years of our marriage my mother-in-law ran our lives and our household.

During World War I, Franklin was Assistant Secretary of the Navy and we lived in Washington.

In 1919 I discovered that Franklin was having an affair with Lucy Mercer, my social secretary. I offered him his freedom, but when he promised that he would not see Lucy again we continued our marriage.

In August, 1921, Franklin caught polio and lost the use of his legs. Helping him regain the use of his legs became a major activity for me. While he was ill, also, I began to give political speeches to keep his name before the public.

When Franklin's strength was sufficiently restored, he gave the speeches again. Then I returned to a more quiet role in the background. In 1928 he became Governor of New York State.

In 1932 Franklin was elected President of the country and I became First Lady. I felt much trepidation during the time between the election and the inauguration, realizing that my days of privacy were at an end. As I became accustomed to my public position I took an increasingly active role in affairs, feeling that I had a responsibility to speak out for those who needed help. Soon, as the opposition to Franklin's policies built, I was made the butt of many of the anti-Roosevelt attacks.

When we entered World War II, I continued my activity, and increased it. But now we were united as a nation and I was not personally attacked. I tried to do as much as I could, traveling and providing a link between the family and the G.I.

In 1945 Franklin died with the War not quite over and much remaining to be done. The Peace still had to be arranged, and Franklin had worn himself out in the fighting. I now became the widow of a president who was revered even more outside of the U.S.A. than within it.

I was saved from the confusions of having nothing to do when President Truman appointed me to the American delegation to the United Nations. I was able to take an active role in it, especially in bringing about the Declaration of Human Rights. I hope that has some effect in future years.

When Eisenhower was elected I was retired from public office, but I managed to continue many of my old interests. In particular I traveled to many countries and spoke to heads of state.

Toward the end I became ill as I had never been before. I would have preferred to pass on more quickly than the doctors permitted. I had already had a long life and I did not appreciate the additional trouble. And so it went.

Chapter 8

The Focus Periods

Vertical and Horizontal Time

Now that we have made our listings both of the Primary and Extended Steppingstones, we are in a position to move deeper into the experiences of our person's life. In practice these two formats for working with the Steppingstones serve to balance each other. The Primary Steppingstones give us perspective and a sense of continuity that includes a person's subjective view of life. The Extended Steppingstones incorporate this and they add to it the facts that can objectively be seen as belonging to each of the periods of the life. This comes from the descriptions of the details of the life that are part of the Extended Steppingstones.

Together the two listings of Steppingstones give us a large view of an individual's life, but it is from the vantage point of only one aspect of time. Essentially the Steppingstones give us a chronological view of a person's life. They take us sequentially *through time* as though by a vertical movement of continuity that proceeds event after event. But there is also a horizontal aspect of human experience that expresses itself *across time*. We must take this into account also when we serve as Journal Trustee for another human life.

Our listing of the Steppingstones reflects the fact that the life of each person moves chronologically from one period or unit of life/time to the next. It is a sequential mode of experience. Pablo Casals, for example, proceeded from his rural childhood to his nascent musicianship, to his professional achievements, to his social activities, to his life in exile, and so on. Similarly the life of Eleanor Roosevelt moved through its Steppingstones from her troubled childhood to her awakened adolescence, to her years of householding, to her involvement with severe illness, to her political activities, and so on. These periods in their lives follow sequentially one after the other. In this sense they express a vertical continuity. At the same time, however, each extends over a length of time that may cover a number of years. This is because each period within a person's life is a unit that is framed by its own context of experience. In a sense it has its own life-span within the larger life of the person. Each *unit of life/time* has a beginning followed by a discernible time of development, then maturity followed by a time of waning, and finally a time of ending. This cycle comprises a full unit of life/time, and a person's life-span is formed by a series of these units, each with a different duration and a different interior pattern.

We draw these together in their chronological sequence when we list the Steppingstones as we work with them both subjectively and objectively in their Primary and Extended forms. The Steppingstones give us a vertical view of time, and they express this in terms of the total continuity of a person's life. We can balance this view and give ourselves a more nearly complete picture as well as a fuller access to our person's life by drawing out the details of the main units of life/time. It enables us to have a view of the horizontal movement of the life *across time* to supplement the vertical view that we draw from the Steppingstones. This is the next step that we take in our Life-Study.

The two listings of Steppingstones that we have made play an essential role in helping us take our next step. To begin, we sit in quietness with the Life-Study workbook open before us. Now we read back to ourselves the listing of Primary Steppingstones that we wrote. We read it back in silence, and then, without a pause, we turn to our Extended Steppingstones entry. Now we read that back to ourselves. We read the two back to ourselves one after another with no interruption between them. We re-read both of them once more, again with no pause between them.

After our second reading we turn to the Journal Trustee Log. This is the section that we use to record and also to develop our own thoughts and perceptions as we carry out our work of Life-Study. It is the place where we record our private cogitations and imaging and where we weigh the various considerations as we make our decisions for how we will proceed in our work as a Journal Trustee. We use the Journal Trustee Log in this way now.

Writing in the Journal Trustee Log, we record the perceptions that occurred to us as we were reading the two listings of Steppingstones. When we read them to ourselves one after another, we did not allow ourselves time to stop and think about our responses or observations or interpretations. We did not think of them consciously or deliberately, but perceptions were forming themselves within us nonetheless. They were forming themselves at the twilight level; therefore they were not intellectual interpretations but twilight perceptions. Now we recall them and we describe them as fully as we can in the Journal Trustee Log. We record the twilight thoughts that came to us while we were reading the two listings of Steppingstones. If images came to us at that time, we record them now as we are writing in the Journal Trustee Log. Presently, closing our eyes in the stillness, we let additional images take shape within us at the twilight level. And we record them here in the Journal Trustee Log.

Choosing Two Life/Time Units

The combination of thoughts and images, observations and perceptions that we have recorded in our Journal Trustee Log may constitute a considerable body of insights into the life of our person. Now we wish to draw upon it for a particular purpose. We recognize that each human life contains a succession of units of life/time. Each unit is a period within the full life span. Each contains its own integral structure of beginnings and developments and maturings and endings; each has its characteristic situations and events. As we move more deeply into the life for which we are Journal Trustee, we realize that one of the ways that we can make contact with the processes that carry the inner continuity of the life is by re-entering the life/time units and reconstructing the events that took place within them. But we cannot work in all the life/time units at one time. We therefore follow a mediating procedure in Life-Study that enables us to gather life-data that will set our active Journal work into motion. We choose two of the life/time units that seem to us to contain varied and significant data that are expressive of the life. And we concentrate our focus on them.

We call these two life/time units the *Focus Periods*. We direct our attention to them, drawing out the facts about that time in the life, exploring and elaborating the experiences that took place then, and beginning the practice of feeding the data from the parts of the life into the integrating process of Journal Feedback. These two Focus Periods play an important role in our Life-Study work because they give us our first substantial resource of data for use in our active procedures. They enable us to set the process into motion and they enable us to practice the basic techniques. For that reason it can be especially helpful for the later development of our Life-Study if we choose two Focus Periods that contain a varied and representational source of the data in the life for which we are Journal Trustee.

The criteria for the two Focus Periods that we choose now at the beginning of our work reflect the purpose for which we will use them. By directing our attention to the contents of two significant periods in the life we seek to provide the horizontal data that will balance and complement the vertical perspective of life/time that we draw from the Steppingstones. As much as possible, therefore, we try to choose periods whose contents are either characteristic of the life as a whole or where the events are discernible parts of a process that is found in other areas of the life as well.

It is usually helpful to choose as Focus Periods two units of life/time that our person felt was of particular significance. In this regard, times of transition can be especially rewarding in the material they provide for Life-Study because they lead us to the experiences that preceded the change, and they also lead us to the experiences that followed the change. In addition they give us access to the experiences of doubt and of searching through which the person passed while moving through the transition. Focus Periods that contain a time of change can have multiple uses and be of great value to us because of the variety of data implicit in their experiences. We can draw much from them.

It is interesting to note that while we may choose Focus Periods which our person felt was important, we cannot always trust the individual's judgment about his or her own life. Sometimes we find that the individual did not appreciate the significance of the events that were taking place at the time. We, on the other hand, having the advantage of retrospect, can know the importance of what was taking place then and we can also recognize the interior processes of change which the person could not be aware of at the time. The Focus Period that we choose need not be a time of particular success in the person's life, nor a time of dramatic failure either. In fact, the outer aspects of the period may not be important at all since we are seeking to reconstruct the continuity of the life as a whole—the inner thoughts and emotions as well as the external events, the high points equally with the low points. Our goal is to make Journal contact with all of these, but sometimes the dramatic events in a person's life can mislead us by drawing our attention away from the interior processes of which the events are only an outcropping. It is essential for us to bear in mind that the dramatic outer events in a person's life are usually part of a continuity of inner events that are active beneath the surface both before and after the outer event occurs.

When we are marking off the boundaries of a unit of life/time that we are planning to use as a Focus Period, it is important that we allow its length to be extensive enough to include the full process of what was taking place, the beginnings as well as the crystallizations. The number of years in a unit of life/time may vary greatly not only from person to person but with the circumstances and time in the life when the unit of experience occurs. The overlapping with other movements within the life may also be important to consider. Nonetheless, it is essential for us to remember that it is not only the exterior events that must be included in a Focus Period but also the interior events from which the outer events derive. As much as possible, we should let the boundaries of a Focus Period reach back in time sufficiently to encompass these sources in an inner process that we can identify.

If one is available to us, it is helpful to choose as a Focus Period a time during which several aspects of the life came together or were at work even though it may have been only in incomplete forms, particularly if it was a period of flux or transition. In this regard, times of uncertainty, times that were experienced in the midst of confusion, can make an especially valuable contribution to our Life-Study, for they enable us to make contact with and begin to draw out the inner processes that were moving beneath the surface of the life.

In general it is good to choose the two Focus Periods from different areas of the person's life. This not only provides a diversity of material but it enlarges our source of the data that express the continuity of inner process in an individual's life. If it is possible to do so, it is usually helpful to choose one Focus Period from an early time in the life and another from the later time. Since each life is unique, and since the relation of each Journal Trustee to his or her person is different from every other and is highly personal, we each have to make our own choice of the two Focus Periods on which we shall concentrate this next phase of our work. It is not primarily a question of psychological judgment but of personal feeling. This is where we begin to express and to shape the Journal Relationship that is building between ourselves and the person for whom we are a Journal Trustee.

Choosing Focus Periods from two different parts of a life, we may find striking parallels and patterns in some periods with the recurrence of similar situations, while there are vast differences and contrasts among the other periods. At this point in our Life-Study we are simply collecting the facts, taking note of them, and describing them as they come to us. When we choose the two periods on which we place our focus, we should not try to anticipate the kinds of events and experiences that we shall find there. We are entering now the detailed side of Life-Study. We should try to approach it with as open a mind as possible, as free as we can be from interpretive concepts, in order that the life-data of the person will be free to speak to us in their own terms.

All these factors and considerations come to us as we are reading back to ourselves the Primary and Extended Steppingstones. An increasing number of observations and responses occur to us as we are writing in the Journal Trustee Log. Numerous thoughts and images and awarenesses of possibilities are stimulated in us. One leads to another as we record them and as we develop them in the Journal Trustee Log. As we are writing, we let our varied thoughts and perceptions stimulate one another and lead on in a self-expanding way with respect to the life of the person we are studying. The content of these thoughts and considerations is without limitation here. It is whatever is called to our mind as needing further reflection. Some of these thoughts may be general in their scope; others may be specific, particularly those in which we seek to mark off the several life/time units that comprise the person's life. It is apparent that the writing we are now doing in the Journal Trustee Log is more than writing. It is a thinking through and an inner experiencing of the work that we are engaged in as a Journal Trustee. We are writing in a broad framework about the life that we are studying, considering the various aspects that are involved in our representing it. We are choosing the two Focus Periods with which to proceed, but we are also doing much more than that. We are exploring our personal concerns and the possibilities of our work as a Journal Trustee. This writing that we do in the Journal Trustee Log is like the tentative trial-and-error work that a craftsman does in the privacy of the workroom, trying this and testing that in order to see what fits and applies and works out best. This is the sense in which the Journal Trustee Log serves as the private workplace for our Life-Study.

Out of our general ruminations and explorations we come to some tentative conclusions as to what are the significant life/time units in the person's life. We are marking off several of them in our mind and in our Log writing. These are the inner divisions that we perceive in the life of the person we represent. Since it is usually true that the persons who are chosen as subjects for Life-Study are complicated individuals whose lives contain a number of phases and nuances, marking off their life/time units turns out not to be a simple matter by any means. We can therefore anticipate that many thoughts and feelings, together with a variety of images, will be stimulated in us as we give our attention to considering the aspects and possible divisions of the person's life. All of these, whatever their content, whether we feel that they are right or wrong, relevant or irrelevant, should be written in our journal Trustee Log. We should record all the perceptions, conscious and unconscious, that move within us now as we are considering that life, our directed thinking and our twilight thinking. We should record all of it without censoring, without eliminating, without editing any part of it. When we read it back to ourselves later on, if we have written it all without omission, we will be able to recognize threads in our thoughts that we can develop into the answers we need as our Journal Trustee work proceeds. We find very often that it is precisely the contents of those entries, which we would have left out if we were acting with careful intellectual judgment, that eventually make the greatest contribution to our understanding, since they open new lines of thought for us.

Writing in our Journal Trustee Log at this juncture serves the particular purpose of helping us choose the two Focus Periods on which we will concentrate the next phase of our Life-Study. It also is a time when we can practice the principles of the creative process in any area of artwork, in this case the artwork of Life-Study.

Naming the Focus Periods

When we have crystallized our decision in the Journal Trustee Log regarding the two life/time units that we choose as Focus Periods, our next step is to turn to the Period Log. This is the Journal section where we carry out the exercises that fill in the range of content comprising each of these periods as we prepare to give them our concentrated attention.

As we prepare to work in the Period Log section now in Life-Study, we should take note of the fact that when we are using the *Intensive Journal* workbook for our own life we use this section with a different type of procedure than we do in Life-Study. In our personal Journal work the Period Log serves as the section where we draw together our feelings and information with respect to the current situation in our life. It is the place where we describe the present period in our life, understanding the *present* in a flexible way that fits our private perception.* In Life-Study, however, the person for whom we are serving as Journal Trustee is not engaged in a present period. We thus have no occasion for using the Period Log in its usual way. We do, however, have the larger task of recapitulating the several periods, or life/time units, that comprise the whole life history of the person. In particular, when we are establishing the foundation of our work in Life-Study and are marking off the two Focus Periods, the Period Log is an appropriate section in which to carry out the several steps in that exercise.

Having identified the two Focus Periods with which we will work, our first step in the Period Log is to set up a separate sub-section for each. This means merely that we take a fresh sheet for each of the Focus Periods, and that we write a few words at the head of each sheet to indicate the general content of the period, something to indicate what period it is. And we also make a note of the date on which we are writing.

As soon as we can, we should give each Focus Period a specific

---

* See Ira Progoff, *At a Journal Workshop*, pp. 64–76, on the principles underlying the Period Log and the ways of working with it.

112

title. We should bear in mind, however, that for our purposes giving the period a title involves more than naming it. The title should convey something of the essence of the Focus Period. It should indicate what that time in the life meant to the person who lived it. The title should be such also that, at least by inference, it gives us a description of the scope of the period. The name should indicate the general contents of the events that were taking place there. As you continue to work with the contents of the Focus Period you may find that with increasing knowledge and insight you wish to refine the name or alter it. You may do that conveniently, especially in the early stages of your work. In that case the name you give a Focus Period at the beginning of your work with it serves as a general hypothesis regarding the events and experiences within it. If you use a provisional name at the beginning, you can adjust it flexibly until you have satisfied yourself that you have found an appropriate term with which to designate the period. Bear in mind that the appropriate name for a Focus Period has a number of useful functions as you proceed in working with the contents of your person's life. The name you choose should have a basic serviceable quality in that it indicates the general time range of the period by means of the contents and events to which it refers. You may wish to consider in this regard the names that are used in the illustrative material of this volume to indicate the Focus Periods with which we work.

For Pablo Casals: "Preparing for a Career"
                   "Exile in Prades"

For Eleanor Roosevelt: "Lucy and Polio"
                      "A Widow and a Person"

For Abraham Lincoln: "Becoming a Family Man"
                     "President in a Civil War"

Chapter 9

Overview Statements

When we have chosen a title and have written it at the head of the sub-section for the focus period, we write a brief descriptive statement that indicates the scope of the events that took place during that time. We wish to give an overview of the period that will indicate the issues, the circumstances, the choices and decisions, and the major events that took place. Sometimes in this brief description we can show how this life/time unit served as a link that connected the period preceding it with events that were to come. In this regard, when we write our overview statement for the focus period we have the benefit of the hindsight of knowing the eventual course and outcome of the life as a whole. In this case, having a retrospective view is a benefit that we can use to good advantage, for it gives us a context of life in which we can place the period. We should indicate this perspective in our overview statement. It is one of the helpful aspects of the fact that, as Journal Trustees, we are carrying out our Life-Study from a point in time just after the death of the person we represent.

The Overview Statement of the focus period that we now write should be brief, no more than a medium-sized paragraph. It should give us an overview of the period, in the context of the life as a whole, referring to its outcome as well as its beginnings. The statement should say just enough to identify the life/time unit, to tell us what was most important in it, and to establish its atmosphere.

As we prepare to write the statement we let ourselves sit in quietness and feel the quality of the period we are expressing. It is as though we are there and have been there through the movement of the entire period. We are telling about a piece of our life as we experienced it in the context of the whole of our life.

For each person and each period the tone and range of an Overview Statement is different. The content of the statement and the mood in which it is presented derive not from an external model but from the feelings that we experience when we place ourselves within the period. It is important to repeat this to ourselves in order that we give full credit to our own individuality as we write the Overview Statement for each Focus Period in which we are working.

We bear in mind that each Overview Statement is to be written from the point of view of our own experiences and perceptions of the life. The following examples are taken from Life-Study Journals.

From the Life-Study Journals

PABLO CASALS

For the Focus Period, *Preparing for a Career*

I have always known I am a musician. From the time that my father first began to teach me, it was clear that I had a talent. The question was whether I could have a public career and earn my living at music. My father was negative because of his own painful experience. But my mother had vision and faith, and she took control of forming my career. Despite our poverty she struggled with determination and guided me with uncanny intuitions. She risked everything, a poor woman at one point contradicting the Queen of Spain, but she was right. Sometimes I think that the way it all happened had more meaning than the music itself.

For the Focus Period, *Exile in Prades*

My time in Prades was really not one exile but two. The first was because of necessity, the second was because of principle, which was a necessity also. But what a terrible irony. It started with me and my countrymen barely escaping from Spain with our lives and then living in despair and deprivation while the totalitarian countries increased their power. Things went from bad to worse and then the tide turned and the democracies won the war. But Spain was betrayed once again when World War II was over. The democracies allowed fascism to continue and I had to continue my exile in Prades as a protest, even if it was the ineffectual act of one insignificant person. From the personal side this double exile ended much better than it began. It began with suffering when I was already well into the second half of my life. And it ended with the Festivals at Prades and with me in my old age going off to Puerto Rico to marry Martita. Yes, it ended much better than it started. But at that point I had only a few years to live.

ABRAHAM LINCOLN

For the Focus Period, *Becoming a Family Man*

This was a period in my life when I tried to establish myself. Previously I had been convinced that I could at least become somebody. Being in the State Legislature helped my feeling of myself. What I wanted was a family. I had hoped for that, and now I took steps to achieve it. But things often turn out to be different from what you had planned.

For the Focus Period, *President in a Civil War*

When this period began I was only offering myself to help solve a problem that had arisen between two groups of good people. I felt that chance and my several weaknesses had placed me in a position to be of help. I think that proved to be a correct judgment. The very fact that I could be elected showed that I could be a mediator. But there were some things that could not be compromised; and the situation itself turned out to be much more complicated and difficult than I had anticipated. The leaders of the Confederacy acted with plans that had been carefully thought through while we in the Union had not been thinking in terms of war. And I had very great difficulty in finding the right generals. The problems of the war became such that I realized that I could not control it. That was when I became reconciled to the fact that whatever happened was in the hands of God. When I died it was no different from when thousands of others had died anonymously on both sides. I probably was spared the most difficult problems.

ELEANOR ROOSEVELT

For the Focus Period, *Lucy and Polio*

This was the time when I faced one difficult life decision after another. After lulling myself into the thought that I had a secure marriage, I found out by accident that my social secretary was having an affair with my husband. My first impulse was to dissolve the marriage, but there were other factors to be considered. After Franklin promised that he would not see Lucy again, I agreed to continue in the marriage. We spent a quiet few years and then, on a family summer vacation, Franklin contracted polio. It was a serious case and we knew that at least some paralysis would be the result. The question was how much and what could be done about it. Franklin's mother wanted him to go back to Hyde

Park and become a country squire. To me, however, this would be a living death. Franklin agreed with me from his own point of view, considering the political plans he had been nurturing, and together we worked to save what physical abilities we could and to maintain as much as possible of his active political life. This led to a special kind of closeness between us as well as to other unexpected developments in my life.

For the Focus Period, *A Widow and a Person*

Franklin's death was a sign to me that I was coming to the end of my own life. However many years might remain to me, I felt that I was entering the closing period. The sense of loss that this gave me was overwhelming at first, but it was followed by a feeling of freedom as I realized that now I had nothing further to lose. In the years that remained to me I could be myself, and increasingly I saw that the United Nations appointment gave me that opportunity. Being myself also meant doing whatever I could to strengthen the goals and the lastingness of Franklin's work. I had a place in the world because I was Franklin's widow, and I never forgot that. But I also was myself. I could speak and act on my own behalf without being concerned about what other people, especially the political people, wanted me to do. I was able to accomplish a great deal in my work at the United Nations and in my travels to other countries, but in the end the political realities prevailed. When the Republican administration took office in 1952 this period in my life was brought effectively to an end.

Chapter 10

The Open Moment Image

Twilight Envisioning at the Start of a Period

Having chosen two Focus Periods and having written an Overview Statement for each of them, we are ready now to do the exercises that are at the heart of Life-Study. From the several life/time units in the life of our person we have chosen two on which we will focus our detailed attention. We have established a place for each of these Focus Periods by opening separate sub-sections for them in the Period Log section of the workbook. Our next step is to reconstruct these periods by filling in and describing the main events that took place within them and their other significant contents. To begin, however, we do not work in the Period Log but in another Journal section, *Now: the Open Moment*.

This Journal section is one that we adapt from our personal use of the *Intensive Journal* process. We use it with different exercises here since it serves a different function in Life-Study. When we are applying the *Intensive Journal* process to our own lives, we use *Now: the Open Moment* to give us a perception at the twilight level of the prospects we have before us in our life as we move into the future. In basic *Intensive Journal* work the main use of this section occurs at the close of a Life Context workshop when we have been engaged in examining closely the recent period in our life. At that point we need a means of drawing together the varied thoughts and feelings that have been stimulated in the course of the workshop since we are getting ready then to make the transition from the present time in our life, which has been the content of our workshop, to our future, which begins as soon as the workshop is over.

When we are at a juncture in our lives, a time of transition or of decision, it can be especially helpful to have a vision of the possibilities of the future that may lie ahead of us. It is important, however, that these actually be *envisionings* and not merely thoughts or mental anticipations. There is an essential difference between envisionings of the future that come by means of imagery at the twilight level and the twilight thinking that may express our anxieties, or alternatively, our hopes. Conscious anticipations can go in circles at the surface of the psyche. But perceptions that come to us in the twilight range can be reflections of the organic process that is seeking to unfold at the seed level of our life. For that reason they can give us an authentic glimpse of the future. We have to remember, however, that perceptions that come by envisioning are symbolic and that we are not to take them at face value. They are not literal predictions, but they can contribute a valuable input to the Journal Feedback process that gives tangible material for the future.

The twilight perceptions that we have in *Now: the Open Moment* have two important qualities. The first is that they are symbolic. The second is that they lend themselves to being used as feed-in material for the Journal Feedback process.

Since the twilight perceptions come to us by imagery, they are symbolic. This means, in the simplest terms, that these perceptions are not actually what they seem to be. Being symbolic, they are referring, or pointing, to something other than what they themselves are. But what they are pointing toward is kept hidden, and is left for us to find out. That is the nature of symbols. The images that we perceive at the twilight level, being symbolic, are not to be understood as being predictive statements about the future but rather as *indications of events that are being formed* and that are now being expressed and represented at a deeper-than-conscious level. That we are able to perceive them and that we know we are to give them serious attention is a contribution of depth psychology; that we can recognize their constructive, formative function at the organic level of our life is a result of *holistic* depth psychology; and that we have a method for integrating these non-conscious factors into the unfolding wholeness of our life is an expression of the *Intensive Journal* process.

In working with this material the main question is for us to find out what the symbolic contents of our twilight imagery are pointing toward. The answer is primarily operational in the sense that it is not a fixed answer but a movement in the direction of an answer which will, in its turn, lead to still another answer. As we feed our symbolic data into the various aspects of the Journal Feedback exercises, we begin to see where the movement of our life is trying to go. One means by which we do this in our personal Journal work is by following the *leads* that come to us through our symbolic experiences. The exercises that we carry out in the *Now: the Open Moment* section are one source of these leads. We use them especially at the close of a Life Context workshop, or whenever we have reason personally to bridge the present and the future in our lives. We seek to place ourselves then in the twilight range of perception, and we let the organic movement of life/time within us disclose itself in a symbolic form.

In Life-Study, as in our personal Journal work, the exercises for the *Now: the Open Moment* section are best carried out at the twilight level. For the purposes of Life-Study, however, we do not use this section at the close of a workshop experience or when we are leaving a unit of life/time. We use it rather to help us enter a new period in the life of the person for whom we are Journal Trustee. This procedure reflects the conception of life/time that is one of the fundamental principles in the *Intensive Journal* process. In the flow of human experience, the point where two periods or units of life/time come together presents an open moment of possibility. At that point the events of the future are still in a formative stage. When events are perceived at that point in their development, they are not being seen in their completeness but in their process as they are moving out of their past into their future. Aspects of this transition are shown to us in the twilight range of consciousness. They are reflected to us at a subliminal level in symbolic forms. That is the imagery of the open moment of transition as it is expressed in life/time. We experience it when we are at the twilight level of consciousness in a receptive mode that allows events to reflect themselves within us. In order for this to happen, we do of course need to be quiet within ourselves, quiet as a mirror is quiet, so that this reflection can take place fully. But there are degrees of twilight perception. We can experience it to a degree that is relative to our inner condition when we are moving personally from the present period of our life into our future, as at the close of an *Intensive Journal* Life Context workshop. And we can experience it in another form in Life-Study when we are preparing to enter a life/time unit in our person's life. That point of entry is a transition in time, and therefore it holds the possibility of being an *open moment* of experience. To reach it we place ourselves in the twilight range of perception, and we let that new Focus Period present itself to us in symbolic forms, in whatever style of imagery it chooses. Thus we gain entry by means of the Open Moment imagery to a period in the life of the person for whom we are Journal Trustee.

This experience of Open Moment imagery that takes place at the twilight level gives us a means of entering a life/time unit. Since we make no judgment of what we find there—and particularly since we restrain ourselves from interpreting or diagnosing the symbolism—it is a neutral means of entry. And since it takes place at a deeper-than-conscious level, it provides an intuitive way of perceiving the contents of the person's life. It places us on the inside of events as they are being formed in the flow of life. Since they are reflected to us in the form of imagery, it is especially important for us to remember that the perceptions we have are symbolic and not literal. The difficulty is that most of us are habituated to believe that things are what they seem to be. Not so. Not so on the outer level of life; still less so on the twilight level.

We use Open Moment imagery as our means of entering each of the Focus Periods with which we are working as a Journal Trustee. We enter each period separately, one at a time. In the subsection that we have set up for it in the Period Log we shall carry out the detailed work of reconstructing the contents of the Focus Period. We have already written its name and its Overview Statement there. For our next experience, however, we move to another section, to the *Now: the Open Moment* section. The work we do here will be in the Twilight Range, and we will describe the imagery that comes to us on the page that we have marked off for it in the *Now: the Open Moment* section. After we have made our entry here we will return to the Period Log to continue our detailed reconstruction of the life/time unit.

We open our workbook to the *Now: the Open Moment* section. At the top of a fresh page we write the name we have given to the Focus Period that we are now preparing to enter. And we write today's date.

Now we sit in stillness. We close our eyes. As the silence deepens, we let ourselves slide inward, back to the point in time when that life/time unit was beginning. We think back in our minds to the events that were actually taking place at that time. As best we can, we let ourselves feel and be in the midst of the context of circumstances as they were at the opening of that period in our person's life. As Journal Trustee we are there on their behalf, and we record in the first person whatever we experience for them. We are there as they were—but our experience takes place in the twilight range. We are there not in memory, and not in actuality, but at the twilight level of perception.

As the silence deepens we are in the atmosphere of the twilight range. We feel ourselves to be in the situation our person was in. We are perceiving their life now as they did at the beginning of that period. At that time they did not know what lay ahead of

123

them, and we now experience their situation with the same unknowing. We are there as they were, and that movement of life/
time of which they were then *on the verge* is reflected to us now in
the form of imagery. The prospective development of their life is
presented to us in symbolic forms by the mode of envisioning.
The various aspects of it are reflected to us in the form of images,
feelings, intuitions, subliminal perceptions of many kinds. Whatever we perceive we take note of and we record, without editing
or censoring, in the *Now: the Open Moment* section.

From the Life-Study Journals

PABLO CASALS

For the Focus Period, *Preparing for a Career*

I see myself as a young boy, perhaps eleven or twelve years
old. I am talking with a man who has a black beard. He is in
charge of an auditorium where a large audience is already filling
the seats. I say to him, "Please let me play." He says, "All right,
go ahead if you want to." Then my hand begins to shake. I find
myself on stage at the center. I am to perform, but I cannot remember the first notes of the piece. I just sit there. Suddenly the
image is different. I am standing on a high box looking over a
podium so that the musicians can see me. I hear someone say,
"Just wait till he is tall enough." I know that my time will come.

For the Focus Period, *Exile in Prades*

I see myself in a country place with many people milling
about. They seem to be confused, not sure of where to go. I am
led into a small cottage where it is warm, but the other people
have to stay outside where it is raining. I sit down on a plain

124

wooden chair. I realize that I shall now have to live in exile here in France under the heel of Hitler. I shall be lucky to survive; but surviving may not even be worth while. I see heavy black clouds blowing in over the mountains. It is about to become very dark. There is a feeling of foreboding. When Franco took power, I did not believe that fascism could last. Now the question is: Can I last? I don't know. But I do know that I must not give up.

ABRAHAM LINCOLN

For the Focus Period, *Becoming a Family Man*

I see a tall thin young man dressed in a business suit sitting on a wooden chair under a tree. The chair is tilted at an angle against the tree. There is a government-type building in the background. The young man's black hat is on his lap. His eyes are closed. He is talking to himself.

"Not much to start with. No social background. No profession. But I do get along with people. Plain people like me. Politicking may be a good way to go. I am here at the State Capitol. And what do I want? I want to have a house that shows that someone who matters lives there; I want a woman to care for it and give it quality; I want to have children. A house and a woman and children will be the sign that Abraham Lincoln has lived and has lived there."

For the Focus Period, *President in a Civil War*

I am sitting in the Congregation at Beecher's Plymouth Church in Brooklyn. Beecher speaks the truth. I know that as I hear him. But it is necessary also to soften the truth, to balance it for those who are not able to accept a single version of what is ultimately true. That must be why God needs servants. God requires mediators to carry out his difficult tasks. Where people are widely apart and obstinate, a mediator is required, perhaps to take the blows of both. Those are God's servants, but it is never for the glory of the servant. It is to carry out a task. If it needs to be done, it needs to be done. If I can do it, I shall do it. Beecher is right about what this country needs, and why God has placed us in this New World. Then I shall offer myself for President, and if it is in the plan of things, so shall it be.

ELEANOR ROOSEVELT

For the Focus Period, *Lucy and Polio*

I see a young woman with an apron around her. She is in her kitchen. Small children are eating bread and jam and drinking milk that she has given them. They are happy and harmonious together. The young mother has a sweet round face, prettier than I ever was. Suddenly there is thunder and lightning and heavy rain. And in the midst of the rain a part of the house is on fire. What shall I do? Who will help me take care of the children? I am in a panic when I hear the fire engines coming. Then an ambulance. I feel that help is here and that I am out of danger. Then the ambulance is opened and they are carrying my husband in on a stretcher. But the house is still on fire. They carry him into a wing of the house that is not burning while the firemen are putting out the fire on the other side. I call the children together and we begin to take care of my husband.

For the Focus Period, *A Widow and a Person*

I see a man sitting with a woman. He is very tired. A cloud covers him and he is gone.

I see myself boarding a ship. A younger man is carrying my brief case but I take it away from him and carry it myself.

I am at a large meeting where I am being called upon to give a speech. Now I am sitting on a deck chair on a ship and I am writing. There is a feeling of tranquility and relaxation as the image ends.

Chapter 11

Signpost Events

The Unfoldment of a Life/Time Unit

We placed ourselves in the twilight range in order to have the experience of an Open Moment image by which we could enter a Focus Period. We recorded that image in the Journal section for *Now: the Open Moment*. It is there for whenever we have reason to refer to it, but we keep it separate from our other descriptions of the contents of this Focus Period. Now we return to the subsection in the Period Log that we have set aside for this unit of time in our person's life. This is the sub-section that contains the Overview Statement that we wrote for this Focus Period.

With our imagery experience we turned our attention inward. We now turn our attention outward to the specific occurrences that took place during that life/time unit. As we proceed in our Life-Study we will want to explore many of the details of this period, especially to see how they fit together with other aspects of the life as a whole. At this point, however, in order to give ourselves a framework for this Focus Period, we take the first step of recapitulating the main events that occurred during this time. We draw together the various happenings that comprise the continuity of movement within this life/time unit, and we mark off the main ones that indicate shifts or changes in the main line of development. These are the Signpost Events. We list them in sequence in order to present to ourselves in brief scope the continuity of the period. Earlier in our Life-Study when we worked with the Steppingstones, first the Primary and then the Extended Steppingstones, we were seeking to give ourselves a perspective in which to reconstruct the person's whole span of life. At this time we are focusing more specifically on particular units of life/time. The Signpost Events are the markers that enable us to get our bearings. With them we can identify the contents and the issues that have had the major effects within the time-frame. In drawing these together now we are placing ourselves in the atmosphere of that period in the life.

A good way to approach the listing of the Signpost Events in a Focus Period is by setting the question to ourselves: What was the event that marked the beginning of that life/time unit? We often find that the Signpost Event that answers that question is also a significant Steppingstone in the life as a whole. When you recall that first event, it will very likely lead you to others that are not as important in themselves as the main Signpost Event, but that derive from it and are integral parts of the situation at the time. Let yourself recall as many of these derivative events as you can. List them and describe as many of their details as you have available.

By answering the question that identifies the first Signpost Event in the period you place yourself in the movement of that part of the person's life. Now you can let the sequence of further events unfold. As one event leads to another, you can retrace the sequence of developments in that period of time. In your first spontaneous listing of the Signpost Events a gap may remain here and there. That will not matter since your first purpose is to establish the context of movement in the period as a whole. You can fill in the gaps at a later time.

In marking off the Signpost Events we may use a concise phrase to identify particular occurrences, but the description of the event can be as extended as we require. Recalling the events and describing them in the first person as a Journal Trustee, we can feel free to experience as much of each original emotion as we can, expressing the feelings and the thoughts that accompany them in what we write.

In elaborating the Signpost Events it is better to be expansive and to say more rather than less. Do not restrict yourself here, but encourage the flow of detail. In this way you may draw a great deal more life-data into the Journal process. As you proceed in Life-Study you will increasingly find—often much to your surprise—that you know more about the life for which you are Journal Trustee than you thought you knew. It seems to be common for many of us to seem to forget but actually to retain small bits of information about another person's life, just as we do with our own. The bits of information are there but they do not show at the surface. They do, however, come to the fore in increasing numbers once we loosen the flow and set things in motion.

You can feed a great deal of material into your Life-Study in the course of enlarging the descriptions of the Signpost Events. Much of it will come indirectly, being drawn in as details that are incidental to the re-telling of the main occurrences. But the effect of these details is cumulative, and they all contribute to the process that places you inside the life of the person whom you represent. In extending your discussions of the Signpost Events, especially in describing the backgrounds and the incidental circumstances, you will often draw on information that you possess regarding the life but that you would otherwise not think of mentioning. Bringing it forth and writing it, however, adds to the material that is consciously available to you, and it enlarges the resources for your Life-Study.

It is essential in our describing these Signpost Events that we understand the circumstances that were in the background of the events when they happened. Whatever they may be, we describe them as fully as we can. As much as possible we reconstruct the events as though we ourselves were participants. We do not make judgments as an outsider; but we write as an insider describing the situation from within.

When you reconstruct the sequence of Signpost Events in a Focus Period, take note of what started the life/time unit. That first question, following upon the Open Moment image, will help you draw together the data for that period in the life. As you proceed you may find that you describe some events in great detail while you mention others only briefly, as though just in passing. It is good to have them all noted in the record, however, even if you say very little at the time of your first writing. Additional details may occur to you at a later time, and you can add them then as you continue your Life-Study.

From the Life-Study Journals

PABLO CASALS

For the Focus Period, *Preparing for a Career*

When I had repeatedly demonstrated my love of the cello and my talent for playing it, my mother determined that she would take me to Barcelona where I could find a teacher competent to teach me more. My father opposed this step as being impractical, but my mother had her way. Thus the first Signpost Event, the one that opened this period in my life, was my move with my mother from Vendrell to Barcelona. My father then visited us every weekend, or whenever he could.

In Barcelona I was able to study with a wonderful teacher, Josef Garcia.

I had my first professional jobs playing in cafés. I attracted some public attention, being called "the little one," and some famous musicians like Isaac Albeniz became interested in me.

Probably the most important event, although it was very painful, was the fact that around this time I went into a deep depression and I had thoughts of suicide. I came out of it, thanks to my mother's perceptiveness, which led to our starting a new phase of life in Madrid. But that was the first time when I asked within myself the fundamental questions about the meaning of life. Those serious thoughts, the questions and the issues that they raised, never left me. These are questions of religion that I shared later with the monks at Montserrat and they were expressed later on in my political life as well. These experiences may be the source of my feelings about integrity and my acting on behalf of all human beings. In my youth when I became depressed it was because I did not want to live a life that was not worth living. And I was becoming convinced that that would be my fate. As things turned out that was not my fate at all. But all the same, the events of my life were often very difficult and painful. I did not realize it at the time, but I really chose it that way.

The next major event was our move from Barcelona to Madrid, leaving my father in Vendrell. This was altogether my mother's decision. Seeing that I had become depressed in Barcelona despite my success there, she decided to make use of a letter of introduction from Albeniz to Count de Morphy. She had been holding that letter for more than two years, but she had refused to use it until she felt that exactly the right time had come. We went to Madrid, and there Morphy became my teacher in history, philosophy, art, everything. He also became my link to the Royal Family, and this led to my being sponsored by the Queen Regent and receiving a scholarship which enabled me to have further music lessons.

I was doing very well at the Court when my mother decided that it was time to make another move. She thought that the time had come for me to establish myself as a cellist. At the Court they were interested in developing Spanish opera, and it seems that they saw me as a possible composer, but my mother saw me as a cellist. Thus we moved on. We went to Paris. Since Morphy and the Queen Regent did not agree with this move, I lost my scholarship. As a result we endured many difficulties in Paris, including poverty and my illness, and we had to return to Barcelona.

At first I felt that I had failed, but suddenly my fortunes changed. My former teacher, Garcia, left Barcelona to live in South America, and I inherited his several positions as cellist and teacher. This was the turning point for me. A great many opportunities came my way, and soon I was able to return to Paris as an established cellist. But this time I went without my mother, who had made it all possible.

For the Focus Period, *Exile in Prades*

This period started in my life when it became clear that the unbelievable was happening. Franco's armies were actually taking over Barcelona. There was nothing to do but to try to escape. I became a refugee from my own country with thousands of other persons, most of whom were in a much more pitiable state than I was.

The main camps for the Spanish refugees were established in the southern part of France. I went there hoping to help and to see what would happen next. I was able to find a place in a cottage with my friend Alevedra and his family.

Many people advised me to go to the United States since I had a number of invitations promising me large amounts of money for concerts. But I felt that I should stay with the other refugees and help as best I could. When word came that Hitler was taking Paris, however, I agreed that it would be best for me to go. Alevedra booked passage on a boat, the Champlain, which we were to board at Bordeaux. We made the difficult trip by land, but when we arrived at the dock we were told that the Champlain had been bombed at sea. So there was no trip to the United States. I took that to be a sign that I was to remain in Prades. So when I returned to Prades it was with the intention of remaining there for the duration of the war.

I gradually settled into the quiet of this country part of France, trying to make the best of a bad situation and waiting for the war to end.

One day during the German occupation some German officers came to my house and said that I was invited to go to Germany to play for Hitler. I immediately said, "No," that I would not do that. Fortunately they accepted my refusal without retaliation and

I was able to continue living as I had been. I was told that my name was on a list. But the war ended before anything else happened.

After the war ended I gradually realized that the western powers had no intention of restoring the Spanish Republic. I decided then not to play in public until the Republic was re-established. Of course my small protest did not change the politics of nations. It did mean, however, that I continued to be an exile in Prades after the war was over.

I continued to refuse to go to the United States to do concerts but finally Alexander Schneider and Mieczyslaw Horszowski had the idea of having a Bach festival in Prades. I agreed to participate. It became an annual event and its effect was to bring at least part of the world to me in my exile. But I did not leave Prades.

In the course of the Prades festivals, Martita, the light of my later years, came to me first as a student and then became my wife. When she agreed to marry me in spite of our difference in age, we left Prades for Puerto Rico.

ABRAHAM LINCOLN

For the Focus Period, *Becoming a Family Man*

When Anne Rutledge died I felt that I would never have a happy relationship with a woman. I had been able to talk about my writing with her, but now that was over. I felt that a part of myself had died.

Being re-elected to the State Legislature gave me confidence in myself. I thought I could amount to something and have an interesting life after all.

Since political office is not a livelihood in itself, I took the step of becoming a lawyer.

I tried to find a wife but that presented problems.

Finally I married Mary Todd, although I had many qualms and misgivings about it.

It soon became very unpleasant for me to be at home with her, and that may have stimulated me to travel and practice in the courts around the circuit.

My life was not happy but my practice of law prospered.

My sons were born one by one, and I found a great pleasure in them as long as they lived.

For the Focus Period, *President in a Civil War*

The Republican Party sent me on a speaking tour of New England in early 1860. The more I talked with people, the more I saw the historic proportions of what we were doing. I realized that circumstances were placing me in a position to do something of consequence.

Passing through Brooklyn, I stopped to hear Henry Ward Beecher give a sermon at his church. I was deeply moved, and it was then that I decided to do what I could, whatever it cost me. If I could resolve the problem by becoming President, I would try.

Once I made the decision, events fell into place. I was nominated with a reasonable expectation of winning.

I was elected but the victory was immediately soured by the secession of the Southern states. I was a President with half a country.

The realization that we were actually in a civil war was a major event in itself. At first I thought, as many did, that we would avoid full–scale fighting. Only gradually did I recognize that we were involved in a full war and that it would take a while to win it.

The first half of the war with its setbacks was a very difficult time. It became apparent that not only were we unable to put down the rebellion quickly but we might actually lose. The possibility that the Union might be destroyed had a numbing effect on my heart. It was a terrible feeling.

In the midst of all my troubles and woes on behalf of the country, my boy Willie died suddenly of a terrible illness. That was a time of darkest despair for me. It was a terrible time for Mary, too. Everything made her life difficult, both outside and inside.

Finally in the Battle of Gettysburg we received a sign that the tide of the war had turned. It was an awesome feeling, as I said in the speech I gave on the battlefield there. After that a strength grew in me as I was convinced that we would eventually win the war.

Any remaining doubts I may have had were overcome when I was re-elected. That was a good time. I felt affirmed and confident that I could complete the task.

The signing of the Peace was like a great sigh of relief. At last it was done. But I had uneven feelings because I knew that the Peace did not finish the work, and that the really difficult tasks remained ahead.

Suddenly they shot me. No, I did not want to be relieved of my duties even though I was weary of them.

They shot me. Just when I was renewing my strength with many hopes, events came to a sudden and abrupt close.

ELEANOR ROOSEVELT

For the Focus Period, *Lucy and Polio*

I was performing a wifely chore of unpacking my husband's bags when he had returned ill with pneumonia from a trip to Europe for the Navy. In the luggage I found a package of letters which were not from me but from my social secretary, Lucy Mercer. I could not help but read them, and that was how I discovered that they had been having a love affair.

After very emotional discussions in which Franklin's mother took a very active role, I agreed to continue the marriage. It was condiditional, however, on Franklin's promise that he would not see Lucy any more. Despite the agreement I felt that the bottom had fallen out of my world.

We continued to live in Washington, D.C. since Franklin still worked for the Navy. In Washington I found myself visiting Rock Creek Cemetery several times and going to the grave of Henry

Adams' wife who had committed suicide during a time of depression. There was a statue by Saint-Gaudens at her grave which spoke to me not only of great inner pain but also of the possibility of transcending pain in one's lifetime. I wondered whether I could ever achieve an inner peace.

While we were on summer vacation in Campobello in 1921 Franklin was taken ill, and we soon realized that it was polio. The paralysis became marked. His illness became the focus of all the family's activities.

Once the illness itself was stabilized, we had a major decision facing us. Should Franklin accept his physical limitations and arrange to live a limited and protected life? Or should he undertake the difficult and painful exercises that would rebuild some of his muscles and enable him to resume an active role? His mother strongly favored the first course. She wanted him to retire as a country squire to Hyde Park. I thought that would be a living death, and instead I favored doing whatever we could to resume an active life. Franklin agreed with me. This was a most important decision for both of us. It called for a great deal of courage on his part, and also a close cooperation by the two of us.

Together with the doctors, Franklin and I worked out a strenuous program to rebuild Franklin's physical capacities and return him to the world. This called for a great deal of strength of will and courage on Franklin's part, but it was not only difficult but very painful for him. We worked together toward the goal we had set. I tried very hard to do my part.

Franklin's political associate, Louis Howe, not only supported me in carrying out the physical therapy, but he had a plan that would retain Franklin's position in the political world. It called for me to step in for Franklin and keep his name in front of the public until his physical strength was sufficiently recovered. This required me to be active in political affairs in a way of which I did not feel I was capable. I gave some terrible speeches at first, but Louis advised and helped me, and soon I discovered that I possessed abilities that I had not suspected I had. We followed the plan that Louis Howe had developed and it worked very well, in some ways better than we could possibly have imagined.

By the time the 1928 political season arrived, we had another major decision to make. But this decision was all Franklin's. His name and position were strong in the New York State Democratic Party, and with Al Smith running for the Presidency, Franklin could become a candidate for the Governorship with a very good chance of winning. The decision he now had to make was whether to continue giving his primary energies to recovering more of his physical strength or whether to accept the progress he had made as the limit of what he could achieve physically and now turn his attention to achievements in other areas of life. It was his decision, and he decided that this was the time to resume an active political role. He chose therefore to run for the Governorship of New York State. It was a fateful decision not only for his life and mine but, as events turned out, for the country and the world as well.

Franklin's decision to run for the governorship was a signal that he was back in the world. It was a signal to me to step back from what I had been doing, that my active political work to keep his name alive while he was recovering his health, was now completed. My public activity was not needed any more, at least not in the same way and with the same intensity. I did not mind the change. In fact, I was happy to see that Franklin had returned to his previous enthusiasm for life, and I felt that I could now enjoy my privacy once more. When Franklin went to the National Democratic Convention in Houston to give his "Happy Warrior" speech nominating Al Smith, I was glad to remain in New York while two of our sons went with him.

For the Focus Period, *A Widow and a Person*

The death of Franklin in 1945 when victory in the war was close but had not yet been achieved changed the course of events not only for me personally but for the whole world.

The personal blow was particularly heavy for me when I

learned that he was not alone in Warm Springs at the time of his death, but was with Lucy Mercer.

After my move from the White House was completed, I was ready to retire into widowhood with very moderate activity when President Truman offered me the opportunity to serve on the first delegation to the United Nations.

The work on the Human Rights Commission leading to the Declaration of Human Rights then absorbed my mind and energies and became a major event in my life.

While I sought peace and accommodation with the Russians in my work at the United Nations, I was caught up in the Cold War maneuvering. I found out in my own experience how difficult the Russian diplomats can be.

I was concerned about the drift of events by the time the election of 1948 came around. I stayed with Harry Truman, however.

My United Nations work continued and I was able to add public lecturing and column writing to my activities. But I encountered some difficulties when I attempted to conduct radio and television programs together with some of my children.

In 1952 I had a wonderful experience in visiting India, but it exhausted me. In the end I was depressed by my experience there.

In 1946 I had rejected attempts to have me run for the Senate in New York State. Now, as there was uncertainty before the 1952 nominations, I had to do the same with respect to my becoming a candidate for the Democratic nomination for the Presidency or the Vice-Presidency. I said "No" firmly. It was not a difficult decision for me to make.

As soon as Eisenhower was elected, I offered him my resignation from my post at the United Nations. He accepted it, and this closed the period of my public service.

Chapter 12

Reconstructing a Focus Period

Setting a Base for Journal Feedback

By recapitulating in sequence the Signpost Events of a period we are able to identify the continuity of movement that is taking place beneath the surface of events. It enables us as Journal Trustees to share the experience of the main occurrences at that time; and thus we can feel the rhythms of change and development that took place then. In this way we build our inner perspective of the life and we form within ourselves a feeling of empathy for our persons as they were confronting the successive circumstances of their existence.

In the framework of concepts that underlies the *Intensive Journal* method, each of these units is seen as a unit of life/time. Each unit moves through a cycle of changes from the start to the end of the period, beginning sometimes with depression, sometimes with enthusiasm, and proceeding through the variations of events and experience. Each person's life-span between birth and death includes a number of these periods, as becomes apparent to us when we consider the listing of Primary Steppingstones that we made. The contents of some of these periods can be of especially great significance for the development of the life as a whole. For

139

this reason an important step in Life-Study is the choice that we make when we choose two of these units of life/time as Focus Periods on which we will concentrate our attention. As we proceed in marking off the main contents of these two life/time units, we shall find that each of these periods gives us a view of one segment of the life as it was experienced at a particular point in time. The two Focus Periods are like windows that give us a view of the whole of the life, but from two different vantage points. Bearing this in mind we try to choose, whenever possible, one Focus Period from an early time in the life and another from a later time. Together, with a range of difference in time, the two periods give us more than a static picture with comparisons in the situations in the life; they give us a feeling for the movement, the changes and developments that have been taking place. By means of the two Focus Periods we can identify the processes at work in the continuity of the life.

Working with the sequences within a life, we are dealing with process, but it is process in two distinct contexts of thought. In the larger sense it is the process that moves through the life as a whole; and in the narrower, more specific sense, it is the numerous *mini-processes* that carry the continuities of development in particular areas of the life.

We seek to identify and work with both of these aspects of process, the general and the special movements through life/time. The interrelationships between the larger unitary process of the life as a whole and the several mini-processes within the life are the main source of the events that comprise an individual's experience. They are the source of the data with which we work in order to re-experience a person's life. When we identify this material we can feed it into the procedures of the Journal Feedback method.

As we apply the Journal Feedback exercises, they lead us from one event in the life to another, following the inner connections and content in a person's experiences. In doing this they tend to activate factors of energy within the life, especially with respect to those aspects of the mini-processes in a life of which a person is not conscious. The use of Journal Feedback carries the main dynamic of the *Intensive Journal* process in its Personal Component, and it plays a comparable role in Life-Study. It gives us a means of active participation in the life for which we are Journal Trustee.

To apply Journal Feedback in Life-Study requires that we work with the interrelationships of the two complementary factors—log and feedback—that build the energy movement in the *Intensive Journal* process. There is a tension, a pull of opposites between them, but the two are also a source of supply to each other. One key aspect of the *Intensive Journal* workbook is that its design reflects the mutual support and dialectic of these two types of sections together with the log and feedback procedures for working with the data of a life.

The log approach is descriptive. It involves gathering data, recording facts of experience as they are perceived, collecting information without censoring or interpreting or altering it. The log approach essentially involves a receptive recording, a neutral gathering of the varied facts of a life with factual, descriptive comments on what has been observed. The feedback approach takes a further step. While the log sections provide the raw material that serves as the starting point, the Journal Feedback exercises have an evocative quality. They encourage one thing to lead to another within the thoughts, the emotions and associations of a person. They build one perception and response upon another. In this way Journal Feedback reflects the accumulative quality of human consciousness. As it adds one inner experience to another it leads to a situation in consciousness in which the sum is greater than the parts. It is thus that we make leaps forward in our awarenesses. Journal Feedback follows this model, drawing its raw material from the log sections and using a variety of procedures—as may be appropriate to the context of the particular subject—to add to the data and to draw out more of their implications.

When it is used in our personal *Intensive Journal* work the back-and-forth movement of this log-feedback combination builds the energy and enlarges the experiences that lead to individual development. In various forms of expression, this is the simple mechanism that carries the dynamic of the *Intensive Journal* process. To get its benefits in Life-Study, however, requires a particular set of procedures.

Our first step is to collect a sufficient store of data for each of the two Focus Periods on which we are concentrating our attention. We draw that information together in brief log fashion stating only the essential facts, and indicating just enough of the details to enable us to put together a picture of the period as a whole. The log data that we record here, in one sense, are filling out the Overview Statement that we made a little earlier. There we were summarizing the period in a general way, but now we speak specifically of each of the contents in the person's life during that time.

To help us focus our attention on each of the significant aspects of the period, we follow a directed series of questions, the *Nine Questions* for reconstructing a life/time unit. Our reason for using a systematic set of questions is that we want to include all phases of the person's experience. The questions serve as a kind of checklist for us, giving us a measure of protection against inadvertently overlooking any pieces of data that might be relevant. We wish to include everything that might possibly pertain to the life.

The basis of the Nine Questions is in the principle of structure that underlies the *Intensive Journal* workbook. The fundamental reason for dividing the workbook into distinct sections is to provide a means of channeling the parts of a life into the movement of the whole of a life. The Journal sections thus correspond to the main aspects of a person's experience set in the context and continuity of the life as a whole, and the Nine Questions that derive from them serve to call attention to each general area of experience. The answers, which we give whenever possible in the form of free-flowing responses, have the purpose of filling in the details for each particular life. Some of the responses provide more of the details of the period. Others draw out more of the implications of the person's life while enlarging our experience as Journal Trustees. The way we carry out the exercise for responding to the Nine Questions varies with each individual's life and the Journal Trustee's relation to it. Its net effect is to fill in the fundamentals of

Life-Study for our person, especially because the response to each of the Nine Questions takes us to at least one and sometimes several sections in the workbook.

The Nine Questions form a guideline for drawing together the facts we need in order to reconstruct a life/time unit. They also give us a means of feeding the relevant life-data into the Journal Feedback process. Our responses to the Nine Questions provide material that fulfills both of these requirements, but it is necessary for us to separate our answers. We have to state our responses in forms that are distinct from each other, varying with whether they have a log or a feedback function in our Life-Study. Now we can practice that together, each of us in terms of the life of the person for whom we are Journal Trustee.

We apply the Nine Questions to both of the life/time units that we have designated as Focus Periods in our Life-Study, but it is usually better to concentrate our attention on one of the periods at a time. In that way we can absorb the distinct atmosphere of each period and be within the emotional tone of each life/time unit when we are responding to the questions. Usually, although not always, the sequences of development become clearer to us if we work first with the Focus Period that occurred during the earlier part of the person's life. There are obvious reasons of chronology for this. Sometimes, however, in special circumstances, it can actually work better for us to start with the later period and to work our way backward.

In the Period Log each Focus Period has its own sub-section. This gives us a flexible space where we can record the range of information that pertains to that time in our person's life. We have already opened a sub-section in the Period Log for each of the Focus Periods with which we are working. That is where we have the two Overview Statements that we wrote, and also the listings of the Signpost Events in which we brought together the sequence of developments within each period. The place for our responses to the Nine Questions is therefore waiting for us, prepared with basic background material. When we are ready to give our concentrated attention to an individual period we will proceed question by question, giving both a log and a feedback response to each question whenever possible. The log responses will be concentrated here in the sub-section of the Period Log while the individual feedback responses will be placed throughout the workbook, each in its appropriate feedback section.

Log and Feedback Entries

Making our entries within the Period Log in the sub-section that we have already started for this Focus Period, we begin our response to each question by stating the essential facts. Since these entries in the Period Log are primarily for the purpose of collecting information, our answers give the necessary data with brief descriptions, some additional thoughts and comments, and explanations when necessary. For example, the log answer to the question about *persons who have an inner importance* in the life may indicate no more than who the persons are and just enough essential facts to identify them. They may also include, but not in detail, some discussion of the relationship with an indication of its quality and significance in the life. The log response is not extensive. Usually it does not need to be more than a few sentences on any given subject since the extended exploration takes place in the course of the feedback entries. In themselves the log responses to each of the Nine Questions are relatively brief. Altogether, however, there are nine of them that are all placed in the same subsection of the Period Log, and this can fill a substantial space. When they are read one after another, these entries in the Period Log give us a composite picture of the unit of life/time. They bring together the variety of aspects of the period, so that we can focus our attention upon it as a whole.

Once we have stated the basic facts in our log entries, we can proceed to write further explanations and elaborations. But we do not write them in the Period Log. These entries take us into the feedback phase of our *Intensive Journal* work. They are our second range of responses to the Nine Questions, and they must be placed not in a log but in a feedback section, for these are the entries that set the feedback process into motion. Each of the Nine Questions involves a different feedback section. Thus, for example, after we have made our first log entry in the Period Log as our response to the question regarding *persons who had an inner importance* in the life during this Focus Period, we turn to the feedback section that corresponds to it. These feedback sections are indicated in our working list of the Nine Questions for a Life/Time Unit, as it is given below. There it is indicated that, for persons who had an inner importance to us, the appropriate feedback section is *Dialogue with Persons*. This means that, after making our basic log entry, we proceed in the feedback section to describe as much as comes to us with respect to the details of the relationship, the events that took place, feelings that may have been involved, and any other aspects of the situation that now seem to be significant.

Just as the log entry was brief, this feedback entry has no limitation in length. It unfolds out of itself, one piece of information leading to another. Since we are writing it in the first person on behalf of the person for whom we are Journal Trustee, there is an associative process that takes place within us that reflects the contents of the life. Naturally, the more familiar we are with the contents of our person's life the more fluid and productive will be the chain of associations that is stimulated in us. For this reason we may find that while it is very helpful to use the Nine Questions as a guideline for reconstructing a Focus Period when we are beginning our work as a Journal Trustee, there is an additional value in using them a second time at a later point in our work when our knowledge of the life is fuller. Whether it is at an early or later stage of Life-Study, these feedback entries express the thoughts, the memories and awarenesses that arise in us as we are considering the particular processes in the life for which we are Journal Trustee. They are stimulated in us while we are in the act of writing our response to each of the Nine Questions.

The entries that we write in this feedback phase of Life-Study are always open-ended. Knowing that we are engaged in an active and moving process, we write each entry with the expectation that it will lead to something additional. We take the view that, as we proceed with pen in hand, we are acting essentially as an intermediary for the contents of the life of the person we represent. We are placing ourselves in the movement of their life, seeking to channel the data of their experiences into their Life-Study Journal by means of our entries. We record this material as it comes to us, in whatever form and whenever it comes to us. We do not edit it as we write it, but we record it as it presents itself. Our responses to each of the Nine Questions build themselves and unfold out of their own content in the course of the descriptions and discussions of life events that we record. We find that, as we continue writing and expressing the experiences of the life, there is a tendency for one thing to lead to another. Further entries are called forth by the entries that preceded them. We are receptive to the inner stimulations that are evoked. Whatever comes to us from within our person's life we feed into the *Intensive Journal* process as an additional feedback entry.

We make each of our Journal entries with the understanding that nothing that we write is to be regarded as final. We are conscious of the fact that all our entries are by their nature partial and incomplete. Each is a small increment added to the larger whole, with more to be added from time to time. Since an entry is only a part of a larger movement, it is not to be judged by itself. We are aware that our entries are each a small contribution to an ongoing process. We know also that the process is in movement not only when we are overtly writing but also when we are in a condition of quiet.

Working with the *Intensive Journal* process in quietness is inherent in our activity. It is essential that we always be ready to resume and extend our Journal entries whenever a further thought or feeling, memory or realization, comes to us. This is true even if—and especially if—we believe at the outset of a writing time that we are only going to add a brief entry. The actuality is that when we begin to write a Journal entry we cannot know in advance whether it will be only a brief entry or whether it will extend itself at length. Since we are working with a process that increases and strengthens itself by self-evoking, we cannot know beforehand. For that reason we deliberately avoid keeping rigid controls on our Journal entries. We let each unfold out of itself. Not infrequently it happens that while a Journal entry is extending itself it overlaps with or repeats something that has been written in another section. These repetitions are unavoidable, but in the course of time they contribute to the larger feedback process. They tend to cluster together in a way that calls our attention to the aspects of the person's life that contained the issues and concerns that were felt to have the greatest importance. This spontaneous repetition of entries contributes to the feedback process. As we do the Journal work of Life-Study it is best to let these repetitions happen without seeking to restrict or regulate them. From the number of them that occur and from the Journal sections where they accumulate we can see not only what is important in the individual's life but also what is significant to us personally as a Journal Trustee. Each entry is contributing data that will eventually be sorted out and given due weight by the self-balancing principle within Journal Feedback.

The common expression, "One thing leads to another," turns out to be an operative factor here as we apply Journal Feedback in Life-Study. It becomes particularly important for increasing the content and generating momentum in our Life-Study because of the fact that, as Journal Trustees, we are working in another person's life. Our responses to the Nine Questions serve to feed the necessary data into the process; and the fact that each of the Nine Questions calls for a feedback entry in a particular section of the workbook stimulates the active interrelationships within the Journal structure that correspond to the interconnections of thought and feeling among the several phases of a person's life. The entries we make in response to the Nine Questions build the Journal Feedback process and lead to integrating effects by means of the diversity of sections in the *Intensive Journal* workbook.

As we add entries and move from Journal section to Journal section, two lines of development are taking place: we are gathering the data that reconstruct a unit of life/time; and we are generating a momentum of increasing perceptions and awarenesses that enlarge our own development. This is one of the valuable results of learning to work with Feedback Leads in the *Intensive Journal* process.

We can now each individually, by making the basic log and feedback responses to the Nine Questions that are listed in the following chapter, provide the data of the two Focus Periods with which we can re-enter and re-experience our person's life. Since our work with the Nine Questions carries the transition between the factual and the feedback phases of Life-Study, we carry out the steps of this exercise in a log-feedback sequence. For each question we begin by making a Log response in the Period Log, using the sub-section that we have already opened for the Focus Period. We follow this with an entry in the particular feedback section that is indicated by the question, letting that entry be as extensive as we require.

These are the steps that we can take now for the Focus Periods that we have chosen responding to the Nine Questions that are listed below. In that list we find that each of the questions, with two exceptions, has listed directly beneath it a "feedback section" indicating the Journal section that bears the closest relation to the contents of the question. It is here that we make our first feedback entry when responding to that question. There may be further Feedback Leads that will follow from that entry and will draw us on to make additional entries in other feedback sections. But that is for a later phase of our Journal Feedback work. At this point the essential step is to make the first feedback entry in the section that is indicated directly beneath the question.

The two questions that do not lead directly back to a feedback section are those that deal with dreams and/or twilight images; and those that deal with connective experiences. These are Question 6 and Question 9. Both of these questions have listed beneath them the phrase, "Corresponding Sections," rather than "Feedback Section." This is because the experiences involved in the answers to these questions are different from the others in that they require an additional entry, which has a partially log aspect, before they can continue to further feedback work.

In the case of dreams and images an additional log entry is necessary in order to draw out and record the details of experiences that may have further feedback uses for us at a later time. Our first entry in answering this question (Question 6) should be a brief introductory response in the Period Log, as it would be for the other questions. In this case we write in the Period Log a brief indication of the nature of the dream or the twilight image. We then turn to the Dream Log or to the Twilight Imagery Log— whichever section is applicable—and there we write as full a description as we can of the dream or the twilight image. We do not add interpretations or commentaries to these descriptions, but only record the dreams and the images as they are known to us. Whenever we can, however, it is good to add to these descriptions a few pertinent facts regarding the circumstances that were in the background of the dreams or imagery at the time they took place.

Having recorded the dreams and images, we come to a further feedback question: to which other section of the Journal (i.e., which area in the person's life) does the content of the dreams or images now lead us? Answering this question may call for some extended reflection, and the place where we record our various considerations in this regard is in either of the two sections that follow the log sections and give the place for working with their contents, the sections for *Dream Enlargements* or *Twilight Imagery Extensions*. From these we go to the other feedback sections, to whichever section we are directed by our consideration of the dreams and the twilight imagery.

At this point we will very likely be brought into contact with symbolic material that is vague and ambiguous, but which we sense to be meaningful for the life of the person. It would be of great value for us as Journal Trustees if we could recognize the messages that lie hidden in the symbolic experiences of our person's inner life. But we also know that we must be wary of reading our own meanings, or our favorite analytical theory, into those symbols. We require a means of moving from the symbols of dreams and twilight imagery to the life-messages that those symbols carry, but without intruding our analytical interpretations into the symbols. Journal Feedback gives us a method of doing this, derived from our experience in personal *Intensive Journal* work where we follow the Feedback Leads as they take us from Journal section to Journal section beginning with the Dream Log. This gives us an effective, non-analytical method of working with dreams, and it is neutral in the specific sense that it provides a method of finding the message of symbols without presupposing any interpretive theory. It simply follows the leads suggested by the dream or imagery material itself, moving within the context of the person's own life-experiences and using the sections of the *Intensive Journal* workbook as the vehicles of conveyance. This is one of the important abilities that Journal Feedback gives us. It uses the Journal sections as the means by which the contents of a person's own life become the context for translating the symbols of dreams and symbols. The purpose behind the extra steps that we take in responding to Question 6 is to make this capacity of Journal Feedback available for our Life-Study.

The other question that requires some extra steps in our Journal work is the ninth, the question that deals with *experiences of connection to a meaning of life*. The subject of this question can be elusive and difficult to handle, especially since it deals with the fundamentals of a person's beliefs. Experiences of connection can be of a religious type and they can also be secular in content. They may express, on the one hand, a spiritual mysticism, and on the other hand, a quest for unity in science or the commitment to a political ideology.

Whatever their content, we should begin our journal work with these experiences, as with the other questions, by making a brief introductory response in the Period Log. Here we state the situation in its general terms. If there then is a specific connective experience for us to report, that requires a further entry in another section. We move to the *Connections* section of the workbook, and there in the sub-section for *Gatherings* we describe the experience as fully as we can. Recording it has the quality of a log entry, but it gives us at once a Feedback Lead. Underlying every experience of connection there is at least one issue of belief or doubt or questing, a concern for a larger truth that will give the person a sense of meaning in life. In the Journal section for *Peaks, Depths and Explorations* we can take that quest a step further, whatever its subject matter may be. The first entry that we make there links the experience to other aspects of the life, and with that we begin a chain of Feedback Leads. Much that has profound possibilities can open in the exercises of the section for *Peaks, Depths and Explorations*. If you find yourself drawn beyond a single entry there, you will do well to consult the full chapter on it in *The Practice of Process Meditation*.*

---

* See in particular Chapters 13 and 18.

Chapter 13

Nine Questions for a Life/Time Unit

The following are the *Nine Questions* that we use as our guideline in drawing together the data for each of the Focus Periods. Essentially these questions comprise a checklist for the essential processes that are present in the continuity of a life. One of their main purposes is to call our attention to each of these processes so that we will not overlook any important area as we re-enter our person's experiences. In addition, our responses to these questions will serve as our starting points for working in the Journal Feedback process. Our responses will be in the form both of Log entries and Feedback entries. The Log entries for responding to each of the Nine Questions will be placed in the Period Log, specifically in the sub-section for the Focus Period that we are reconstructing. The Feedback entries will be placed in the appropriate section that is indicated following each of the questions.

1. Who were the *persons who had an inner importance* to you during this unit of time? Describe the relationships, including both the pleasant and the unpleasant aspects.
Feedback Section: Dialogue with Persons

2. What were your *work projects and activities* during this period? What were your long-range goals and your short-range goals? What happened to them? Which came to a dead end? Which were completed? Which were halted and then resumed at a later time? Tell the feelings and the experiences that were involved in these.
Feedback Section: Dialogue with Works

3. What was *the physical condition of your life,* your health and illnesses, your sensory life, your sensual life, your overall relation to your body and its uses during this period?
Feedback Section: Dialogue with the Body

4. What were your *social attitudes* during this time, your beliefs, loyalties, antagonisms? What was your relation to your family, your nation, your historical roots? Were changes taking place in your social or philosophical orientation during this time?
Feedback Section: Dialogue with Society

5. Were there *events that occurred in your life* at this time that were striking in their impact and that brought about sharp changes in the circumstances of your life? Were there events that seemed to have a fateful or mysterious quality? How did this feel to you at the time, and in the times that followed?
Feedback Section: Dialogue with Events

6. Are you aware of having *sleep dreams or twilight images* during this period of your life? Are there any that stand out from the others with respect to their symbolism, the insights they gave you, or possibly the predictions they made?
Corresponding Sections:
Dream Log: Twilight Imagery Log
Dream Enlargements: Imagery Extensions

7. Were there *persons who inspired you,* persons from history or mythologic times, or persons living in your own time, in whom you felt a quality of wisdom that was especially relevant to you?
Feedback Section: Inner Wisdom Dialogue

8. Were there *intersections of decision* in your life during this time? Considering that you chose to take particular roads and left other roads untaken, how do you perceive the consequences now?
Feedback Section:
Intersections: Roads Taken and Not Taken

9. Did you have any experience of *connection to a meaning in life* during this period? Did you feel a lack of meaning in life?
Corresponding Sections:
Connections; Peaks, Depths and Explorations

Some of these questions may not apply to your person while others will draw forth a great deal of material both as brief log entries and as extended feedback responses. You will be able to give only a partial response at this time to some of the questions even though you know that there is much more to be said on the subject. In those cases the brief feedback entry that you make now will serve as a door opener, marking off a sub-section to which you will add further material at a later time. In each case you should not feel yourself to be under pressure to write anything more than what you are comfortable with. As a Journal Trustee you need to feel free to write as much or as little in the form of a Journal entry, whether log or feedback, whenever a further perception or experience comes to you regarding the life of your person. It is not necessary to make a large or complete entry at any one time. But a number of small entries that are spontaneously stimulated can have a substantial overall effect. There may be specific aspects of the life where you feel that you have not yet gathered sufficient information to enable you to write with sureness in a feedback section. Even in these areas, making a first feedback entry, however brief it may be, can be very helpful in setting a process into motion. At the least, even if it contains a minimal response to one of the Nine Questions, a first feedback entry has the effect of establishing and naming a sub-section, and thereby it opens the door for further Journal Feedback in that area of the life.

As you respond to these questions, it is important to bear in mind that there is no single correct way to recapitulate and describe any human being's life. In Life-Study the basically correct way is only to respond to each of the questions in terms that you feel to be the most appropriate and the most honest by the light of your present understanding. As you proceed in making your Journal Feedback entries, one experience will lead to another and gradually, by its self-integrating procedures, the continuity of your Journal work will itself lead you to understandings and to an authentic inner relationship between yourself and the person for whom you are Journal Trustee.

The point to keep in the forefront of your work as a Journal Trustee is that, while the events that you emphasize and the forms in which you recapitulate them may be individually variable, the principles that enable us to establish the inner movement of a life are definite. It is these that must be maintained and carried through in order to reach the results of our *Intensive Journal* work in Life-Study. We have considerable leeway for our personal subjectivities, but the principles of our Journal work are objective in the sense that they are the *operative* principles. When we follow them step by step in their appropriate sequence they build the cumulative *integrative* effect that is the special capacity of the *Intensive Journal* process. Since these operational principles are neutral with respect to the subjective contents of each life, they do not affect our personal judgment regarding the individual. It is, however, essential that we maintain the identity of these principles in operation; we do this by means of the interplay between the log and the feedback factors. Our responses to the Nine Questions supply the life-data for the log and feedback entries.

The next four chapters contain excerpts from Life-Study journals being maintained on behalf of Pablo Casals and Eleanor Roosevelt. For each person, responses to the Nine Questions are given with respect to two Focus Periods, one from an earlier time in life, another from a later time. These excerpts can be viewed as illustrations of how a Journal Trustee may use the Nine Questions as a means of feeding life-data into the Journal Feedback process. By no means, however, should they be regarded as models. As long as you bear in mind the fundamentals of Journal Feedback, especially the necessities of the Log-Feedback relationship, your responses to the Nine Questions can reflect your individual perceptions as a Journal Trustee.

If it should happen by chance that you are a Journal Trustee for one of the persons whose Life-Study Journal is excerpted here, for Pablo Casals or Eleanor Roosevelt, you will very likely find that the responses you give to the nine Questions are different from those that are given below. You may find that you have even chosen to mark off different units of life/time as the Focus Periods with which you are working. In that case, do not be influenced by the illustrations that are given here. Stay true to your own perception. It is inherent in Life-Study using the *Intensive Journal* process that each individual working as a Journal Trustee will have his or her own angle of vision, and it is essential that this be expressed. That is one reason why the excerpts from a Life-Study Journal that are given here are not intended as a model to be copied but are presented as illustrations for purposes of discussion and to indicate some of the forms of response that we can use in working with the Nine Questions.

Chapter 14

Excerpts from the Life-Study Journal of Pablo Casals: I

An Early Focus Period: "Preparing for a Career"

Note: The excerpts given below from a Life-Study Journal of Pablo Casals are for the Focus Period in his life designated as "Preparing for a Career." It covers the years during which Casals was becoming established as a professional musician.

Material from this Focus Period has already been given in Chapter 9 for the Overview Statement, Chapter 10 for the Open Moment Image, and Chapter 11 for its Signpost Events. Those exercises provide background for the responses to the Nine Questions given here.

Where the entries below are marked as appearing in the *Period Log,* it is implicit that they are from the sub-section there that is set apart for this Focus Period, "Preparing for a Career." Where feedback entries are made in addition to the *Period Log* entries, the specific Journal section and sub-section are indicated in each case.

Question 1. Who were the *persons who had an inner importance* to you during this unit of time? Describe the relationships, including both the pleasant and unpleasant aspects.

Period Log Entry

These were childhood years and my mother and father were still the most important persons in my life. They were more than parents to me, for they both actively contributed to shaping the work of my life. Often they disagreed with each other in their view of what I should do, and I was caught in the middle. But I had my own definite opinion of what I wanted to do. My mother and father disagreed, but they were both my closest friends as long as they lived.

Feedback Entry in *Dialogue with Persons:*
Sub-section for *My Father*

My Father was a musician who played the organ at church services and also gave lessons, but he was not able to make much of a living at it. This influenced him in his thoughts about my future when he wanted me to be apprenticed to a carpenter. He was only trying to protect my livelihood, for he loved music as much as I do. He was the first person to teach me music when I was very young, and he always did whatever he could to help me improve in it. Music was what we shared and what we did together, especially when I was very young. During this period the things I had to do in developing my career increasingly took me away from him, and that was very painful. I think that his asthma and other ailments became worse during this period, and it may have been related to the frustrations of his life.

Feedback Entry in *Dialogue with Persons:*
Sub-section for *My Mother*

My Mother spoke of herself as "the wife of a poor man." That is how she thought of herself. She accepted that in a stoical way and as the will of God, although she was not a church-attender. She loved music and as soon as she realized the nature of my talent she resolved to take it as far as it could go. She believed in me altogether, and she was willing to risk everything for this belief. She endured very difficult conditions and we suffered through great poverty together. Most of the time it was I who was the weak one and became ill when the situation was especially difficult, but she remained strong.

One main trait of my mother that always impressed me and had me somehow in awe of her was her capacity of knowing intuitively just what was the right thing to do. She could anticipate the future. She had these intuitions which you might say were instinctive to her. They came to her very strongly so that she was absolutely certain about them even when other people—who you might think were more knowledgeable about the subject—had a contrary opinion. She was absolutely insistent when she had one of these intuitions. But she almost always proved to be right in the end. For example, when my father said that I would not be able to earn my livelihood as a musician, she opposed him without compromise and insisted on taking me to Barcelona where I could find an advanced teacher and begin to get work as a musician. She turned out to be right. And later on, when she felt that Count de Morphy and the Queen Regent were trying to develop me as an opera composer rather than as a cellist, she was adamant in opposing them and in taking me to Paris. We had many difficult days then, since my scholarship was taken away as a result of her attitude. But in the end she proved to be right. She was a remarkable woman with tremendous strength. I always thank God that she was my mother.

Question 2. What were your *work projects and activities* during this period? What were your long-range goals and your short-range goals? What happened to them? Which came to a dead end? Which were completed? Which were halted and then resumed at a later time? Tell the feelings and the experiences that were involved in these.

Period Log Entry

Music is my work and the main activity of my life. It always has been. I never had a question about it. But there was serious question as to whether it would be economically possible for me to do my work. That was decided during these early years.

Feedback Entry in *Dialogue with Works:*
Sub-section for *Music*

I have never thought of my music as being work in the sense of it being an unpleasant activity that I did because I was forced to. On the other hand, I cannot say that I have played music because I decided that I wanted to. Would you say that a bird wants to fly? What else can it do? I am a musician. Yes, I am a human being too; that is true. I am a human being who is a musician. That is what I am. So if it looks as though I am working at music, I am not really working. I am only doing what it is my nature to do.

On the other hand, it is true that work, difficult work, has been involved in my music. It has involved great effort, sometimes painful effort. I was born in a sense as a natural musician. But it has required a great deal of effort and discipline, hours and hours of practice which sometimes I loved and sometimes I did not love, in order to become as good a musician as I possibly could be. I know that when a bird flies, it just flies. For a bird there is no such thing as being a good flier or a bad flier; at least I don't think so. But for a musician it is different. There is the question of becoming good enough. There is the question of becoming as good a musician as you possibly can be.

There is also the fact that I know that at different times in my life I have had different feelings about being a musician. During the period when I was preparing for my career I felt that I was a musician, but I did not know for sure. I had to find out for myself, and then I had to prove it to others.

In addition there was a great doubt that arose in me because of the disagreement between my mother and father. After all, my father was a musician, too. Very much a musician. But he was not able to make much of a living at it. That was why he wanted to apprentice me to a carpenter. My mother said that I was a good enough musician to make my living at it, and even do more than that. But she herself was not a musician. I thought she was right but I was not absolutely sure. Perhaps she only thought those things about me because she was my mother. This was the big question for me during the early years when I was preparing for my career. Was I really capable of being as good a musician as she thought I could be? I did not want to disappoint her, and sometimes that made me very nervous. But gradually, as so many good things began to happen to me one after another, I became convinced that she was right. Even so, I would still get terribly nervous before each performance. I would shake, my hands would get wet, and I became afraid that I would forget what I had to play. That nervousness became like a habit that never left me. Probably after that I could not play without it.

In this early period of my life I had to settle the question of whether music would actually be the main activity of my life. At first there was the definite feeling that I am a musician and that music is what I want to do in my life. Then there arose the doubt of whether I am good enough as a musician to succeed in it and to make my livelihood at it. Could music become my career? Or could it only be my hobby? I did not like that distinction, but during the arguments between my father and my mother I wondered about it quite a lot.

Eventually that question was settled in my mind and in my whole feeling of my life. I knew for sure that I was a musician and that I would have a career as a musician. It was only a question to me of how the details would work out. And also a question of when.

But something further is important. After I became convinced that I am truly a musician, it became a question of: What for? I had proved something to myself personally, but now the question was whether there was something even more important that I had to know about.

Two large questions then formed themselves in my mind. One was, if it is clear that I am really a musician, if I have proved myself, what is the best music that I can play, or that I can compose?

And the second question was, since I am really a musician, and since music is not something isolated but is important as a part of the whole of life, how should I use my abilities as a musician to contribute to the lives of other human beings in the world?

I began to be concerned about these questions very early in my life, for it was quite early in this period that people's responses to me convinced me that I am really a musician. These larger worries began right after my first significant successes in Barcelona. I think they were an important factor in the period of my depression when I almost committed suicide.

At that time I had only one project in my life, and it included everything that I did. It was the basic task of establishing myself as having a career as a musician. And that meant becoming a cellist and establishing myself as a cellist. That meant also that my primary task was to play music as a cellist as absolutely well as I could. And that remained the goal of my work all my life. Later on I had other goals in my work as well. Composing was a main one, but I had to keep it as a hope in the back of my mind while I was concentrating on becoming a cellist.

The other goal of my work was to become a conductor. In the early years I could not even allow myself to imagine that. But the feeling for it was there at the very beginning, and as events moved along I realized that it might actually be a possibility. I found myself thinking about it more and more often. Eventually, of course, conducting became an important part of my work as a musician.

Question 3. What was *the physical condition of your life,* your health and illnesses, your sensory life, your sensual life, your overall relation to your body and its uses during this period?

Period Log Entry

My main attitude toward my body at that time was that it was not important. But of course it was essential. It would have been very difficult for me to play the cello without my body and without a certain natural strength that my body has always had. But I did not think about it at the time. I just took it for granted. There were other aspects of my physical life that I became more aware of and that became more important to me later on but that I did not pay any attention to during this period.

Feedback Entry in *Dialogue with the Body:*
Sub-section for *Life History of the Body*

I have never been a physical person in the sense of putting physical things first, but I have used my physical abilities considerably in various ways. My music depends upon my physical senses. I suppose I would not be a called a sensual person. But in some ways I have been. And if I was not a very sexual person, perhaps, that may have to do with other factors in my life, factors other than my body. I don't know. We could look at that some time.

I was small as a child and I always remained small in height. Perhaps because of the food I ate or did not eat as a child. I never grew to be much taller than my cello. They used to call me "the little one," but that was not really because I was a short person. At that time I had not yet finished growing, even though I did not grow much taller. They called me "the little one" because I was a young, small boy, about ten years old, playing solos in a café for adults. In those years I was with older people most of the time, so I grew accustomed to thinking of myself as a little person. And I remained a little person always.

I think I was quite strong in those early years, especially my arms and shoulders. I was very good as a wrestler with other boys my age. I did not like to beat the others, but I did not enjoy being a loser either. I did not lose very often in wrestling.

Once I became actively engaged in playing music professionally, I had many demands on me, performing and practicing and studying all at the same time. But I found that I had a great capacity for endurance. Extra energy always seemed to be there when I needed it. Probably the source of that was more than physical. My love of music has always been a source of strength for me, and my desire for it in those days was very, very strong. I have always found that music stimulates great energy in me. I have been able to respond to very trying challenges if music is involved. But other emotional pressures could weaken me, and at those times I became a victim of illnesses.

That happened when I lost my scholarship from the Royal Family and my mother and I were stranded in Paris. We were living in great poverty without any money and in very squalid conditions. I pushed myself by trying to work at more than one job at a time in order to be able to stay in Paris. But I became ill. I was not strong enough to bear up under the emotional pressures. Even my love of music could not enable me to do that. But when I returned to my native Spain my health returned. Yes, but it was more than Spain that brought my health back. I received great new opportunities for my music at that time, and I am sure that those encouragements helped me become physically strong again.

Question 4. What were your *social attitudes* during this time, your beliefs, loyalties, antagonisms? What was your relation to your family, your nation, your historical roots? Were changes taking place in your social or philosophical orientation during this time?

Period Log Entry

Questions of social belief were not important to me at this time in the sense that I was not thinking about them. These things were not in my mind. But my feelings of loyalty were there nonetheless, and they were getting stronger all the time. In later years they would be of tremendous importance in my life, and this is when they must have been developing beneath the surface of events. But I was not aware of them at the time. I was just trying to find my way in the world.

Feedback Entry in *Dialogue with Society:*
Sub-section for *Music and Society*

During this period I was primarily wondering about my career and wondering what my life would become. Where social beliefs were concerned I was still a youth. I mean that at that time I believed in whatever my father and my mother believed in.

In retrospect I can say that they were correct in what they believed in, and I always continued to agree with them. They believed in Spain and Catalonia and especially they believed in the people. My mother's father had suffered greatly in fighting for the freedom of Puerto Rico against the Spanish colonial government. And she believed in freedom for the common people, the working people. So did my father. And so did I. And all three of us believed in music as an expression of the people. I tried to give those beliefs a further practical expression by linking freedom and music later on when I had the opportunity as a member of the government of the Spanish Republic. But in the days of my youth when I was exploring the possibilities of a career in music and was hoping for one, I did not know much about this. Gradually I came to understand how important music is for the social life of mankind.

As I reflect on it further I realize that in the course of developing my career I was taken to all levels of society. And my beliefs were tested by this.

I began as the son of poor people. I belong to the common people, and that is where my loyalties have always remained. But I was taken in by the Royal Family, supported and cared for, and helped by them, not only in my career but in my personal life as well. They did things for me for which I can never repay them. I came to love the members of the Royal Family as persons. And yet my loyalties always remained with the common people from which my own, original family came.

I did not think about it at the time. I mostly did things from a kind of instinct then. But I did feel a conflict of emotions underneath. In fact, when my mother decided that I should leave the Royal Family and go to other countries to study, I felt an emotional pull that almost made me stay. So it was a good thing that my mother had such a strong, insistent will.

For a while during this period I was pulled between the two different social classes. I could be in both because music belongs to all social classes. But the terrible events of later years overcame this conflict.

Question 5. Were there *events that occurred in your life* at this time that were striking in their impact and that brought about sharp changes in the circumstances of your life? Were there events that seemed to have a fateful or mysterious quality? How did this feel to you at the time, and in the times that followed?

Period Log Entry

There have been a number of events in the course of my life that seemed to be coincidences, and yet they had to be something more than that. But I cannot say exactly what. At the time they happened they each seemed to be so strange as to be impossible and unbelievable. But when I think of things in the context of my whole life, I see that nothing could be any different than it was. It was most unusual for a poor boy like me to become so close a part of the Royal Family. And yet it happened.

Many events happened in my life, especially in the early years, that seemed like magic. And yet they were all natural. But it was also a great mystery to me. I do not know what to say about it except to say, "Thank you" to God. And I say that even though I am not a religious person in the usual sense.

I think of two events in particular that seemed to come out of the blue and to happen without warning as though by pure chance, and yet they had a tremendous influence on the direction of my life. The first is my finding, it seemed by chance, in a music store some manuscripts of Bach's music that I had not known existed. The other is the remarkable chain of events that led to my being supported and virtually adopted for a while by the Royal Family in Madrid.

Feedback Entry in *Dialogue with Events:*
Sub-section for *Finding Bach's Manuscripts*

An event that seemed to be just happenstance and yet was much more than a coincidence for me occurred when I was just beginning to make my way in music. It was a particularly fateful event for me. I was eleven or twelve years old at the time and I was playing at the Café Tost in Barcelona. They had just started to permit me to play solos one evening a week, and as a result I needed new material.

My father used to visit me in Barcelona one day a week, and that day he brought me my first real cello. That was a great day for me. Then we went shopping in a music store looking for new solo material. I was just rummaging through a pile of sheet music when suddenly I came upon some old manuscripts. It was Bach's *Six Suites for Violincello.* Before that I had not even known that Bach had written solo music for the cello. Now this became a great source of inspiration to me. It gave me a sense of direction in my music. And it was a tremendous challenge. It took another twenty-five years before I felt competent to play those pieces in public. But I feel that those sheets of music were placed in my hands because they were meant for me. At the time I thought it was chance, and that I was just lucky. When I was young I thought a great deal in terms of luck. At that time I was so excited by finding the music and in thinking about what I had to do in order to learn it and master it that I did not consider anything else about it.

Feedback Entry in *Dialogue with Events:*
Sub-section for *Being with the Royal Family*

It was certainly a remarkable turn of fortune that took me into the Royal Household. There were, however, a series of events, some of them apparently chance events, that led up to it. After I had begun playing solos at the Café Tost in Barcelona, the word began to spread in musical circles that a talented boy was playing cello in that small café, and musicians began to come to see for themselves. Among them was a well-known musician of the time, Isaac Albeniz. After the performance he came up to talk to me and to my mother and he offered to be of any help to us that he could. He said he would write a letter of introduction for me to Count de Morphy who was closely connected with the Royal Family and who might very possibly become personally interested in me. In a few days the letter did come, but my mother felt that this was not the right time to use it. Something said, "Not yet," to her. So we waited. For about two more years she held that letter without using it while I played in Barcelona. Finally, when she saw that I was in a state of depression and she felt that something had to be done, she decided to use the letter. And that was precisely the right time. We went to Madrid with that letter of introduction, and we arrived just at the time when Count de Morphy was available. He saw us and took me under his wing. He became my teacher in all the general and philosophical subjects that I needed to study and he arranged for me to play for the Queen Regent. When she was favorable to me, I was invited so often that I became like one of the household, and I received a scholarship with enough money to support us in whatever we needed at the time. It was a remarkable event and a remarkable change of fortune. Again I could only thank God for it.

Question 6. Are you aware of having *sleep dreams or twilight images* during this period of your life? Are there any that stand out from the others with respect to their symbolism, the insights they gave you, or possibly the predictions they made?

Period Log Entry

Those types of experiences came to me from time to time all through my life, but I did not keep a record of them. I might recall some of them later on if something we are discussing reminds me of them.

Dream Log Entry

It occurred in a later period but I do recall that on two separate occasions, first when my father died and then when my mother died, I was on tour in Switzerland when I was told in a dream that the event of their death was about to happen. Each time I returned home and it turned out to be true.

Twilight Imagery Log Entry

I do not recall specific twilight images at this time, but I do recall that when I was in Paris, the philosopher Henri Bergson used to invite me to come and talk with him and he would ask me a great deal about the intuitive experiences I had in relation to my music. Much of these would be related to this question of twilight images, but I do not remember the details at this time.

Question 7. Were there *persons who inspired you,* persons from history or mythologic times, or persons living in your own time, in whom you felt a quality of wisdom that was especially relevant to you?

Period Log Entry

There were several such persons, and some of them recurred to me at different points in my life. I think of two who were especially important to me during this period: El Pau and J. S. Bach.

Feedback Entry in *Inner Wisdom Dialogue:*
Sub-section for *El Pau*

El Pau was an old Catalan sailor who lived in the town of Vendrell where I was born. When I was a small boy he would tell me stories of the sea. How true they were I don't know. But I have always thought of him as a person who was detached from the squabbles of the world and who was free therefore to be a person of wisdom. Whatever wisdom he had was, of course, a wisdom of nature, since he was not educated in any formal way. But sometimes, as the years passed and I was away from Vendrell, when I wanted to think of home I would sit quietly and think of him. Then I could feel something of the wisdom of Catalonia come to me, a wisdom of nature and of the sea. El Pau has represented that to me.

Feedback Entry in *Inner Wisdom Dialogue:*
Sub-section for *J. S. Bach*

Johannes Sebastian Bach is another person who has had a great importance to me. Bach has served as a master for me both in music and in life. The actual events and styles of our lives were very different, of course, but I have often felt that I understood in a close and intimate way what he was trying to do. That is why it was so important for me when I found the manuscripts of his *Six Suites*. Studying them over the years was for me a means of carrying on a personal communication with Bach. I sometimes felt as though I had received a letter from him in that music store.

Question 8. Were there *intersections of decision* in your life during this time? Considering that you chose to take particular roads and left other roads untaken, how do you perceive the consequences now?

Period Log Entry

There were a number of crossroads during that early period in my life since the main developments were still uncertain. The direction of my career was not yet clearly shown, and most of the decisions that were made at that time were made without being sure of what the actual outcome would be. They were mostly based on intuition, mainly my mother's intuition, and certainly there were roads that we did not take that could have had valuable results. Sitting where I am now after the activities of my life are over, I feel that it could not have been other than as it actually was. Nonetheless, the fact is that there were some very interesting possibilities left unexplored along the roads not taken in my life.

One road I could have taken is the one my father had recommended for me as being more practical, which was to try to make something other than music my career. Another intersection was the decision to leave the Court in Madrid.

Feedback Entry in *Intersections—Roads Taken and Not Taken:*
Sub-section for *Vendrell or Barcelona*

One road that I did not take was to stay in Vendrell as a boy instead of going to Barcelona to study. In that case I would have followed my father's advice, for he thought that the sensible thing for me to do was to become apprenticed to a carpenter. He wanted me to have a secure vocation and to play music only for my own pleasure, and not for my livelihood. Even to conceive of that is unthinkable to me now. It would have meant that I would not have become Casals. My life would not have happened. And yet for many years I struggled with the guilty feeling that it was my decision to try to make music my career and to earn my full livelihood at it that was the source of the great friction between my mother and my father. I would have given anything to have eliminated that discord, but I could not change the commitment that meant my life to me.

Feedback Entry in *Intersections—Roads Taken and Not Taken:*
Sub-section for *Leaving the Court in Madrid*

An intersection of decision that had great consequences in my life involved the situation that developed in my relation with Count de Morphy and the Queen Regent Maria Cristina. I was receiving a royal scholarship and I was studying everything educational with the Count as well as music at the Conservatory. Then my mother had the intuition that it was time to leave Madrid. So that is what we did. But it led to a great many difficulties. In the end, however, it had much better results than could have been anticipated.

I have sometimes wondered how my career would have developed if I had remained in Madrid with the Count and the Queen Regent. They were nurturing me as a composer more than as a cellist. That was very interesting to me. From the point of view of my personal tastes and desires I would have enjoyed exploring that path, even though my interest was not in opera as theirs was. Actually the road not taken in my career and the one that I constantly kept trying to take—and eventually did take to a considerable degree—was that of a conductor. There might have been more of that more easily achieved if I had taken the road that the Count de Morphy and the Queen Regent pointed out for me.

There was also a result of that decision that could not have been anticipated but that had some very significant effects on my life afterwards. It was an aspect of our experience that we would have avoided if we could have, but the eventual result of it was for the good. It was painful at the time, but in the end it was beneficial. I am thinking of the fact that when I was receiving support from the Queen Regent I was protected from the problems of the world. As a consequence, I was becoming sheltered and actually cut off from many of the harsh realities of life. But that changed rapidly when we were in Paris and our royal stipend was cut off. Then it was left to me to earn enough money for my mother and the other children who were with us in Paris. For the most part I was not able to do that. Our situation became very difficult then and I had to struggle as best I could in the harsh Paris music world. There can be no doubt that I learned a great deal more about the realities of human beings in the course of my struggles in Paris that I would have learned had I stayed in the shelter of the Court in Madrid. The protections of the Court would have been much easier, and considerably more pleasant. But the struggles in Paris were a much greater teacher. I also think that the amount of varied cello playing that I had to do in the circumstances I was subjected to in Paris contributed to my ability to conduct an orchestra in later years. And I know that I made a number of friends in Paris who eventually became important in my life and work. But who can tell what lies at the other end of a road not taken? It is interesting that when I was in contact with Count de Morphy and the Royal Family years later, even when my Republican sympathies were clearly known, our friendship was still cordial.

Question 9. Did you have any experience of *connection to a meaning in life* during this period? Did you feel a lack of meaning in life?

Period Log Entry

I have experienced a lack of meaning in life, and that was when I did not wish to live any longer. But at later times I did experience meaning in life, in different forms and degrees, strongly enough to place energy and purpose and commitment in my life. That has involved music, and other human beings, and something more, something mysterious as well. It is difficult to limit this to any one period in my life. But after a certain point it was always there, and it continued and developed through all of my life.

Connections—Log Entry

During this period when my primary concern was to establish my career, the main understanding that came to me of what may be involved in an experience of connection to life was negative; it came through the absence of such experiences. During the latter part of my teen years I had the experience of feeling altogether disconnected from life. I could see no reason to keep on living. Nothing was important. Nothing mattered. I was playing my music in a café in Barcelona. People were responding well to me. But that made no difference at all. I did not feel connected to anything. At that time I felt altogether depressed, no energy, no desire. I was seriously thinking of suicide.

Then everything changed. My attitude changed. My feeling for life changed. And what changed it? At that time it was not a mystical experience of connection to life. No, not as I remember it. It was simply that at that time my mother decided to make use of the letter of introduction from Isaac Albeniz to Count de Morphy. Then the two of us—with the other children as well—went with that letter from Barcelona to Madrid. It was a strange event done without preparation. It was one of my mother's intuitions, and it came at just the right time from several points of view. From my point of view it came just when I needed it most. When Morphy accepted me and offered to sponsor me to play at the Court, I saw my life in music being revitalized. All at once my depression was gone. I felt reconnected to life. It was clear that music was the center of my world, but the possibility of actually having a career was the link that made the connection for me to the world of reality.

There have been other experiences of connection in my life that were of a deep and affirmative nature in contrast to my experience of depression. But I think of that time of depression as particularly important because, by the absence of an experience of meaning in life, I realized how important such an experience can be. Some of the affirmative experiences of connection involved my relation to the monks of Montserrat. Others involved my relation to the music of Bach. I am not clear as to the details. But I am sure as to the time in my life when they took place. I would prefer to wait a while before I attempt to describe them further here in this Journal.

Feedback Entry in *Peaks, Depths and Explorations*:
Sub-section on *Music as My Connection to Life*

My underlying sense of life is a connection to universal realities by means of music. That is fundamental, for music is the basic connector. Music has always been there in that way for me as the connective link to life, but it has not always been able to provide a meaning in life for me. At the beginning, before I had established my career, I knew that I felt very good when I played music. But I could not say more than that. The main thing was that I wanted to be considered good enough as a cellist so that I could call myself a musician and make my living as one. I think that if I had been asked at that time I would have said that if I could be a musician that would be the meaning of life. I felt that I would not need more. Later on I found that I did need more. Most of the time, however, music was able to be the vehicle for me, as it was when I wrote music for the monks at the monastery of Montserrat, or when I conducted the Workingmen's Chorus later on. In the early years the security that I sought in music was nothing more than a personal need. I was primarily looking for a career, and that is what music gave me. Only later on did I recognize that music involves much, much more. Then it gave me more, and I experienced much more by means of it.

Chapter 15

Excerpts from the Life-Study Journal of Pablo Casals: II

A Later Focus Period: "Exile in Prades"

Note: The excerpts given below from a Life-Study Journal of Pablo Casals are for the Focus Period in his life designated as "Exile in Prades." It covers the years in Casals' life during and just after World War II.

Material from this Focus Period has already been given in Chapter 9 for the Overview Statement, Chapter 10 for the Open Image, and Chapter 11 for its Signpost Events. Those exercises provide background for the responses to the Nine Questions given here.

Where the entries below are marked as appearing in the *Period Log,* it is implicit that they are from the sub-section there that is set apart for this Focus Period, "Exile in Prades." Where feedback entries are made in addition to the *Period Log* entries, the specific Journal section and sub-section are indicated in each case.

Question 1. Who were *the persons who had an inner importance* to you during this unit of time? Describe the relationships, including both the pleasant and unpleasant aspects.

Period Log Entry

This was such a critical and difficult period in my life, in which external events placed such a great pressure on me and in ways that could not have been anticipated, that intimate personal relationships hardly seem important. And yet without them I could not have made it through this period. Considering the persons who had an inner importance to me, I think of those who enabled me to survive the time and those who made it even more difficult. I think of my mother, Joan Alevedra and Alfred Cortot.

Feedback Entry in *Dialogue with Persons:*
Sub-section for *My Mother*

Even though she had died several years earlier *My Mother* was very important to me in the exile part of my life, especially during the first part of it. She was mercifully spared the pain of the events that took place then, but I continued to feel her presence. During the formative years of my life, and particularly during the years when I was developing my career, she was the person who made the major decisions. After she died, whenever there arose the need to make a difficult decision, I would imagine her as being present, and I would ask the question of what she would have done if she were here in this situation. This practice was very helpful to me. After Franco had forced us to leave Barcelona under dreadful circumstances, there were many times when I had to make immediate life-or-death decisions. I tried to make them with the combination of good sense and intuition that she had possessed, for it was her decisions that had saved my career many times in the past. And now I needed her abilities to save my life. It happened again and again.

Feedback Entry in *Dialogue with Persons:*
Sub-section for *Joan Alevedra*

Joan Alevedra was the Catalan poet, who with his wife and

children went into exile in Prades with me. We had known each other before, but now we were bound in a great unity of friendship and commitment. We were devoted to our countrymen who were suffering, and we shared the same ideals.

When I was ill he was especially concerned for me and he was very helpful. There were many practical details to take care of because of the difficult conditions in which we were then living, and he took care of many of them for me as though I were part of his family. I was amazed that so sensitive and spiritual a poet could keep his mind on practical things so well. But those were the necessities of the times.

I am especially grateful to Alevedra for taking me into his family and helping me cope with my physical necessities during those difficult times. Even more important was the way he helped me meet the spiritual necessities of life during those times. Without him I do not think I would have survived because I would not have had the will to survive. And I believe that together in those circumstances we learned a great deal about the meaning of life.

Feedback Entry in *Dialogue with Persons:*
Sub-section for *Alfred Cortot*

Alfred Cortot was an old friend in France and a musical colleague with important government connections. He could have helped us when we were refugees but he became a collaborator. After the war he apologized and I accepted his apology. I said that I forgave him, but I am not so certain of my feelings. I think of him as a person, but there is a principle involved in his actions, and I never stopped wondering about it. It is a question I have never answered. How can it be that there are persons who love music and the arts, who spend the main part of their lives in these activities, and yet they deliberately do evil to other human beings when they have the opportunity?

Cartot represented to me the person with a musical soul who did evil to others even though he knew it was wrong and that it contradicted the rest of his life. I try to understand such persons and even to sympathize with them. After the war I shook Cortot's hand, but I am not sure that I truly forgave him. After all, when he refused to help me in France under Hitler it almost cost me my life. In that case I would not have been able to shake his hand in forgiveness when the war was over. Cortot had an outer importance to me because he almost cost me my life. But his inner importance to me is even greater. His life represents to me the unanswered question of evil in the world, especially the question of people who do evil to others even though they have music in their souls.

Question 2. What were your *work projects and activities* during this period? What were your long-range goals and your short-range goals? What happened to them? Which came to a dead end? Which were completed? Which were halted and then resumed at a later time? Tell the feelings and the experiences that were involved in these.

Period Log Entry

When the democracy collapsed in Spain my personal goals as a musician also collapsed. So also did my social goals of making music a part of the life of the common people. During this time I did not feel I could have the luxury of thinking of myself as a musician. I could think of myself only as a refugee together with my fellows, and I could only suffer with them. This was a terribly difficult and painful period in my life. But I learned something in the midst of it that I had not known before. My music became more than a means of earning money for myself. It became a connection for me to society. And later, when I had the experience that led me to write *El Pesebre,* it gave me a spiritual connection as well.

Feedback Entry in *Dialogue with Works:*
Sub-section for *Music and Society*

By the time Franco had made his military moves, I had already established myself as a musician. More than that, by that time I was very likely the best known musician in Spain. This was only partly because I was recognized as a cellist. My position as a cellist did not depend on Spain. My concerts were all over Europe and America, so you could say that my recognition as a cellist was international. And you certainly could say that I earned my living at it. I had received an unbelievable fortune in money over the years, much more than I had ever imagined I could earn; I tried to use, at least some of it, in a social way.

My position as a musician in Spain by the time Franco came, however, was additional to all this. After World War I, I spent a large part of my time in Spain trying to develop the idea that music is not just for performances by talented individuals but that it is to be participated in by all the people. This is what led me to form the Workingmen's Chorus in Spain and also the Pau Casals Orchestra, both of which were based on participation by ordinary people. These had succeeded, although at great cost to me both in time and money since I personally financed them. With my concerts I earned the money that was necessary in order to do these things. The people themselves were enthusiastic in taking part in these activities, and this is what was important to me. It was clearly being demonstrated that music can play a large role in the life of a society and that all the people can be included. This was the point that I wanted to prove in the years after World War I.

The social programs of music stood on their own feet, and when the republican government came to office in the elections I was given a portfolio in the government to develop music still further. We had great hopes then. I especially was full of optimism and plans. And then the terrible thing happened when Franco dissolved everything in a bloodbath.

Feedback Entry in *Dialogue with Works:*
Sub-section for *Helping the Spanish People*

When Franco destroyed the republican government and the free way of life in Spain, everything changed in my life. All my friends had to leave Spain, for we now had to be refugees from our own country. I was different from many of other Spanish people to the degree that I had an option. I could go to another country, for I had many offers from England and America to play in concerts for large fees. The alternative to doing this was to link my fate with that of my countrymen and be with them as a refugee. I chose the latter.

When I made this choice my primary work and activity became not music but doing whatever I could to help the Spanish people. If I had gone to another country, I could have spent my time playing music; but now I felt that the main thing I had to do was help the other Spanish refugees who had come to the southern part of France, and to help them in any way I could. Unfortunately I found that it was I myself who was often in need of help, especially for physical and emotional reasons. I was not always as strong as I thought I could be.

Once the turmoil had begun to settle and we could realize what had happened—that Franco's military power with Hitler's support was going to remain in Spain for a while—I saw that I had a new work before me. It was not primarily music, at least not for the time being. I had the task of getting supplies, money, anything that could be of help, considering the great needs. In order to do that, I wrote letters, I gave concerts, I did whatever I could to raise money for the refugees. At this point there was not even the thought of re-establishing our democracy in Spain. It was just a question of staying alive as refugees who had been forced to flee their country leaving everything behind.

Now for the first time in my life music was not my main work and activity. It was just a means for my work of helping the people with the hope of eventually restoring democracy in Spain. This had now become the main artwork and commitment of my life, at least for the time being.

Feedback Entry in *Dialogue with Works:*
Sub-section for *Writing "El Pesebre"*

Before my exile from Spain, music had clearly been established as the work of my life. In many ways it had become my life. But when I had to live in Prades, my life changed altogether. Of course the physical conditions of my life changed. That was part of the ordeal, and it made everything very difficult. But even more difficult and confusing to me was the fact that my primary work activity had changed. My music was no longer my main activity, and it increasingly seemed that this situation was going to last for quite a while. The atmosphere of the war was felt everywhere. It was becoming a way of life and I was being forced to the conclusion that it was not going to end nearly as soon as I had hoped. In fact at that time no one could tell when the war would end. No one could even be certain that we would win it.

This opened a very frightening possibility, and the thought of it was very upsetting to me. It led me into a very dark depression. The latter part of 1942 and the first half of 1943 were particularly difficult times. Supplies for food and heat ran very low. I was sick a large part of the time. Rheumatic pains, probably from the lack of heat in the cold and damp, made it increasingly difficult for me to play. And without my music I felt that I could not last very long. The physical conditions were driving me to despair. What would the outcome be? What was the meaning of it all? These thoughts brought to the fore of my consciousness something that I had always sensed, that music by itself is not enough, that no art by itself is enough.

In the midst of these feelings I heard my friend, Alevedra, read his poem, *El Pesebre (The Manger)* when it won first prize in a local competition for Catalan poetry. It was a series of poems about the Nativity that he had written some years earlier to sing at Christmas with his little daughter. Now it seemed to me to express the spiritual essence of the struggle that we were in. I resolved in that moment to set the whole of that poem to music, and I eventually did so even though it took me more than two years to complete it working under those conditions. Writing the music for that poem enabled me to feel the profound universal truth of the fundamental Christian experience. And something more important happened. Feeling that great truth, and also feeling the commitment to complete that work in a way that would do honor both to the poem and to its great subject, I had a personal work that was strong enough to carry me through the difficult times that lay ahead. It was a musical work of the spirit, and it gradually built the strength in me to overcome my despondency. I think that the work of composing *El Pesebre* came to me just in time.

Question 3. What was *the physical condition of your life,* your health and illnesses, your sensory life, your sensual life, your over-all relation to your body and its uses during this period?

Period Log Entry

When the trouble with Franco became serious I was already in my early sixties, but I had possessed good health and strength for my activities until that time. Naturally it was a terrible pressure on my body when I became a refugee. It had that effect on everyone. At first I did not think I would survive it; but it seems that I did. The strength came from somewhere.

Feedback Entry in *Dialogue with the Body:*
Sub-section for *Life History of the Body*

When I went into exile in Prades I was having severe headaches and dizzy spells. But I was much better off than the people in the refugee camps. I was just over sixty at the time, but my health had been good until then.

My hands had a tendency to tremble at that time, and that made it difficult for me to play my cello.

Frequently during this time I became so ill and weak that I could not do much to help the others. I was not able to stand up physically to the terrible pressure of events.

I had a tendency to become suddenly very fatigued then. This continued all through my later years. But I found that if I rested a little bit at such times, I seemed to bounce back with renewed energy. This pattern continued for many years, but I noticed it first when I came to Prades. Perhaps the terrible emotional pressures brought it about. After a while I came to regard these sudden feelings of fatigue as a warning sign, and I was grateful for them. I honored them whenever I could. Perhaps that was one reason why I was able to continue living for so many years.

The condition of the Spanish refugees in the camps had a very depressing effect on me. These were really little more than concentration camps which the French government had only begrudgingly allowed us to have. The sick and the dying were everywhere. Whenever I visited the camps, as I felt I had to do to be of whatever help I could, I was physically ill afterwards.

As these conditions continued and as I realized more and more that I could do very little to be of help, I began to feel irrelevant to life. For the first time in my life I felt old and essentially useless. This was a psychological attitude, but it had the effect of depleting me of my energy and it made me feel physically weak. Only later on, as the tide of the war turned, did my strength begin to come back. When it did, I became quite energetic again.

Question 4. What were your *social attitudes* during this time, your beliefs, loyalties, antagonisms? What was your relation to your family, your nation, your historical roots? Were changes taking place in your social or philosophical orientation during this time?

Period Log Entry

The government of the Spanish Republic had given me great reason to hope, and it had given me the opportunity to do a great deal with music among the working people. I had conducted regular concerts and ongoing musical programs with the working people as participants. Now all of this was destroyed. In Prades I could only try to maintain my faith that one day music and the people would be together again.

My fundamental loyalty was to Spain and to the Catalan people. But not just to the Catalan people. I felt that the important thing about the Spanish Republic was that it was a wonderful expression of freedom for everyone; and when the Spanish people lost it, everyone lost it. Somehow it had to be regained.

That time in Prades was terrible, but during it I developed the belief that music can be a vehicle for peace and unity among human beings everywhere. That became the motivation for the activities of the later years of my life.

Feedback Entry in *Dialogue with Society:*
Subsection for *Spain and Mankind*

As the war proceeded, a shift in emphasis seemed to take place in my thinking. I became more of a universalist. I think I always had had these feelings, but now they became clearer.

When Franco took over the government and forced so many people in Spain to flee for their lives, my sympathy was with the Spanish people. Naturally I was one of them. But that was not the reason for my sympathy. It was not because they were Spanish but because they were losing their freedom. I felt this in an intimate way because the government that was falling was my own government. I had been part of it and I had placed my personal hopes in it. I had even had an official position in it where I could try to do good things. Now it was being destroyed, and it was as though my own family was being destroyed.

This was the way I felt about Catalonia also. It was my own family, my own people. And it was part of Spain, which was also my own people. So if I had nationalist feelings for Spain, it was more like having a special sympathy and concern for the troubles of the people in my own family. If I would not worry about them and try to take care of them, who would?

But while I was in Prades a further development took place in me. I still worried about Catalonia and about Spain, as I always continued to do. But I became more and more concerned for peace among all human beings regardless of their nationality. Perhaps this was because I saw that the war had brought terrible suffering to all the nations of mankind without distinction. Apparently there were many other people around the world who also had this perception. This desire for unity among all human beings eventually led to the idea of the United Nations. It is what I believe in, but I hope it is not a vain belief.

Question 5. Were there *events that occurred in your life* at this time that were striking in their impact and that brought about sharp changes in the circumstances of your life? Were there events that seemed to have a fateful or mysterious quality? How did this feel to you at the time, and in the times that followed?

Period Log Entry

The fundamental event that changed my life at this time did not happen to me as an individual, but it affected me personally a very great deal. My life as an individual had been proceeding much better than I could possibly ever have hoped. My career was going well internationally; I was well accepted by the Spanish republican government; and I was also warm friends with the Royal Family. Everything was good in my world until Franco came along with Hitler's support. Then things turned upside down. My life was completely changed. This was my destiny, and not my destiny alone. It was the destiny of all persons who live in this period of history, so there is no point in complaining. The question is what kind of response does a person make to the events of history. I made my response.

At first I resented and resisted the events that were happening. I was very angry at the way my country was betrayed by the western democracies that had pretended to be her friends. I never stopped being angry about that; and I kept on making my protest for a long time. Finally I tried to act in a more affirmative way than by protesting.

Feedback Entry in *Dialogue with Events:*
Sub-section for *Fascism and the Event of My Life*

The coming of fascism to Spain was an event that changed my

life altogether. It was a disaster for me and for civilized humanity. There is no question about that. But it was not the end of the world. We suffered, but some of us survived and we worked to remake the world for peace and humanity again.

This leads me to realize that while certain events had a great effect on my life, no one event finally determined my life. There were a series of events that happened to me, and also that happened inside of me. Perhaps I could say that that series of events formed the one event that is my life. I mean, in the sense that the whole life of Pablo Casals as a person is a single event in the whole movement of the universe.

The event of the first part of my life, which included several smaller events, was the basic fact that I was able to establish myself as a musician. The events of my life were such that I could make the transition from being a poor country boy in Spain to traveling the world as a musician. That was the first and basic event.

Then, the next really interesting event was that, after World War I, I could begin to do what I had always wanted to do, which was to give music to the people. The political situation in Spain at that time (in addition to the money I earned giving concerts) made it possible for me to form the Workingman's Concerts and the Pau Casals Orchestra. My friendship with the Royal Family did not hurt in this, and after a little while I was able to be in the republican government to do more things to give the working people a greater contact with music. The fact of having a government that would help me develop music for the people made this a wonderful time in my life. It was so full of hope and possibilities for the future.

Then everything turned around. Suddenly there was the threat of having a government that only wanted to keep people under control and to fight other people. There was no feeling for people as persons to play music or think or be in science or the arts. So naturally we had to fight that. Soon there was a civil war and we were betrayed and we lost and we had to run from the country in a terrible condition. That turnaround was the event of fascism in my life. It was also a main event in the lives of all my countrymen. And it led to another event, the war that reached all over Europe.

That was an event that affected everybody. Everybody paid dearly for the fact that fascism was allowed to come to Spain.

But now, as I think of it in retrospect, I see that all of this suffering and disappointment led to another event in my life that may have been the meaning of it all. My loyalties had been to Catalonia and to Spain, and I was interested in music for the Spanish people. When Franco came, I naturally was loyal to the Spanish people. I thought of them first because I saw their problem as my own problem. But as the World War involved everybody in its suffering I realized that the problem is not for one nation but for all mankind. At that point I recognized more about the spirit in all beings, and I saw music as an expression of this unity. I think that this recognition was the great event of my life.

Dialogue with Events:
Sub-section for *The Ship That Was Bombed*

When I first went into exile in Prades, there were many opportunities for me to come to America where I could expect the people to be very friendly to me. There was something inside of me, however, that influenced me to stay with my countrymen in exile. Finally when Hitler took Paris and it looked as though he would move right down to the Mediterranean Sea, I agreed to come to America. Actually, at that point there seemed to be no alternative if I was to survive at all. With my friend Alevedra I booked passage to go by ship. It was to leave from Bordeaux. We made all the arrangements and with his wife and children Alevedra and I made the trip to Bordeaux. But when we arrived we found that there was no boat. It had been bombed out of existence while crossing the Atlantic. So that was the end of that.

I took that event as a sign that the place for me to be was still in Europe. We did not try to make other arrangements to come to America even if we could have. But we went back to Prades where I then stayed for a long time.

Question 6. Are you aware of having *sleep dreams or twilight images* during this period of your life? Are there any that stand out from the others with respect to their symbolism, the insights they gave you, or possibly the predictions they made?

Period Log Entry

During these years my sleep dreams were seldom anything else than nightmares. They were reflections of what I saw around me. In the early times in Prades I would be sure to have these nightmares after I had visited friends in the concentration camps. But my experience of twilight images has always been more peaceful.

By that time in my life I had found my own way of having twilight images, or their equivalent, in various forms. The main method for me was to begin each day by playing something by Bach. I would become quiet and centered while I was doing that, and sometimes good, new creative thoughts would come to me. A good example of that is when I was trying to compose my oratorio, *El Pesebre,* amidst the terrible conditions of Nazi occupation, raids and terror. I would begin my day by playing Bach, and that would put me in a twilight atmosphere in which I could compose despite the external circumstances.

If I can recall specific dreams and twilight images, I will make the further entries to record them and describe them.

Question 7. Were there *persons who inspired you,* persons from history or mythologic times, or persons living in your own time, in whom you felt a quality of wisdom that was especially relevant to you?

Period Log Entry

There were two people who very frequently came into my thoughts when I felt weak and when I needed to remind myself of the importance of the tasks that lay before me. These persons helped me maintain perspective and I could renew my determination when I placed their image before me. They were Fransesc Maciá, the great Catalan leader, and also Beethoven.

Feedback Entry in *Inner Wisdom Dialogue:*
Sub-section for *Fransesc Maciá*

During the difficult times in southern France I constantly held the thought and saw the image of Fransesc Maciá. It had an effect for me like my playing *The Song of the Birds*. It reconnected me with the Catalan past and with deep historical sources of strength. Maciá had dedicated his life to Catalonia and for that reason the Catalan people called him "The Grandfather." Thinking of him was like thinking of my mother. I could put the question to them of what they would do in this situation, and their answer would always remind me of the principles that a person must be true to.

Feedback Entry in *Inner Wisdom Dialogue:*
Sub-section for *Beethoven*

During the days when warfare and destruction of all kinds were going on around me, I remembered Beethoven and the way he kept his faith. He continued with his music through the years of violence. I realized that Beethoven had found a way to retain sanity in insane times while staying true to principle. I saw that as the great task for those of us who had the painful destiny of living in terrible times. It is essential that we not give up our beliefs, and that we not lose our personal commitment to the activities in life that we value. Whenever a moment came when I did not feel the strength of music, Beethoven reminded me. I turned to him often in order to reconnect myself with the principles in my own life to which I knew I must remain true at all costs. Fortunately I had not only had the thought of Beethoven as a person, but I also had his music. This reconnected me and sustained me.

Question 8. Were there *intersections of decision* in your life during this time? Considering that you chose to take particular roads and left other roads untaken, how do you perceive the consequences now?

Period Log Entry

This period of my life, this time under the Nazis, was full of life-or-death situations, one after another. Any moment could involve an instantaneous decision that might become a final moment. At the beginning I was frightened by this. It made me quite nervous. After a while, however, I came to the conclusion that there was no point in thinking about it. I would just live with it and try to act by my inner principles as much as I could. In a sense there were no intersections in personal life during this period because the main events were fixed by the circumstances of history. As individuals we did not have a future for which we could plan, so we could live only from moment to moment.

In my situation, however, there were some opportunities for a choice; but I chose not to take them. Had I chosen to, I could have left the problems of Spain behind me and gone to America. But I did not. And later on, I could have accepted the invitation to go to Nazi Germany to play. But of course I did not do that either. In refusing those choices, I was making one definite choice. I was choosing to stay with my own people and let their destiny be my destiny.

Feedback Entry in *Intersections—Roads Taken and Not Taken:*
Sub-section for *The Question of Coming to America*

I suppose I had a choice to make when it became apparent that Spain was destined to go through a period of very difficult turmoil. It was clear that much physical suffering lay ahead. I received many offers for concerts in the United States. My friends recommended that I go to America and that I try to remain there as long as the trouble continued in Spain. But I felt that I belonged with my people. Perhaps I would be able to help. And even if not, I wanted to be with them. I wanted to suffer what they would suffer. I did not really feel that it was a choice to make. I felt it was a fact of my life, like being a member of a particular family.

Feedback Entry in *Intersections—Roads Taken and Not Taken:* Sub-section for *Saying No to the Nazis*

When I was living in Prades after Hitler had moved his armies into France, some Nazi officers came one day to invite me to come to Germany to play. Of course a Nazi invitation was not just an ordinary invitation to be lightly refused. But I told them that no, I could not go. I am sure that I did not think about the alternatives before I answered them. I did not consider it to be a choice at the time. I suppose it was a crossroad of decision, but I did not feel that I had a decision to make. It was a matter of principle. I gave health as the reason, and that is probably why they accepted my refusal without reprisals. I just said no at the time, and I did not become nervous about it until afterwards.

Question 9. Did you have any experience of *connection to a meaning in life* during this period? Did you feel a lack of meaning in life?

Period Log Entry

At the beginning of this period of exile, and all through the events of the war from the bombings in Spain to the destruction in the rest of Europe, I felt that the meaning in life was being destroyed. This so distressed me that there were periods when I would not leave the darkness of my room. Eventually I could remain sane only because my music gave me a connection to more than myself. This is when I thought of Beethoven a great deal. And my morning work with Bach, whenever it was possible, became more important than ever.

The first half of 1943 was particularly bleak because the war was not going well. Hope was low for me and for everyone. My physical fatigue was becoming emotional fatigue as well, and I realized that this would pose a great problem if it went too far. I was becoming very depressed and I felt that my life was without meaning. Then I heard my friend Joan Alevedra read his Catalan poem, *El Pesebre (The Manger),* and I was so deeply moved by it that I resolved to compose the music for it. It took me more than two years to complete it. But in many ways composing *El Pesebre* was a turning point in my life. Probably it saved my life. In any case, it gave a connection with meaning once again.

Connections—Log Entry:
Sub-section for *My "El Pesebre" Experience*

The experience that led me to begin composing the music for *El Pesebre* was a most important event in my life. It had the effect of renewing my life. In that sense it gave me a rebirth even though I was in my middle sixties at the time. Since I lived another thirty years after that, I think it is possible that this experience is what gave birth to the next thirty years. It was certainly the seed of whatever sense of meaning and purpose I had in my life during the remaining years.

The original experience that led me to make the decision to try to compose the music for Alevedra's poem was a very important event in my life. Something of great consequence happened within me at that time. But I realize also that the experience of writing the music over a period that extended far more than two years in the midst of dreadful conditions also contained many important experiences and new understandings for me. I had to read and re-read the poem, consider and reconsider what my friend saw in the original Christian events that he was telling his daughter about. And this went deeper and deeper into me. Although the poem was in the Catalan language, it took me beyond Catalonia. Although it was Christian, it took me beyond Christianity. It took me to what is universal in the human condition. Probably this is why when I realized later on that it is the survival of the human species that is at issue as a result of the so-called advances in armaments, it was natural for me to dedicate *El Pesebre* to the hope that the human species would find a means to live in harmony and avoid another war.

In order to re-enter my *El Pesebre* experience, I have gone back over the events of the time as far as I remember them. I know that my feelings before it happened were of dreadful despair. I was becoming exhausted by the deprivations and the failures in the war, and I was losing hope. The way it began then was very simple. It was in the midst of what amounted to a family affair. My closest friend had won a small award and I was listening to him read the poem that won the prize, realizing that it was a poem he had written a few years before for his small daughter whom I knew well. It was a Catalan poem about the events that lie behind Christmas. Everything about it was elementary and involved things that I had known about all my life. But gradually I realized that I was experiencing it all in a new way. I was filled with emotion at the sound of my friend's voice and the thought of him with his daughter in the home they had lived in back in Barcelona. I know I thought of how different things were now, but I did not really resent it. I saw a light of meaning in everything that was happening. I felt a light in the darkness, and I felt reconnected with my own life. Somehow in that moment I became convinced that regardless of what would happen to me personally, that light of meaning in life would remain in the world. That changed my life altogether. In a way it meant that I did not have to live because the meaning in life would be there anyway. But in another sense it gave me a meaning in life and it gave me what to live for. It made me free to work without fear to keep that meaning in the world.

Afterwards as I worked at composing the music and found myself engaged in creating a full oratorio, I came to many points where the power of my original experience grew weak. Sometimes it seemed to have left me, and at those times I felt unable to continue with the composition. That was when I became especially grateful for my close connection with Bach. By playing his music I could place myself in a quiet and creative atmosphere, and I could resume my composing. Perhaps of even greater importance, when I played Bach's music during the time when I was composing *El Pesebre* I could feel the spiritual ground of what Bach touched in his own experience. This was a wonderful communion with him, and it was a further part of my experience of reconnecting with a meaning that renewed my life. Sometimes the process of writing it among those difficult conditions was tedious. I would become weary and despair of ever completing it. But it was also being done as a gift for my good and beloved friend. Each Christmas I had some more to play and sing for him. That was my present to him. And the thought of this with its personal feelings helped strengthen me and keep me going. Writing it was thus a very personal act. And it was much more than personal as well.

Chapter 16

Excerpts from the Life-Study Journal of Eleanor Roosevelt: I

An Early Focus Period: "Lucy and Polio"

Note: The excerpts given below from a Life-Study Journal of Eleanor Roosevelt are for the Focus Period in her life designated as "Lucy and Polio." The period covers the years from her matrimonial crisis into her time of political activity.

Material from this Focus Period has already been given in Chapter 9 for the Overview Statement, Chapter 10 for the Open Moment Image, and Chapter 11 for its Signpost Events. These exercises provide background for the responses to the Nine Questions given here.

Where the entries below are marked as appearing in the *Period Log,* it is implicit that they are from the sub-section there that is set apart for this Focus Period, "Lucy and Polio." Where feedback entries are made in addition to the *Period Log* entries, the specific Journal section and sub-section are indicated in each case.

Question 1. Who were the *persons who had an inner importance* to you during this unit of time? Describe the relationships, including both the pleasant and the unpleasant aspects.

Period Log Entry

I suppose it says a great deal about my life that the three main persons who had an inner importance to me during this period were people about whom I had mixed feelings. This was true with respect to Franklin, and also about Lucy Mercer, of whom I had been fond, but whose conduct surprised me. I had less ambiguity about Sara Roosevelt for, as my mother-in-law, she had always been a problem to me. There was a fourth person about whom I developed consistently affirmative feelings and about whom, after I overcame my initial misgivings, I had no reason to feel any further ambiguity. That was Louis Howe. But then, I am not sure that Louis had an inner importance to me in the sense that the other three did. There is no question about his effect on my life, however, for it was very great and we eventually became very close friends. His effect on my life was as surprising to me as it was constructive.

Feedback Entry in *Dialogue with Persons:*
Sub-section for *Franklin*

I think it is correct to say that I fully loved *Franklin* when we were married. I felt just too lucky to have such a handsome man of my own social class want to marry me, especially since I thought of myself as being ugly. When I came to know his mother, however, and to live in the midst of that relationship, often feeling that the marriage placed me under the control of my mother-in-law, I saw that there was another side to the story. I did not feel quite so lucky then, but I did place my complete trust in Franklin as a person. This was particularly so because I had borne six children with him and we had lived through many family ordeals together. I was finally feeling safe in my life, but when I found the letters from Lucy I felt that I had been deluding myself.

It is possible that I overreacted at the time. Perhaps that was part of the social attitudes of the time. I understand now that Franklin required something that I could not give him. And that may have been harmless, even beneficial in the long run, if I had understood it correctly. But I reacted terribly. I began to feel once again, and in even stronger terms, the old feelings of being worthless and useless. That was what led me to think of suicide. It was only Sara's cold, pragmatic argument that a divorce would ruin Franklin's political career that led me to stay with him. I did not commit suicide but let life go on.

Life went on, but things were different. My feelings toward Franklin were cold. We were separate persons altogether. At least at the beginning. My emotions toward Franklin were very confused then. I did not know what I felt. I was just keeping on as I had agreed to do.

Then came the cataclysm of his illness. It was sad to see, and I really became very sorry for him. It was terrible to see his physical weakness and his frustration as he tried to do things and his muscles simply would not obey him. And then there was his great pain. I found myself feeling it with him. I felt a sympathy, but it was more than just sympathy. It became a closeness. I tried to give to him and to help him in every way I could. In that circumstance I felt that there could be no holding back. I suppose also, though, that I felt secure with him once again. This time I knew that he needed me whether I was beautiful or not.

Even though I had loved Franklin very much, often very blindly, I had been realistic about his personal traits. I had seen how ambitious a person he was, and I recognized how much he wanted to make a place for himself in the world. Against that background of knowledge, it was an especially terrible thing to see how he was suffering inwardly as it became increasingly clear to him that his sudden illness was destroying all his carefully nurtured plans. Before this, I had had very mixed feelings about the ambitious side of Franklin, but now I truly suffered with him. I wished for him to be able to re-establish his life as much as possible in the way that he had wished it to be.

After a very difficult period the decision was made to try to restore as much strength to the weakened muscles as possible, and then to try to resume a political career. That was of course Franklin's decision ultimately, and it depended on him to carry it through. He was the person who had to feel the pain and do the difficult exercises day after day. I did what I could to help. I really tried to share the burdens in every way I could. In the end, and through the years, that probably became the keynote of our relationship. We shared very closely. Franklin knew that he could count on me. Perhaps he also felt beholden to me, although whatever I gave I gave freely and asked nothing in return. It may be, though, that something more became part of our relationship over the years, especially later when he carried burdens that were even greater than polio.

For myself, I developed a tremendous respect as well as sympathy for Franklin during his years of making a comeback from polio. I had to respect, even to admire, the determination with which he bore the pain and carried out the exercises to try to recover the use of his muscles.

Feedback Entry in *Dialogue with Persons:*
Sub-section for *Lucy Mercer*

I suppose that *Lucy Mercer* was "the other woman," and that makes it very difficult to consider her in a clear-minded way. After all, she had worked for me as a secretary, so I had not considered her to be a rival. In retrospect I think that my reaction to discovering the events that had been taking place had much less to do with her than with my own feelings about myself. Lucy was the occasion for me to remember my old self-doubts. And she was also the occasion for me to realize that what I had thought to be a safe relationship with Franklin was mostly an illusion.

In this sense Lucy was merely a situation in my life, and she did not really have an inner importance to me as a person. But she did have an inner importance to Franklin, and this, as I discovered, did continue over the years. In this sense I did feel that there is an indirect connection between Lucy and myself that is important in some way. I feel it is like a part of my life that I never lived but that I think I would have liked to live. There were times when I felt deprived of that romantic possibility in my life. When I married Franklin I pretended to myself that marriage and children had given me romance. But then Lucy took it away from me, and I could no longer pretend to myself. So Lucy made me a more honest person.

Feedback Entry in *Dialogue with Persons:*
Sub-section for *Sara Roosevelt*

Sara Roosevelt was my mother-in-law. Once I became married to Franklin that was a basic fact of my life. Perhaps that was the basic "better or worse" of the marriage vow I took. The events of this period in my life brought about a basic change in my relation to her. From my point of view the change was for the better, but it came about as a result of some very painful events.

From the very beginning of the marriage Sara had been a very domineering mother-in-law. She had always dominated Franklin, and when he married me I was an easy mark for her domineering tendencies. Of course it was she who had the money, and she knew how to use it. She had taken over our household from the start. She actually bought the furniture and hired the servants while we were away on our honeymoon. And I accepted all of that. My only desire was to please her, and that set the tone of things. When the affair with Lucy came to light, it was she who made the decision for what was ultimately done.

I reacted very emotionally, but she was very calm and calculating about it all. Once again she had power because it was she who controlled Franklin's purse strings. She was still the source of the largest part of his income. By her calculation Franklin's political career would come to an end if we divorced. Therefore we must not divorce. She said that if we did she would cut off her supply of money from all of us. We must keep up appearances and continue as before. I was forced to agree, but I extracted the promise that Franklin would not see Lucy any more. I do not know for sure, but it is possible that Sara and Franklin winked at each other when Franklin made that promise. In any case the situation was settled according to Sara's opinions and her determination as to what we should do. I know that Franklin's relation to Lucy did not raise me in Sara's eyes. She continued her practice of dominating me in every way she could.

That was a low point in my life as a wife, and my mother-in-law's attitude toward me made it humiliating as well as painful. But the circumstances changed when Franklin became ill with polio.

When it became clear that the disease had atrophied the muscles, the question became what to do next. As usual Sara had a definite opinion and was ready to take events into her own hands. There was an alternative to Franklin's political career, she said; he could go into a semi-retirement and become a country squire on his estates in Hyde Park. All of us could live together in the semi-isolation of the country, and Franklin's paralysis would not be a serious drawback, and therefore not a serious concern, under those circumstances. She saw this as a convenient way to solve a difficult problem, but I saw it as consigning Franklin to a living death. At that point, which was actually the critical decision of his life, Franklin rejected his mother's view of what he should do. He opted for doing whatever he had to do medically or by physical exercises, no matter how painful they would have to be, until his use of his body was returned to him, at least sufficiently to enable him to have a life in the world once again. I had told Franklin that I would do everything I could to help him if this was his decision, but the decision itself was up to him. The effect of his decision was to choose my help and to reject his mother's direction. This had a very important effect on all our future relationships. The work of restoring his physical capacities while keeping his name alive politically brought me exceedingly close to him in many practical and intimate ways on a day-to-day basis. It is ironic, but when he became so seriously ill physically I became more his wife than I had ever been before. Finally I replaced his mother.

As this period moved on I felt the increasing strength of my relationship with Franklin because of what I was doing with him. And this allowed me to feel much stronger in relation to my mother-in-law. She was still domineering in her ways whenever she had the slightest opportunity. That was the kind of person she was, and I knew that that could never change. But Franklin had chosen to fight for his active life rather than go into retirement, and I was the person who helped him do this. Now when Sara's domination was more than I could bear I was strong enough to say what needed to be said and to do what needed to be done. In relation to Sara I was strengthening my muscles much as Franklin was.

Feedback Entry in *Dialogue with Persons:*
Sub-section for *Louis Howe*

When Franklin first brought Louis Howe home I did not like him. I am afraid that I was given to hasty opinions in those days based on superficial attitudes. Louis gave the appearance of a person who neither washed nor changed his clothes very often, and his manners were not as fine as I thought was proper. For those reasons mainly I took a dim view of him, but I discovered that I was very wrong.

He was a journalist and Franklin had made him a close personal advisor especially in matters that related to politics since the early days in Albany. I first came to appreciate Louis' great intelligence and sensitivity during the 1920 campaign when Franklin ran for Vice-President. He took a warm personal interest in the problems that I had at that time as a candidate's wife and he taught me many things that proved to be of great help through the years. I learned to trust him, and he became an increasingly close friend over a long period of time.

When Franklin became ill, Louis was steadfast in his help and support. Once we could see the full extent of the physical damage that the polio had done to Franklin, Louis designed a plan by which Franklin would work to regain his physical strength while I would do whatever I could to keep Franklin's name alive in the political world. I would do this until Franklin was able to come back and take things over on his own. Louis said that he would show me what to do and that he would give me all the help I needed. That is exactly what he did. He was true to his word.

This was the quality of Louis that I valued so greatly. He was sensitive to a person's problems and realistic about what was needed to solve them. He did not look for easy answers. He was honest about the facts and he had not only great courage but persistence in carrying out whatever he felt needed to be done. Perhaps the most important thing about him is that when Louis said he would help, he did help. I had met many glib, facile people in the political world—many of whom were cleaner and much better dressed than Louis—who would promise to do many things, but they never did them. But Louis always did what he said he would do. He was sincere. Yes, that is the right word and that is what I appreciated so much about him. Especially he was sincere to me, and I needed that kind of friend over many years. When situations arose where I needed help, Louis really gave it whenever he could. He was there, really there. He helped Franklin greatly during the time of illness. And he helped me help Franklin the best I could. This was the basis of the trust between us.

Question 2. What were your *work projects and activities* during this period? What were your long-range goals and your short-range goals? What happened to them? Which came to a dead end? Which were completed? Which were halted and then resumed at a later time? Tell the feelings and the experiences that were involved in these.

Period Log Entry

When this period began I thought I was well settled in the work of my life. I felt that I had fulfilled my major role in bearing my children. I was vaguely dissatisfied with the content of my life as a wife, but that was in a way that many women are. I felt that I was too dependent on my husband. That made me restless and rather irritable. I wanted to be independent and do something on my own, or so I said. But the truth is that I did not really want to be independent, and I did not want to have to do things on my own. I was actually afraid of those situations. I tried to avoid them, and sometimes I literally forced myself to do them, as when I did volunteer work. Occasionally, when I could not avoid it, I even gave a public talk. At first these experiences were dreadful.

Everything that I dreaded was forced upon me, however, by the strange turnings of events during this period. When I found out about Franklin's affair with Lucy Mercer, the very thing that I had been complaining about most, namely, my being a dependent housewife, was put in jeopardy. And I was thrown into a great emotional confusion. Then, when Franklin contracted polio, the relation of dependency was reversed. In many ways, Franklin became dependent on me. I know that I was necessary to him at that time. I felt that I was needed, and that enabled me to do things that I had been afraid of trying before.

The main activity that had an inner importance to me was being a wife, specifically, being Franklin's wife. This led to many other things, especially the work of helping him get back the use of his body. But that was part of being his wife. It also led to another work that was less clear and important then than it became later on. That was my being a political person in my own right. I did not have any idea of the things that it would lead me into, but it all started then.

Feedback Entry in *Dialogue with Works:*
Sub-section for *Being Franklin's Wife*

I could say that my work during this time of my life was being a housewife. But that was not really true. I was never much of a housekeeper, partly because I did not like to do it. Other things came into my mind and I wanted to do them. And besides, I always had servants taking care of the house. That was part of my social background. My role was to manage the servants, and I have never liked managing other people. I have never liked telling other people what to do, so the fact that I had to have servants has never been pleasant to me. I often found myself thinking of the servants as part of the family, as part of my family and not as people who worked for me. I did not enjoy taking care of the house. Often I would rather do things myself than have other people do them for me.

If I did not think of myself as a housewife, I did very much think of myself as a wife. I took that very seriously as something that was very important for me to be good at. And not just being any wife. I was Franklin's wife. That was my special role and I considered it to be my special opportunity in life. That is why I was so earnest about it when we first were married, and why I was thrown into consternation when I encountered Sara's domineering ways. I felt that I was not going to have a chance really to be Franklin's wife. I think that is a main reason why I was so devastated by learning of Franklin's affair with Lucy. I felt that I had failed in the one work that really mattered to me.

Part of being his wife was the fact that I bore Franklin's children. There was a special intimacy in that, not so much the sexual side of it as all the things that followed from it once the pregnancy became visible and a new person was brought into the world. I think the intimacy and the sharing were the greatest in the case of the infant who died. For the rest, Franklin kept his distance from the details. But he did like the role of being father of the family, and he enjoyed its becoming larger and larger. I was glad to do that for him. As I think of it now I realize that I mainly bore the children out of my desire to be a good wife to Franklin. But something further developed from it. I realized that I was a mother. I had not thought about that very much before, but gradually I realized that it was a very important part of my life. I came to see that being a mother was a work that had a great inner importance to me. During this period the work of being Franklin's wife went through great changes. When I found out about his affair with Lucy, I thought that it had come to an end. I felt very despondent about it, and about everything else in my life. Naturally I felt very cold toward Franklin. I felt that the emotional side of our relationship was over. But then came the polio. Being Franklin's wife then meant helping him regain the use of his legs and helping him become able to resume an active role in the world. That brought us together again and, in its way, it was at least as intimate as anything else had ever been.

Feedback Entry in *Dialogue with Works:*
Sub-section for *Being a Mother*

I never thought of being a mother as a work in my life. In fact, when I was young there were many times when I doubted whether there would be an opportunity for me ever to become a mother physically. When I did become a mother, I experienced it as part of being a wife. I saw being a mother as part of what a wife did. I was giving Franklin a family. But the years have made it more than that.

After the situation of Franklin's affair, I realized that my being a mother was not something that I had done simply as Franklin's rib. It was a definite creative act on my part. There were five living human beings who were now in the world as a result of what I had done, and I felt both a love for them and a responsibility to them regardless of anything that Franklin might do. It was very pleasant for me to find whenever the occasion arose that they had special feelings toward me just as I had very special feelings toward them.

One of the effects of the crises during this period of my life was that I realized how important a part of my life being a mother was. And I realized that it was quite separate from Franklin even though it was closely related to him. I also realized that being a mother was not the whole of my life, that there were other things that I could also do, even though a large part of my emotional life was connected to my being a mother.

Feedback Entry in *Dialogue with Works:*
Sub-section for *A Political Woman*

When this period began I was suffering from the vague dissatisfaction and restlessness plaguing many modern women. I complained of the fact that, as a wife, I was too dependent on my husband. I did not feel that I had my own identity. It probably was nothing more than the usual vague complaining that is characteristic of many women. I did not really want things to change, for I still had the attitudes toward marriage and family and a woman's role in it with which I had been brought up. That was part of the social class into which I had been born, and it was also the generally accepted attitude of the whole culture around the time of the first World War.

I felt vaguely restless and the usual prescription for that was that I needed something more to do, something outside the home. That meant volunteer work, and I had been accustomed to that. There was a strong feeling in me, however, that a woman did not need to be limited to a dependent role and that I could develop a great deal more of myself. But at that time I did not feel sufficient strength in myself, nor did I have a strong enough motivation. I did, however, take part in women's organizations, although only in a minor way. That gave me something to do, but I did not give a large part of my energy to it.

When Franklin became ill with polio the situation changed. He was a well-known figure at the time for he had been the Democratic candidate for Vice-President in 1920. Even though he lost, the outlook for his political future was very good, for he was still a young man and now he had attracted national attention. But everything came to a stop when he was paralyzed by polio in 1921. The critical point occurred when Franklin decided that he would devote all his energies to recovering the use of his body in order eventually to return to political life. Then Louis Howe developed the plan that called for me to take an active political role in order to keep Franklin's name before the public until he himself could take over. At that point I could step into the background again, but until then I would be required to be active as a political woman. As a good wife I agreed to do that, but I was actually terrified of the kind of speechmaking that it would require.

Louis Howe helped me through the worst times of it, which mainly were at the beginning. I did many things for the Democrats nationally, especially for the women's groups. It seemed to be successful, for I found that I could be effective in organizational work. I did it strongly for Franklin until he was able to become active again and run for Governor of New York State in 1928. Then I stepped into the background again.

During those years when Franklin's illness held him back, I had a strong taste of political life. It caused me to make some very unflattering judgments of some high political figures; but I mostly kept those judgments to myself. Basically I enjoyed the activity.

Question 3. What was the *physical condition of your life,* your health and illnesses, your sensory life, your sensual life, your over-all relation to your body and its uses during this period?

Period Log Entry

My health has always been good. It is difficult for me to think of times in my life when I suffered an extended illness. Infirmities of the body seemed never to interrupt the conduct of my life. Even when I carried and delivered children—six in all, although only five lived—I did not become sickly.

On the other hand I cannot say that I was particularly strong. I was not a notably good athlete. I was not drawn to athletic activities. It is merely that I was gifted with a good serviceable body that did not become ill.

I do not know what to say about other aspects of my body. We did not speak about sexual things when I was a young woman. I thought I was functioning well enough in that regard until the situation with Lucy arose. After all, I became pregnant often enough. But apparently that was not all there was to it.

Feedback Entry in *Dialogue with the Body:*
Sub-section for *Life History of the Body*

As a young person I was generally healthy and seldom ill.

I rode horseback and danced and swam. I used my body in ways that were socially appropriate.

My adolescent years were particularly difficult because I thought of myself as being ugly. I would recall the fact that my mother had called me "Granny" and that would make me feel sad about my looks. After I became a mother, however, I did not worry about it; at least, not until the Lucy affair.

When Franklin became ill with polio my main concern was that I have sufficient physical strength to take care of him properly. I did have. My physical stamina was very useful then. And also for the many public appearances that I had to make as part of Louis Howe's political program.

Question 4. What were your *social attitudes* during this time, your beliefs, loyalties, antagonisms? What was your relation to your family, your nation, your historical roots? Were changes taking place in your social or philosophical orientation during this time?

Period Log Entry

A basic fact of my life is my social background. I was born into the well-to-do social class of New York State, but their accustomed activities did not suit my temperament very well. As a young girl I accepted the attitudes of the social class into which I was born. But something in me did not like them. So it did not require a great deal of prodding to set me in protest against them. But I had no ideology. I only wanted fairness and decency for people. When I think of my relation to society with a small "s," it comes in two parts. One is the part of society that gave itself a capital "S" and against which I was in rebellion. The other is the aspect of society that includes all human beings and that seeks to give everyone a fair chance. I was gradually working my way from one to the other, but I believe that the second one was in me all the while.

Feedback Entry in *Dialogue with Society:*
Sub-section for *My Social Background*

My father was President Theodore Roosevelt's brother and that gave me a heritage to which I have always felt connected. I was conscious of my uncle's social progressivism, especially after my education in England under Mlle. Souvestre. But I was also under the influence of the select social class into which I was born. It presented me with many rules and requirements, and although I rebelled against them I usually obeyed them nonetheless. This placed a strong ambiguity in my life. I felt the pull of conflicting social attitudes. During this period when my marriage was in crisis and when I was beginning to become politically active, these divergent attitudes had a great effect on me.

Feedback Entry in *Dialogue with Society:*
Sub-section for *Political Rights*

I have been working for women's rights and trying to do what I can also to ameliorate the hard lot of people in the working class. I have not felt able to do much, and I realize increasingly that ladies who try to work in the social and political field are not treated seriously. There is not much that they will be allowed to do more than keep themselves busy. I would like to be able to do more. The more I am active in political work, the more I see what needs to be done. But I have to keep in mind my own limitations.

Question 5. Were there *events that occurred in your life* at this time that were striking in their impact and that brought about sharp changes in the circumstances of your life? Were there events that seemed to have a fateful or mysterious quality? How did this feel to you at the time, and in the times that followed?

Period Log Entry

Two unexpected events stand out in my mind as having a most

striking effect on my life during this period. The first is my discovery of Franklin's affair with Lucy Mercer. It had a devastating impact on me. But perhaps I overreacted.

The second event is Franklin's becoming ill with polio. His paralysis and the effort to counteract it changed the life of everyone in the family. For several years it was the main factor in my life, and it led to activities that I would never have undertaken otherwise.

Feedback Entry in *Dialogue with Events:*
Sub-section for *The Lucy Affair*

As I go to write about it I am not sure which had the greater importance: the fact that Franklin had the affair with Lucy or the fact that I accidentally discovered it.

In retrospect I can see that the affair did not mean that much in itself. But the discovery of it sent shock waves through me and led me to question the very foundations of my life. But after a while things settled down. It is very possible that, given a large perspective of life, I overreacted at the time. But that was the way I was then. Perhaps my reaction changed things more than the affair itself. It becomes less and less important in the larger view of things, especially when I think of Franklin's physical illness that followed a few years afterward.

Feedback Entry in *Dialogue with Events:*
Sub-section for *Franklin's Contracting Polio*

Franklin became ill with polio during the summer of 1921. He had been working very hard at the time and his body was undoubtedly overtired when he contracted the illness. Probably the major event in his life preceding it had been his campaign for Vice-President on the Democratic ticket in 1920. He had felt let down after the defeat, but it had not been unexpected. During the early part of 1921 he had mainly been engaged in gathering together the pieces of his career and getting his financial affairs in order after the several months of concentrating on the campaign.

As far as our personal relationship was concerned, it was cool but cooperative at that time. I had gone on the campaign train with him in 1920 and we were working together to maintain our family life. In fact, the place where he contracted polio was at our summer home in Campobello. He came there to be part of the family, but he was physically worn out when he arrived.

When we realized the nature of the illness it was a great shock to us. It was misdiagnosed at first, but soon we perceived the extent of the problem. This was certainly an event that changed Franklin's life, and changed my life as well.

The personal difficulties between us now became inconsequential. What did anything else matter if Franklin was so seriously ill? At first he was fighting for his very life, and we felt that he needed the support of all of us to give him the will to get well. When it became clear that he would survive, the task became for Franklin to regain the use of his body. That depended on his willpower alone, and on his dedication. It was a terrible ordeal. I would not like ever to see another human being suffer such pain and personal torment. But the fact is that Franklin emerged from it with a strength within him that I do not believe he possessed before. He emerged from his illness as a very strong person.

As for myself, there were two important consequences of the event of Franklin's illness. One was that we had a closer working relationship in our life together. The other was that, being sent out into the political world as Franklin's representative during his illness, I built an active life and developed capacities that I never would have undertaken otherwise. In that unexpected way also Franklin's illness became a turning point in my life as well as his.

Question 6. Are you aware of having *sleep dreams or twilight images* during this period of your life? Are there any that stand out from the others with respect to their symbolism, the insights they gave you, or possibly the predictions they made?

Period Log Entry

I am aware of having dreams of my father from time to time, but I never paid much attention to the details. I do not know whether there was anything else of significance in the dreams. I understand the dreams to mean that I loved my father very much and that I missed him. But I already knew that and I did not need dreams to tell me so.

In general I tried to base my life on commonsense and the realities of the world around me. I did not pay much attention to dreams and things of that kind.

Question 7. Were there *persons who inspired you,* persons from history or mythologic times, or persons living in your own time, in whom you felt a quality of wisdom that was especially relevant to you?

Period Log Entry

There are two persons to whom I would turn for inner guidance at this time in my life. One is Mrs. Henry Adams (Clover Adams) who had died by her own hand and was buried in a Washington cemetery. The other is Mlle. Souvestre, the headmistress of the school I attended in England during my adolescent years.

I do not know the details of Clover Adams' life, nor what it was that led her to take her own life. At her grave, however, there is a statue of her by Augustus Saint-Gaudens commissioned by her husband. This statue expresses a profound quietness. Perhaps she achieved this quietness only in death, or only in the conception of her that the sculptor projected. Perhaps it was a conception of her that her husband projected to Saint-Gaudens. I do not know. What I do know is that when I became despondent and was despairing of my life when I learned of Franklin's affair, I would often go to the cemetery and sit beside the statue. I found peace there, and eventually I regained my strength. I felt at that time that Clover Adams would be a person who would understand whatever personal problems I might have. I suspect that there is very little that I could experience that she had not already experienced. But I believe the artist was correct in showing her in a profound state of peace. Sitting near that statue I could feel the peace communicate itself to me.

The other person to whom I would turn for inner guidance is Mlle. Souvestre. When I first came to her school I was a frightened girl, accustomed to being an outsider who was not accepted by others. I was also a person with no appreciation of the values and beliefs outside of my particular social class. She showed me that there is more to the world than I knew about at that time. She gave me an appreciation of other people, and she also enabled me to begin to value myself.

In this period of my life when I was beginning to take an active role in political life, I often found myself thinking back to the things that Mlle. Souvestre had taught me. She had made me aware of the fact that women are capable of becoming fully developed individuals and making a full contribution to society. When I married Franklin I let myself forget some of what she had taught me, for I was altogether intent on becoming a good wife for him within our social groups. But Franklin's affair awakened me to many things, among them the importance of women developing themselves.

Question 8. Were there *intersections of decision* in your life during this time? Considering that you chose to take particular roads and left other roads untaken, how do you perceive the consequences now?

Period Log Entry

These were years in which decisions were made that affected not only my life but the others in my family. The decisions were made under the pressure of circumstances.

When I learned of Franklin's affair with Lucy, I came very

close to breaking up my marriage. That would have had far-reaching consequences. But I did not do it.

When Franklin became ill with polio, I made the decision within myself to help him do whatever he decided to do. When he needed help to regain his physical strength, and when he needed me to help him politically in order to carry out Louis Howe's plans, I was already committed. I could not have done otherwise, and I would not have done otherwise.

Feedback Entry in *Intersections—Roads Taken and Not Taken:*
Sub-section for *Retaining the Marriage*

I was on the verge of breaking up the marriage when Sara intervened with two considerations. One was that to end the marriage would also end Franklin's political career. The other was that she would cut off Franklin's income and this would affect everyone, especially the children.

The first consideration turned out to be more important than I realized at the time. Who can tell what would have happened in the world if Franklin had been forced out of politics and had not been President at the time of the Great Depression and the Great War? And who can tell how my personal life would have developed if I had left Franklin? And how the lives of the children would have developed?

Sara's financial arguments and her control were very persuasive at the time, and I bent to them. These were practical considerations and not matters of principle. When I became more active in politics, I saw more and more how such practical considerations tend to override matters of principle. It was a great question for me, but I came to accept it.

Question 9. Did you have any experience of *connection to a meaning in life* during this period? Did you feel a lack of meaning in life?

Period Log Entry

I cannot truly say that connective experiences or awarenesses of meaning came to me during this period. But I know that some large and fundamental questions were forming within me. These were questions that I had not been asking before.

When Franklin's affair with Lucy came to light, I found myself asking what the meaning and purpose of a person's life is. That was the time when I would go to sit at the statue of Clover Adams in the cemetery. I do not know that I ever received an answer, but the questioning was started.

Later in this period when I became active on Franklin's behalf in political circles, I found myself wondering more and more about the fundamental questions of social justice. I was becoming increasingly concerned about more than women's rights but the right of all social classes to have the ability to take care of their families. My questions about social justice became much larger and more important to me than they had been before.

Feedback Entry in *Peaks, Depths and Explorations:*
Sub-section for *The Question of Meaning in Life*

My personal disappointment with Franklin leads me to wonder about the meaning and purpose of a person's life. Is there any meaning? I do not know. But in reading certain poems, or when I sat at the statue of Clover Adams at her grave, I have felt a great quietness and peace. Then I have thought that perhaps it is in those feelings of peacefulness that the meaning of life is to be found.

Feedback Entry in *Peaks, Depths and Explorations:*
Sub-section for *Social Justice*

As I work in the field of politics and find it to be more and more rewarding personally, I come to understand how the great issues in our country's history have been resolved. It seems to be largely a matter of bargaining, of dealing and negotiating. You give me this and I'll give you that. I feel it vaguely, but it seems to me at this time that something much more fundamental is at issue here. It is the question of what is really the right and fair way to treat people of all classes. I like to think that this is what my Uncle Theodore was trying to get at, although he could not finally succeed. And that is what Mlle. Souvestre was trying to communicate to me back in school. I had a sense of it also when I did the volunteer work in the settlement house in lower Manhattan. I sensed that the injustices there were fundamental and were much more than a matter of the advantage gained by one political group or another.

The more active I am in the political field, the more I see the importance of the fundamental question of social justice, and the less I see the politicians addressing it. At this point I do not see very much that can be done about it.

Chapter 17

Excerpts from the Life-Study Journal of Eleanor Roosevelt: II

A Later Focus Period: "A Widow and a Person"

Note: The excerpts given below from a Life-Study Journal of Eleanor Roosevelt are for the Focus Period in her life designated as "A Widow and a Person." It deals with the years following the death of Franklin Roosevelt. It covers the years from her matrimonial crisis into her time of political activity.

Material from this Focus Period has already been given in Chapter 9 for the Overview Statement, Chapter 10 for the Open Moment Image, and Chapter 11 for its Signpost Events. Those exercises provide background for the responses to the Nine Questions given here.

Where the entries below are marked as appearing in the *Period Log,* it is implicit that they are from the sub-section there that is set apart for this Focus Period, "A Widow and a Person." Where feedback entries are made in addition to the *Period Log* entries, the specific Journal section and sub-section are indicated in each case.

Question 1. Who were the *persons who had an inner importance* to you during this unit of time? Describe the relationships, including both the pleasant and the unpleasant aspects.

Period Log Entry

Franklin's death leaves me a widow with five grown children. In one sense it can be said that I have a great many friends. When I ask myself, however, about the persons who have an *inner importance* to me, I find that the number is not large at all. It also makes a significant point about the nature of my friendships. There are several people about whom I care very deeply as friends. Nonetheless, if I ask who are the persons who have an *inner importance* to me at this point in my life, I find that the answer has to be given in terms of my immediate family. It is Franklin and my five children, Anna and James, Elliot, Franklin Jr., and John.

Feedback Entry in: *Dialogue with Persons:*
Sub-section for *Franklin*

Franklin has been laid to rest with profound general mourning and amid a great deal of fanfare. And I remain here.

Now the pressure of events is gone and the pain is healing. Now, however, I have discovered that he was with Lucy Mercer and not with me at Warm Springs when the end came. Others knew, but I did not know. All of it says a great deal to me that I did not let myself believe. It had undoubtedly been true for a long time.

Now that Franklin has died there is nothing to be done about any of it. The only question now is how much I let myself continue to dwell on it. I shall not let myself think about it, at least not if I can help it. The country is still at war and I have a responsibility as far as that goes. And beyond that, there are many possibilities that Franklin's work opened that have not been fulfilled, and some that have not even been developed. Once the war is ended there will be a great deal that needs to be done, not only in his name but because the world requires it. There may not be much that I can do, but I shall try. I shall be true to his work, even if he could not be true to me. It is strange. I feel very close to it, and it seems to be something more than personal.

Feedback Entry in *Dialogue with Persons:*
Sub-section for *Anna*

Now that Franklin has died I realize that Lucy Mercer visited at the White House while I was away. *Anna* was part of it. She helped her father arrange his tryst, and she did not tell me about it. I suppose I should be angry with Anna, but I sympathize with her. She was placed in a terrible dilemma that was not of her own making. She was caught in the middle of something, and it was not her fault. It was unfair to her, and I hope that she has not suffered too much because of it.

I felt very sad over the break-up of Anna's marriage to John. My attempt to conduct a radio show with Anna was interesting, but it was not a commercial success. The radio stations dropped it, probably for many different reasons. Many people have said that the main reason for my doing the radio program was to try to help Anna recoup her finances. There is certainly considerable truth in that, but of course that could not make the program a success. I am very concerned about Anna's troubles, both personal and financial.

Question 2. What were your *work projects and activities* during this period? What were your long-range goals and your short-range goals? What happened to them? Which were halted and then resumed at a later time? Tell the feelings and the experiences that were involved in these.

Period Log Entry

Now that I am a widow I am free to see in terms of my own thoughts and judgments what are the work activities that I truly feel to be important. It seems to be the first time ever that I feel free to ask myself what I truly care about without having to be concerned about other considerations

The test of my caring about a particular work activity lies in the fact that I myself choose to do it, and that I am not impelled to

220

do it because someone else wants me to. Many of the things that I have done in the past were not so much because someone else told me to do it as because it was the thing to do. And also because there was some part of me also that wanted to do it. Perhaps that describes how I became a mother.

The fact is that I became a mother not once but several times. It has absorbed a large part of my life, and it is an authentic part of me. I am a mother and I have continued to be concerned as a mother. Now, in addition, I am a grandmother; that also is very important to me. I feel a great concern and love and caring for my own children and my grandchildren. But I have observed in recent years that the feelings that stir in me when I think of the impoverished people in the world are feelings like a mother's feelings toward her children. I feel a mother's concern for the hungry people of the world. In that sense my most continuous work, even in the public field, is my being a mother.

Feedback Entry in *Dialogue with Works:*
Sub-section for *Being a Mother*

I am more than a mother now. I have become a grandmother several times and find that it is a very pleasant experience. It extends my feelings of mothering but without giving me the specific responsibilities of being a mother.

As I have moved into the public sphere, my private role as mother has fallen increasingly into the background. Perhaps it is my increasing age and the fact that I am Franklin's widow, but I have found in my travels that people respond to me as a mother. And I find myself feeling toward them in that protective way. That was true in India especially; but not only in India. I have my personal children. They belong to my private life, and I naturally feel a special connection to them. But I also have feelings of mothering, protective feelings, toward people who are not my own physical children. Since I have a public life as well as a private life, I often feel myself to be acting as a mother in my public life. And then I find myself caring about people so much that I feel heart pain, more than I can bear sometimes, when I see the suffering of helpless people in the improverished countries. This was particularly the case in India, so much so that I had to leave.

In India I could not bear it, and I could not take the responsibility of it. That is the difficult side of being a mother: the responsibility of it. I certainly did not feel satisfied with the way I have fulfilled my responsibilities to the children of my private life. I do keep on trying. But when I realized that a great many of the people whom I visited in the course of my travels have seen me as a mother to whom they look for help in solving the terrible problems of their poverty, the responsibility became too great to bear. I know that I am not able to fulfill their expectation, and I certainly do not want to mislead them. I realize that I have been seen as a kind of public mother in my travels during this period. On one level it is very flattering. On the other level it has been a source of great pain to me.

Feedback Entry in *Dialogue with Works:*
Sub-section for *Being a Public Person*

I have lived my life in public view since 1929 when Franklin became Governor of New York State. The situation became more prominent in 1933 when he was inaugurated President. I have had many years in which to become accustomed to it.

At first I was fearful of living my life in public view. And perhaps with good reason. But in this latter period after I became a widow, I have realized that the nature of my life is that I am a public person. Even with Franklin gone, I myself have made it that way. The question is not whether I am a public person, but whether I can do it well and fulfill its responsibilities.

There has been a change in my life over the years. When I was young I did not want people to notice my life. I was very insecure then and my life was not worth noticing. Besides, I was only involved in personal affairs then. But now the issues apply to more people than to myself, from the Declaration of Human Rights to the means of alleviating hunger in the undeveloped countries. If I can say or do something that will be helpful I am willing to be on public view. If not, I can still have my own opinions, but it is better for me to function as a private citizen.

Question 3. What was *the physical condition of your life,* your health and illnesses, your sensory life, your sensual life, your overall relation to your body and its uses during this period?

Period Log Entry

My basic health continues to be good through this period and my energy level continues to be high. Nonetheless, I find it necessary to rest a little more and I have been subject to some minor illnesses, especially in the course of my travels. Also, my dark moods return occasionally. They come more than they have for a while. But they do not last very long.

Feedback Entry in *Dialogue with the Body:*
Sub-section for *Life History of the Body*

Although my energies continue to be strong in this period since Franklin has died, I find that I have the need to rest more than I did before. I find that I tire occasionally, but with a little rest I am able to keep on going.

My general health continues to be maintained even while I travel into countries with very different climates and customs of eating. On at least one occasion, however, I have been walking around with what the doctors say is a case of pneumonia. But my basic strength seems to have absorbed it, and I have been able to continue my work.

Occasionally during these years I seem to be subject to a recurrence of the dark moods that have bothered me from time to time. But I have been able to overcome them by throwing myself into my work and trying to do good for people.

Question 4. What were your *social attitudes* during this time, your beliefs, loyalties, antagonisms? What was your relation to your family, your nation, your historical roots? Were changes taking place in your social or philosophical orientation during this time?

Period Log Entry

As Franklin's wife, I had an opportunity to learn a great deal about society at the practical level where governments operate. Occasionally I was even able to exert some influence although it was seldom of much consequence.

When Franklin died I had an opportunity to reach out directly to society through the United Nations. This was certainly a wonderful experience for me, and also a great frustration. The great interest and commitment of my life has been to society, and in this period I was able to reach out to the nations of the world. But I cannot say that the results were what I would have wished.

Question 5. Were there *events that occurred in your life* at this time that were striking in their impact and that brought about sharp changes in the circumstances of your life? Were there events that seemed to have a fateful or mysterious quality? How did this feel to you at the time, and in the times that followed?

Period Log Entry

The event that started this period in my life was Franklin's death. That left a great void and altered my whole life situation. It caused me to see very clearly how much my position in life was derived from the fact of my being Franklin's wife. There was a pain in that, for I have always wanted to be myself, an independent person. And yet I had to acknowledge how much of my life was based on his. In a way I was a symbol of Franklin for many people, and I felt that as my personal responsibility. Even with Franklin dead,—in fact, especially now that Franklin had died—I felt that I owed it both to him and to the people who cared about him to represent him as truly as I could. I tried to do this in the United Nations and in my travels, but it brought me to the ultimate question of my life: Was I Franklin's widow or was I a person myself?

Feedback Entry in *Dialogue with Events:*
Sub-section for *The Event of Franklin's Death*

When Franklin died it brought to the fore the whole question of my relation to him. In that sense I have to consider not only the event of Franklin's death but the larger, encompassing event of our relationship as a whole as it extended over so many years. There were so many good aspects to my life with Franklin, and also so many painful difficulties. I feel a tremendous ambiguity when I reflect on my relationship with Franklin.

There was the great joy of getting married to Franklin.

And the disappointment, even panic, when I discovered that his mother would run the household.

There were the satisfying feelings of bringing a family of children into the world, and the troubles that went with that.

There were the feelings of security in being a wife, and the restlessness that came with my feeling that that did not give me enough to do that mattered in the world.

There was the shock of my discovering Franklin's affair and the confusion that then came into my life.

There was Franklin's terrible illness and my sharing his heroic efforts to overcome the paralysis that it brought.

There was the glare of living in the White House and also the possibility of doing some good in the world.

There were the awesome responsibilities that he carried as Commander in Chief during the Great War, and my being close to those burdens even though I did not share them.

And there is the emptiness of finding that he is gone. I am Mrs. Franklin Roosevelt, but without the Franklin. It is a terrible loss to me. But in a certain way I sense that it is also a freeing. For him and for me as well.

Feedback Entry in *Dialogue with Events:*
Sub-section for *Travels in India*

My visit to India lasted about a month. I was greeted warmly everywhere and treated most graciously. More than that, I felt a great warmth from the people, I could even say a feeling of love. And I found that I was feeling a special warmth and love toward them. But that became a problem to me. I saw the extent of their poverty, and I felt a tremendous compassion for them. They seemed to sense that I had this warm feeling toward them, and quite naturally, since they saw me as coming from wealthy America, they expected me to be a source of help to them.

They had great expectations of what I could do for them and would get for them to alleviate their poverty. But I did not have any power at all. They had expectations that I could not fulfill. Perhaps they were misleading themselves. And perhaps I was misleading them without intending to. Finally I came to the conclusion that this was indeed what was happening, that I was misleading them by my interest in them. When I realized that this was the case I had a terrible sinking feeling and I felt that I had no choice but to cancel my trip and return home. I could not bear the thought that inadvertently I was misleading those poor people.

The realization that my desire to do something good and helpful for the people might actually have a negative effect for them had a devastating effect on me. It threw me into one of my dark and depressed moods. I thought that I had grown past them, but a dark mood took hold of me at the time that I decided I had to cancel my trip to India. I found myself thinking—and with good reason—that if my going forth to people to be helpful to them had an effect that was the opposite of what I intended, there was no point in my doing it. And then I had the thought that if that was true there was no value and no meaning in what I was doing. In that moment the work I was doing became pointless to me.

I had no answer to those thoughts nor to my feelings of darkness and depression. All I could do was to try to stop the thoughts. At the time I had a number of details to take care of, protocol visits and other things that were necessary to do in order to make my preparations for returning to America. Doing these tasks drew me out of the depressed state into which I had fallen. The questions that had been raised, however, did not go away.

Feedback Entry in *Dialogue with Events:*
Sub-section for *Family Arguments*

From time to time when the family is assembled, intense family arguments erupt. The arguing is especially strong among the three middle boys. It has a very upsetting effect on me personally, I suppose it is a reflection of something in them that they are not able to fulfill in their lives. But I know that there is more to it than that. I feel that it is something for which I am responsible. Perhaps that is why it upsets me. I would like them to be happy and harmonious with one another. And yet I know that they have each had their failures which seem very great to them because they had such expectations. And I feel powerless in the face of it because I do not know what to do.

Question 6. Are you aware of having *sleep dreams* or *twilight images* during this period of your life? Are there any that stand out from the others with respect to their symbolism, the insights they gave you, or possibly the predictions they made?

Period Log Entry

I am not aware of dreams as a significant part of my life, at least not dreams in the way that people usually speak of them. I do not recall having dreams in my sleep. Probably I would not be interested in finding their significance even if I did remember them.

During these recent years, however, many people have called me a visionary. Usually, of course, they call me that with a very derisive tone; but there may be a truth in what they say deeper than they know. Actually I am glad to be a visionary, if that is what I am, but I want to be a practical visionary.

I recognize that being a visionary is a kind of dreaming. My vision is, in its way, a dream of all the races of mankind living together in peace. Perhaps that is only a hope, but it underlies all the things I try to do despite the many disappointments I have had.

Question 7. Were there *persons who inspired you,* persons from history or mythological times, or persons living in your own time, in whom you felt a quality of wisdom that was especially relevant to you?

Period Log Entry

When I was engaged in the United Nations work and found myself increasingly in confrontation with the Russian delegates, my thoughts would go back to my uncle, Theodore Roosevelt. I felt that he had a hopeful vision of the possibilities of life for human beings, but that he also was realistic about the practical difficulties that are encountered. During the years that followed World War II, when so many difficult situations arose that called my idealistic hopes into question, my thoughts went back to my uncle. I wondered whether he had experienced the conflicts of feeling that often arose in me during my United Nations days. And I wondered how he would have dealt with the Russian intransigence while still seeking to build peace in the world.

Question 8. Were there *intersections of decision* in your life during this time? Considering that you chose to take particular roads and left other roads untaken, how do you perceive the consequences now?

Period Log Entry

There were a great many choices placed before me during this period when I was placed on my own and was able to take an active role in life. Probably the most important choice was a road that I chose not to take. I chose not to become a candidate for public office.

The opportunity to make that choice was first offered to me in 1946, and it arose again strongly in 1952. The possibility was implicit in between those times, but those were the two main occasions. When I considered it, I concluded that I could continue to be a public person which gave me in various ways a platform from which I could say what I thought. But if I became a candidate I would lose a great deal of that freedom. I therefore decided to take a middle course and I declined to become a political candidate, whether for the Senate, or for the Vice-Presidency, or whatever. Once I had thought about it carefully and made my decision, my mind was clear about it, and I did not waver.

In retrospect I think it was a good decision that probably enabled me to preserve my strength for a number of additional years.

Question 9. Did you have any experience of *connection to a meaning in life* during this period? Did you feel a lack of meaning in life?

Period Log Entry

My experiences of connection came mainly from perceptions of life that were negative. I saw the disconnections that people experience in life, but somehow it caused me to feel more connected to the people.

For example, when I traveled to the various countries in the world I saw the extent of the poverty and the ignorance in so many of the nations. I also saw, and was somewhat overcome by, the deep and blind antipathies that whole nations and races feel toward one another. I saw it among the Indians and the Pakistanis, and among the Arabs and the Israelis, and among the various races, the blacks and browns and whites and yellows. People do not see each other as people, but only as members of a race toward which they have a blind hatred. And then there are the conflicts of the economic and political systems, the democracies and the Soviets. My feeling is that the terrible divisions among people are because of the poverty and the fear, and because people are desperate and do not know what to do.

As I have traveled over much of the world and seen these problems at first hand, I have had a sense of being overwhelmed by the disconnections among mankind. It has made me increasingly apprehensive that it will all end in warfare in which large masses of human beings will be destroyed. Realizing the extent of the disconnections among mankind has been a terrible experience for me, but, for all the disconnections among the peoples of the world, I have a feeling of connection to them all, especially in this later period of my life.

Especially when I was in India I was deeply touched by the poverty of the people. I had strong feelings of warmth toward them, very much like the feelings of a mother for her children. As I became older, especially after Franklin died, I found that I had a feeling of motherhood for all people. Sometimes it would become very strong, and then it would make me feel depressed when I would realize that the problems of the people were largely insoluble. Eventually I tried to protect myself against having these feelings.

I saw people around the world doing foolish, self-destructive things, but I could not be angry with them any more than I could be angry at my own children when they did foolish things. In some way I felt connected to them, and even responsible for them. I felt that my own deficiencies were the cause of their foolishness. I felt that, in those times when they looked to me for help—as though I were in a position to help—the way the Indian people looked to me for help when I visited them. They thought I represented the American government, but that was not the case. I realized that I was giving people false hopes. I felt that I was misleading my children when I was in India and was with all those imploring people. I felt such love for them, but I knew I could not help them. And in the United Nations I wanted so much to be in harmony with the Russians and with all the people who feel they are identified with Communism. I wanted so much to establish cooperation among us all so that there could be peace on earth and we could work together to overcome the poverty and suffering of so many millions of people. And when I realized that there was not going to be harmony between us but only meanness and nastiness, I felt a terrible sadness. I was not angry but I felt a great sorrow, a great loss. It depressed me. It was much as though I realized that my children were going to fight among themselves and there was nothing I could do about it.

Nonetheless I could continue to love them and seek to draw them together so that, even if they were bound to be contentious with each other, they would at least not destroy one another.

That feeling of love for people which I felt very much as a mother also extended to society. I think it is the heart of the feelings of connection that I had during this period of my life.

Feedback Entry in *Peaks, Depths and Explorations:*
Sub-section for *My Concern for Mankind*

I was born to a degree of wealth and economic security. That has always been assured to me, even if happiness has not necessarily come with it.

When I realized that there are people who live all their lives in great want, I became concerned for them. This first occurred when I was a schoolgirl in England. Mlle. Souvestre was the primary influence on me then.

My concern continued when I returned to the United States and did volunteer work in the slums of New York City.

During the depression years of the early nineteen thirties I felt great pain and sympathy at seeing the families of the unemployed.

When I became First Lady I tried to do what I could, but I found that it was not very much. It was certainly much less than people thought I was doing.

After the War, I had great hopes that good things could be done in the rehabilitation of the destroyed countries. But I was overwhelmed when I discovered how much poverty there is in the world.

I wanted to do so much, but I realized that there was very little that I could do.

My feelings were very strong and the pain was very great. Eventually I concluded that I had to protect myself against these feelings since there was nothing I could do about them.

Chapter 18

After the Nine Questions

In the Journal Trustee Log

In responding to the Nine Questions, we have drawn together many pieces of information in the two life/time units that we are using as Focus Periods. The answers that we gave to each of the specific questions are necessarily incomplete. There is much more to be said and explored in each area of the life. But the composite of all the answers that we gave gives us a large resource of data. We now have the information and a perspective that enables us to consider the life as a whole. Setting the two Focus Periods in sequence while leaving spaces open for the intervening periods in the life, we can develop a sense of the timing with which the movement and the various changes took place. As we carry out this phase of our Life-Study, we clarify for ourselves what our own perception is of the life to which we are giving our *studied attention*. We may now have a fuller experience of the implications of the life, both affirmative and negative, than we had before, and we can look deeper into the question of what are the implications, the larger meanings, of the life for which we are Journal Trustee.

There are two main sequences of exercises with which we work at this point in our Life-Study. We work first in the *Journal*

Trustee Log, and then in the section for *Meetings.* We begin by examining the material that we have collected in answer to the Nine Questions, drawing our several responses together in contexts that will enable us to consider the parts of the life in relation to the whole. These integrations help us crystallize our fundamental understandings of the life in the Journal Trustee Log. We can then express these understandings and explore them further in the *Meetings* section. The exercises that we can now carry out in these two sections help to strengthen and deepen the Journal Relationship that has been building as we have been doing our work as a Journal Trustee.

The Journal Trustee Log is a section of the Life-Study Journal that has multiple uses. We have already made entries in it at several points in our work. All of our varied uses of it, however, have reflected the one basic function of the Journal Trustee Log. It is the Journal section that is set aside for the entries by which the Journal Trustee can express the problems and questions that arise within the work. In the other Journal sections (with the exception of the *Life-Study Research* section and *Meetings*) we are speaking only on behalf of the person for whom we are a Journal Trustee. In the Journal Trustee Log, however, we are speaking for ourselves as we are in the midst of our Life-Study. It is the section where we record our thoughts and images, the feelings and perceptions that occur to us. We record them here as our work proceeds for two main purposes: to sort out the data in order to help us make our decisions and to build a record of the whole process as it is evolving within us.

We have already used the Journal Trustee Log to record our experiences of Twilight Imagery when we were establishing an atmosphere of depth at the beginning of our Life-Study workshop. Since that first experience of Twilight Imagery we have continued to use the Journal Trustee Log to record any additional experiences of Twilight Imagery that came to us in the course of our Life-Study, even if these experiences were very brief and seemed to happen by accident. At a later point in our Life-Study, when it was necessary for us as Journal Trustees to consider the relationship between the Primary Steppingstones and the Extended Steppingstones in choosing which two life/time units we would use as Focus Periods, the Journal Trustee Log also served as the place where we set forth the pro-and-con considerations by which we reached our decision. Now we have another situation in Life-Study that calls for us to work in the Journal Trustee Log. Having responded to the Nine Questions with respect to the two Focus Periods that we chose, a substantial amount of data has now been gathered in the Life-Study Journal. It is there for us now to reflect upon and comment on in the perspective of the whole of the life. We do this in the Journal Trustee Log.

To carry out this step in Life-Study we begin by opening the Journal to the Journal Trustee Log. We sit in silence. After our extensive detailed work in responding to the Nine Questions, it is good to begin this aspect of our work in the Journal Trustee Log with a sustained pause. This gives us an opportunity to renew our capacities of deep inner perception. With the Journal Trustee Log open before us, we may sit in silence with our eyes closed, letting twilight images appear before us. Being receptive to these images, we observe and record them in the *Journal Trustee Log*. We may also wish to set an atmosphere for this introductory Twilight Imagery by means of readings of Entrance Meditation.* However we choose to proceed, we treat this as a time of quietness and reconsideration during which we will make our judgments and decisions regarding our next steps as a Journal Trustee.

After we have settled in quietness and have recorded whatever imagery has presented itself to us, we begin by making a brief entry in the Journal Trustee Log. This is a summary entry that states in a few sentences our perception of the Life-Study work that we have done so far. It describes what we feel we have learned of our person's life, and it states an overview of the observations we have made up to this point.

* See *Appendix B*, p. 288 ff.

The Earlier Focus Period

After we have completed this first entry, which has the effect of putting us on record to ourselves after we have written our responses to the Nine Questions, we have an important piece of reading to do. It may in fact be a substantial amount, for our next step is to read back to ourselves the Log Entries that we have written in response to the Nine Questions.

In the *Period Log* we marked off a separate sub-section for each of the two Focus Periods, and it was here that we entered a brief response to each of the Nine Questions. These are the *Period Log Entries* that were noted in Chapters 14 to 17. In this volume we have followed the procedure of presenting the responses to each question in sequence, first the log response and then the feedback response. This has a particular value for demonstrating the way that the responses were made. In the actuality of our Journal work, however, all the *Period Log Entries* were written one after another in the Period Log within the sub-section that contains their particular Focus Period. These Log Entries are therefore all assembled in one place while the Feedback Entries are scattered throughout the various feedback sections of the Journal. As we now return to the Period Log section we are able to read in sequence and in a single sitting all the Period Log Entries that we made for each of the Focus Periods. As we read them back to ourselves together, we can feel the wholeness of the unit of time of which they all are expressions. And we recognize also that each of the entries reflects a different aspect of the same period in the person's life.

We begin with the earlier of the two Focus Periods and we read back to ourselves, together as a unit, all the Period Log Entries that we wrote for that period. Writing them separately, each as a distinct aspect of the Focus Period, made one impression on us. Reading them back to ourselves as a unit will have quite another kind of impact. The composite of the log entries that we wrote in responding to the Nine Questions enables us to perceive both the wholeness of the period and the movements of change that took place within it. We can recognize a context now that was not apparent to us when we were responding to the questions one at a time.

Thoughts and feelings, observations of many kinds, stir in us, and we describe them in the *Journal Trustee Log*. There are many things to say, and we say them each in our own way. One way to begin, however, is to state directly what is taking place. We may start this entry in the Journal Trustee Log by saying:

"As I read back to myself the log entries of the earlier Focus Period, I recognize that . . ."

With that as our starting point we continue the sentence, recording our observations and thoughts as they come to us.

Reading back to ourselves these log entries may stimulate in us a great deal of thought and emotion. Images may arise as well. We write them all as they occur to us. We do not judge them, nor censor them, nor edit them. But we do articulate them as fully as we can. We express them in written form in the Journal Trustee Log. A flow of ideas and perceptions regarding the Focus Period was stimulated by our reading back to ourselves the composite of the log entries. Now we stimulate it and extend it in the course of writing our further perceptions. We are encouraging a flow of consciousness within ourselves with respect to the person for whom we are Journal Trustee. The Journal Trustee Log is the place where we record the stream of consciousness that now comes to us as we read back to ourselves and record our responses to the Journal entries for the earlier Focus Period.

The Later Focus Period

Responding to our reading of the log entries for the earlier Focus Period, we let our line of thought and observation extend as far as it wishes with respect to the log entries for that earlier Focus Period. When we feel that we have expressed all that is relevant for the time, there is a second step for us to take. We return to our readings in the Period Log, but now we go to the sub-section that we set apart for the later Focus Period. All the responses to the Nine Questions are together there. We can read them back to ourselves as a unit, one after another. We do this now, reading them to ourselves receptively, perhaps more than once, as we allow a composite impression to form within us regarding this Focus Period.

As we read, we find that we have new perceptions regarding this time in our person's life. Additional thoughts and observations come to us to be recorded as further entries in the Journal Trustee Log. When we wrote our response to our reading of the various log entries that we had made for the earlier Focus Period, we began with a simple descriptive statement telling of the material that we had been reading in the Life-Study Journal, and we then added a statement of the thoughts and other responses that arose in us. We do the same now with respect to the second Focus Period. For this period we may lead into our response with the phrase:

"As I read back to myself the log entries for this later Focus Period
I recognize that . . ."

We summarize what we have read, and then we add the various lines of thought and feeling, emotions and imagery that have been stimulated in us in relation to the contents of this second Focus Period. Once again we are encouraging a flow of consciousness simultaneously on the level of our intellect and at a twilight depth. We let thought and imagery add to each other. Twilight thinking and twilight imagery come together to form a stream of entries, expressing our response to the composite of log entries for the later Focus Period in the life of our person.

A Private Workplace

We are now using the Journal Trustee Log in the way that gives it an active, recurrent role in Life-Study, especially from this point onwards. We are using it now as our private workplace where we can consider, as though in our own Journal, the various aspects and implications of the exercises that we have carried out in our person's life. Here in our privacy we record the facts, describe them, consider them and make our decisions as to what to do next.

In the earlier phases of Life-Study there is little need for a private workplace of this kind. That is because in the early stages of Life-Study we are not called upon to consider the material and decide upon next steps. For the most part, the core exercises are each necessary and there is no leeway for choice before certain basic data have been accumulated. We did, however, have need to make a decision at the earlier point in Life-Study where we were choosing the life/time units on which we would concentrate our attention as Focus Periods. Several considerations had to be taken into account in making that choice, and they were individual considerations for each of us. For that purpose at that time we used the Journal Trustee Log as our private workplace where we recorded the various factors, considered the pros and the cons, and made our choice.

At other times during our Life-Study we have used the Journal Trustee Log as the place where we have recorded our Twilight Imagery experiences. And we maintain it as the place where we record not only the sustained experiences of Twilight Imagery that come particularly at the start of workshop sessions, but also the brief, almost casual experiences of Twilight Imagery that seem to come as though by happenstance while we are in the midst of other activities in the course of our Life-Study work. We have used the Journal Trustee Log in that way because of the general function that it fulfills for us all through our Life-Study. As a general rule of thumb, when material for an entry occurs to us in the course of our Life-Study work and we do not know where to place it, the Journal Trustee Log is the section where we record it. Later on, we will reconsider it and place it in whatever other section is appropriate.

The present point in our Life-Study presents a situation, however, that requires the specific use of the Journal Trustee Log. We have worked in the life of our person and we have developed in a Journal format the details of two periods in that life. We have considered each of those periods, working out our own judgment of what is involved in them. We have done this in the Journal Trustee Log where our considerations are available to be drawn upon in any further decisions that we may need to make.

Now we may add another consideration. Having reconstructed the events and the changes in the life that took place during those periods, we are in a position now to set the two periods in their chronological sequence and in their relation to each other. We have assembled two series of entries in the Journal Trustee Log. One expresses our experience in reading back to ourselves the Log Entries for the earlier Focus Period; the second is our response to the entries of the later Focus Period. Our response to each period is in the form of a substantial stream of consciousness—thoughts and feelings, insights and images, perspectives and understandings. In each case it reflects our degree of participation in that period of our person's life. Having done that much, we can now express our perception of the life, its lines of development and the issues that we have felt to be present beneath the surface of events. Whatever questions we have been holding and nurturing while we were carrying out the core exercises can now be stated. This point in our Life-Study completes a phase, specifically the phase in which we work with the Nine Questions and the two Focus Periods. It is therefore a good time, as we sit in our private workplace of the Journal Trustee Log, to delineate as fully as we feel called to do the various aspects of the life that we have discerned until now. This is a time to make our basic statement to ourselves regarding the life of our person. In a little while we will be able to explore this statement further when we have our experience in Meetings.

Chapter 19

In a Journal
Relationship

The Place of MEETINGS

The entries that we made in the Journal Trustee Log built a stream of thoughts and twilight perceptions that drew us toward conclusions, or at least toward a definite trend of understanding regarding the life of our person. Increasingly we are developing a perspective that gives us a way of recognizing the inner continuity of the life. But would he—or she—agree with us? How would the persons whom we are studying respond to our point of view? What would they say to it? Would they have some important information to add? Or a comment that would be helpful to our understanding?

In literal terms these questions can have no answer since the persons whom we are discussing have already died. But literal answers are not the whole of the matter. In the course of our *Intensive Journal* programs we have worked with twilight perception in several forms and have found that it often does serve to supplement the conventional modes of cognition, especially in ways that show the meaning of the events that are taking place in a person's life. Our most affirmative experience with twilight perception comes not from the specific pieces of information that it may give us but from the larger sensitivities and life-understandings that it builds, often in symbolic terms, from which we may draw our individual inferences. By means of twilight perception with its intuitive qualities, we can reach beyond literal knowledge and sometimes touch a wisdom of life at deep levels of cognition.

Especially for those of us who have come this far in Life-Study and have experienced the empathy of reconstructing another person's life by making Journal entries in their name, the possibility of gaining additional knowledge of a life at twilight levels is very substantial. With our background of knowledge we can use the experience of Journal Dialogue at a twilight level as a means of reaching a deep understanding of our person with a particular insight into the wisdom of their life. Now that we have articulated our perception of the life for which we are Journal Trustee, having crystallized our view of its main periods and their relation to each other, we possess a point of view that can serve as a basis for discussion with our person. We can share our view with them, draw forth their response, and open the possibility of a continuing mutual interchange of feelings and ideas. Having done our work in the Journal Trustee Log, we have laid the foundation for a step that can draw together much of what we have done in our experience of Life-Study.

We now turn to the Journal section of *Meetings*. To do our work here we adapt a procedure that plays an important role in the personal component of the *Intensive Journal* program, but we develop it here in the context of Life-Study. In our personal *Intensive Journal* work we use the section of *Inner Wisdom Dialogue* to establish a Journal communication with a person who has a special significance to us. In that case, although we usually choose an individual whom we hold in high regard, we have not entered into the details of that person's life as we have in Life-Study. We approach the person there in terms of the general quality of their life and the quality of their consciousness as we seek guidance from them in terms of our own life-circumstances and concerns. The dialogue discussions that we have with them take place in the twilight range of consciousness, and we find that they often give us access to an awareness that is greater than our personal understanding. When we adapt this procedure to our work in Meetings, we bring more specific knowledge to the exercise. We are therefore able to deal in it with a more definite subject matter. We are able to establish a more personal relationship in Meetings. These differences have important consequences as we proceed.

Working in the Meetings section we have a situation toward which all our Life-Study has been leading. We are meeting in direct relationship with the persons for whom we have been working as a Journal Trustee. It is as though we are sitting side by side with them in an atmosphere in which each of us can speak with freedom and without reserve. It is our opportunity to discuss all that has been building within us. We have a personal meeting, but our communication will not take place in the physical forms of speech. It is communication by means of Journal Dialogue. Now our Life-Study Journal serves as our instrument as we use the *Intensive Journal* process to evoke a flow of thoughts and perceptions of all forms and without restriction of content at the twilight level.

In using this aspect of the method of Journal Dialogue we begin by speaking into our Journal. We state whatever we have to say, but instead of speaking it aloud we write it in the Meetings section of our Journal. Now the second person in the dialogue can respond. In the silence at a twilight level it is as though we hear them speaking by an interior ear. Whatever we seem to hear them say, or whatever we *just know* that they are saying to us interiorly, we record on their behalf in the Journal. We do not edit it, nor correct it, nor try to improve upon it, nor try to make it "correct" in any way. We just record it as it seems to us to be spoken. And we record it following the statement that we write on our own behalf. We write their name at the head of their statement, as we wrote our own name at the head of our own words. We thus have two statements by two persons, one following the other and each referring to the other. It is the beginning of a script. We have set a dialogue in motion, and our Journal is the carrier of it. Now in the silence we can let the dialogue script continue. We respond to the previous statement, adding something of our own. That, in turn, draws a response, a further statement as well. And so it goes, as a dialogue script builds in momentum and in content.

Now on the twilight level, sitting with the person for whom we are Journal Trustee, what shall we discuss at the start of our Meetings experience? When we were working in the Journal Trustee Log we let a stream of consciousness build. In the course of it we articulated our view of each of the Focus Periods and their relation to the life as a whole. That took place on the twilight level, but it was altogether contained within our own realm of thought. In that sense it was a *twilight monologue*. It dealt with another person's life, but that other person did not know of it. Now we can tell them. In our Meetings exercise we can recapitulate the line of thought that developed in us as we worked in the Journal Trustee Log, and we can state the conclusion that we reached. In doing this we are sharing our experience with the persons for whom we are a Journal Trustee, and they can respond to it. They can add to it, raise questions about it, stimulate further questions within us. Now what was a monologue when we were working in the Journal Trustee Log has become a *twilight dialogue* that can open in many directions as we continue with it. This is an important aspect of the Meetings exercise.

The step from a *twilight monologue* to a *twilight dialogue* has a number of consequences. Of the greatest importance is the quality of personal feeling that it generates at interior levels. As we tell the experience we had when we worked in the Journal Trustee Log, telling it to the person for whom we are a Journal Trustee, an openness of communication enters our relationship. It becomes easier for us to speak at the twilight level, and easier for them to speak. It becomes easier also, and more natural, for an open-ended, unfolding dialogue script to take written form.

It is taking place at the twilight level where it is not visible by physical perception, but the fact is that an acquaintance is being deepened as the experience of Meetings proceeds. The measure of it is the freedom of communication back and forth that now takes place by means of interior experience and that comes to written expression in the Journal. The flow of entries, words spoken and responded to at the twilight level, builds the momentum of a dialogue and increases the freedom of interior speech between persons who now are open to one another. The momentum of *twilight dialogue* flows past all boundaries and blockages that individuals might imagine and construct as separations between themselves. It is important to note this and to bear in mind that the momentum of speech and response at the twilight level builds an energy of communication that gives the dialogue a self-generating form. If the momentum dwindles, self-consciousness will enter the experience and soon the Meeting will be taking place not at a twilight depth but at the surface of the mind. There at the surface its energy will decrease until it ceases to be a viable experience at all.

In this we see the operational essence of the Meetings experience and the building of Journal Dialogue at the twilight level. Opening the inner gates and freeing the flow of thoughts and feelings builds a momentum that goes beyond self-consciousness. If the movement is free and strong, self-consciousness is at a minimum. And vice versa. Underlying this is the equality of relationship. That is why, when we re-tell in Meetings our experience in working in the Journal Trustee Log, and when we tell it in an honest and ungarnished way, we not only draw forth a spontaneous response but we build a momentum of Journal Dialogue. Now on the twilight level one thing leads to another as though of itself. Having moved beyond self-consciousness, many additional truths can be told to us and shown to us. Now, in the atmosphere of the twilight level we will be able to hear them, and able to see them.

There is an increasing fluidity in the Journal Relationship that develops between ourselves and the person for whom we are a Journal Trustee. The knowledge that we had of the life was helpful at the beginning. It started our discussion. But now we have gone far beyond that. We find that we can discuss in our twilight dialogue subjects that we did not know we knew; but as soon as we become self-conscious about it, the dialogue goes away. It is interesting in this regard as a bit of practical experience that if we try deliberately to avoid being self-conscious in our Journal Dialogue, that effort itself produces self-consciousness. Therefore we find that trying to do it properly will not work at all. On the other hand, simply not-trying will not work either. The way that does seem to work is to be spontaneously involved in what we are doing, in this case our Life-Study.

When we tell our experience in Meetings, we may become so involved in what we are discussing that we forget ourselves. Forgetting ourselves in the spontaneity of our talk, we soon realize that a response has been given to us, also in spontaneity. At that point the dialogue process has clearly been set into motion and is moving of its own strength. If we let its momentum build, it will continue and deepen at the twilight level. More and more, things that we could not anticipate will be told to us. We may find, for example, that the memory of facts that we did not know about will be spoken in the Journal Dialogue in the course of Meetings. That may happen if we do not look for it. Many things may be said in the course of these *twilight dialogues,* some of them profound discussions of wisdom in life, some of them inconsequential chatterings. We let them all come without judgment and without censorship. Those that are relevant will give us Journal Feedback Leads and will eventually take the form of additional entries in other Journal sections. Thus they will integrate themselves into the *Intensive Journal* process and become part of our Life-Study. Those that are irrelevant or inconsequential will simply drop away unused. We can therefore feel free to record everything that comes to us in the course of our Twilight Dialogue, knowing that it will all be sorted out in the end.

Whatever the content of these Meetings, their effect is a deepening of our personal relationship within the context of the Journal. Once that relationship has been established at the twilight level, the door is open for continuing dialogue. After that, even small, seemingly unimportant contacts help to keep the door ajar, and can therefore be exceedingly valuable. As the back-and-forth flow of the Journal Relationship continues, a momentum builds that deepens the level on which all our future Meetings can take place.

Many interior events may occur while we are engaged in the Meetings section. In the course of Twilight Dialogue many experiences become possible. But we do not think of them in advance, lest we become self-conscious and thereby cut the process short before it can generate sufficient momentum to sustain itself. It is especially important for each of us that, as we establish our individual relationship with it, the twilight ground of Meetings remains accessible to us as a place to which we can freely come in future times.

The Twilight Dialogue Exercise

We now come to the experience of Meetings in the Life-Study Journal. With our workbook open before us, we sit in silence. We remain in quietness, letting our Self become still. Our eyes closed, we see—or feel—the presence of the person for whom we are Journal Trustee. Perhaps we actually see him, or her, visually on the inner screen of the mind's eye, but that is not necessary. If an image of the person comes to us, we sit in stillness with it. Primarily it is a quality of the person's being that becomes present to us. We feel their presence and we sit in stillness, our eyes closed. Our Life-Study Journal is open to *Meetings*.

Presently something stirs within us and leads us to speak, but at a twilight level. We write our words instead of speaking them aloud. As our person is present with us, we tell them the experiences that we have had in studying their life and in making entries on their behalf in the Journal we keep for them. We may speak about the experiences we had in the Journal Trustee Log, and any other aspect of our Life-Study. Events come to mind, and we speak of them. As we recall them and as they come to us, we describe the thoughts and feelings that have arisen in us from time

247

to time, or that are present in us now at the time of writing. We tell our person about it, just describing the events and telling our experiences in a matter of fact way. We can feel relaxed in what we are telling—and in what we are writing. We can let it flow, as though of itself.

After a while we may feel that our person also has something to say. Perhaps it is a comment to add. Perhaps it is a larger statement. The floor is always open for them. Now as we sit in silence we feel that they are speaking, and we write the words for them. We mark off a segment in the Journal, and we put their name at the head of it. Thus we write in their name the things they seem to be saying. As they speak, and we speak afterwards, and they speak again, the *twilight dialogue* gradually takes on the appearance of a script. But we let that form itself as it wishes in its own timing.

Now we write for our person the things we feel that he, or she, wishes to be saying. It may be a little; it may be a great deal; it may be nothing at all. There is nothing in particular that need be said by anyone at any time. But if, or whenever, something wishes to be said, we let it be written, whatever it may be. We may speak, and we write it. When our person speaks, we also write it. Gradually a dialogue script unfolds, giving expression to the Meeting that is taking place and is building a Journal Relationship between ourselves and the person for whom we are a Journal Trustee.

Chapter 20

The Basic Steps in Life-Study: A Review

We have now carried out the basic exercises in Life-Study. We have drawn together the life of a person who is significant to us, and we have established both the foundation and an operational framework for building a Journal Relationship between the two of us in the future. We may continue and deepen that relationship in our own timing, perhaps calling upon it in response to new circumstances and questions that may arise in our life. Now that we have done the basic work, the Journal Relationship that we have begun is part of our life. We can draw upon it whenever we feel that it can help solve a problem. We can add to it at other times simply for the pleasure and understanding that it gives us, just as we would enjoy a meeting with a valued friend.

We can enlarge this Journal Relationship while we are also establishing additional Journal Relationships with other persons. This is the open-ended quality of Life-Study. It expands the range of the resources that are available to us for deepening our inner experiences at a personal level.

In carrying out the core exercises of Life-Study for the one person whom we chose we have also given ourselves a model that we can use whenever we wish to become a Journal Trustee for another person. The material that we have gathered by our Journal entries and exercises up to this point provides the essential foundation and framework for Life-Study. It is necessary to follow the same steps on behalf of each person for whom we wish to serve as a Journal Trustee. There is much more that we can experience and that we can add upon this base, especially as we are able to extend the procedures of Journal Feedback and Process Meditation within the context of Life-Study. These Journal experiences can contribute a great deal to our lives as they expand the scope of our awareness and enlarge our contact in historical time. They are, however, part of the advanced uses of the *Intensive Journal* process. In this volume we have described the basic exercises of Life-Study, laying the foundation for our work as a Journal Trustee and providing the framework by which the several feedback procedures can be carried further in each aspect of the person's life. We have noted that the basic work of Life-Study differs from the personal use of the *Intensive Journal* process in some significant ways, primarily because of the fact that here we are studying a life other than our own. The advanced use of Journal Feedback in Life-Study, however, follows procedures that parallel the personal practices of Journal Feedback. As we proceed in Life-Study, we find that we can adapt the techniques of Journal Feedback as they are described in volumes that are directed to the personal use of Journal Feedback. A particular instance of this is the material dealing with personal and transpersonal feedback leads in *The Practice of Process Meditation.*★ Additional volumes are now in preparation describing the specific application and variations of Journal Feedback both in Life-Study and in the personal use of the *Intensive Journal* process.

In order to enjoy the fruits of *Intensive Journal* work, it is necessary to do the planting first for each of its components. We have done that in this volume for the Life-Study Component as we have carried out the basic exercises for being a Journal Trustee. Let us now review the steps of Life-Study as we have experienced them here.

We began by choosing an individual to whom we felt drawn

★ Chapter 17, p. 272 ff.

by a sense of personal significance and inner connection. We then declared ourselves to be a Journal Trustee for that person. In doing so, we were making a commitment, a commitment to ourselves. We were committing ourselves to set up a Life-Study Journal for our person, and also to make entries in the workbook to provide both a foundation and a framework for future work in that person's life. We were undertaking to provide a foundation of life-information that would enable us to re-enter our person's experiences, and we were undertaking to establish a framework of Journal sections and procedures that would enable us to extend our Life-Study into an ongoing Journal Relationship. We have now fulfilled all sides of that commitment. We have set up a Life-Study Journal and we have written the entries in it that provide both a foundation and a framework for further Life-Study experience.

After choosing our person, we set up a Life-Study Journal in their name. With this Journal as our instrument, making entries in it in the first person on their behalf, we carried out the Life-Study exercises in the atmosphere of a Journal Workshop. We took steps to establish that atmosphere and to enter it by means of some brief practices of Entrance Meditation and by developing our familiarity with Twilight Imaging in relation to our work as a Journal Trustee. At the start of our Journal Workshop we encouraged the experience of Twilight Imagery and we recorded the experiences that came to us in the Journal Trustee Log. As additional Twilight Imagery experiences have come to us from time to time in the course of our Life-Study work we have recorded them also in this Journal section.

In the Journal Workshop we first gave our attention to re-capitulating the outlines of movement in the life. We did this by taking over the Steppingstones concept that is used in the Personal Component of the *Intensive Journal* process, and by adapting it to the needs of Life-Study. The exercises that we carried out here called for us to list the Steppingstones of our person's life in two formats, the Primary Steppingstones and the Extended Steppingstones.

The Primary Steppingstones enabled us to experience the

thread of continuity moving from birth to death in our person's life, each Steppingstone being briefly and concisely stated. The Extended Steppingstones similarly recapitulated the life, but they did so in greater detail. This listing contained a larger number of Steppingstones than were included in the listing of Primary Steppingstones, and the contents of each Steppingstone were described more substantially. Working with the Steppingstones, we developed a view of the sequence of events within a life. The Steppingstones gave us a chronological perspective, but they also incorporated a dimension of *life/time* which, in the *Intensive Journal* structure of concepts, provides the link between the subjective perception of individual events and a method of working with these events tangibly, operationally, almost objectively. Our listing of the Extended Steppingstones opened the door for us into the possibility of our working with this life/time dimension of our person's experience.

The Primary Steppingstones and the Extended Steppingstones together enabled us to reach into the aspect of a human life that is a sequential continuity. There is a chronological quality to a human life that is perceived as a vertical movement of time. The two listings of Steppingstones reflect this and make it possible for us to identify the unity of development in the life as a whole.

Marking off the vertical, or sequential, movement in a life led to the realization that there is another aspect of experience that must be taken into account. Each Steppingstone refers to a unit of time in which a number of contents, thoughts, relationships, circumstances co-exist side by side. Complementary to the way that the Steppingstones moved vertically *through time,* these contents are placed *across time*. They are the horizontal composition of each of the periods in a life. In reconstructing a life these horizontal contents are essential for an adequate description of a period. Sometimes we find them occurring in more than one period, and that indication of a continuity moving within the larger process of the life is often a significant fact for us to feed into our Journal Feedback exercises.

To identify the varied factors in the life we took a selective approach. Considering the Primary Steppingstones and the Extended Steppingstones in relation to one another, we chose two periods in the life on which to concentrate our attention. We chose these two Focus Periods from among the several life/time units that were disclosed to us by our listings of the Steppingstones. We chose one from an earlier time in the life, the other from a later time. Various factors of thought and observation had to be considered in making our choices, and we recorded the pros and cons of these considerations in the Journal Trustee Log. The choice of the two Focus Periods and the subsequent entries we make in describing their contents play an important role in the basic work of Life-Study.

When we designated the two Focus Periods, we gave each a descriptive name and opened a sub-section for it in the Period Log. Working in these sub-sections we assembled descriptions of the main aspects of each of the Focus Periods, making our entries in response to a sequence of Journal exercises. The effect of these exercises was to put together a composite picture of the main periods in the life, and also to establish a framework for our future use of the Journal Feedback procedures. At this point in our work we were laying the foundation of our Life-Study by reconstructing in detail the two Focus Periods that we had chosen, one from an earlier and one from a later time in the life.

After naming each of the Focus Periods, we wrote an Overview Statement describing the period as a whole. This contained a summary of the period, indicating the tone of the events that took place within it and marking off the events with which the period began as well as those that ended it. Our Overview Statement thus defined the outer boundaries of the period and took note of the external events.

Our next step in Life-Study took us inward. Working in the Journal section, *Now: the Open Moment,* we used the Twilight Imagery method. Envisioning ourselves as the person for whom we are a Journal Trustee, we placed ourselves at the very beginning of each of the two Focus Periods. At the twilight level of experience we then let images come to us in which the quality and movement of the life at that time were reflected. Thus we formed a perception of the period from a point within it and also from a point outside of it. With our Imaging experience in *Now: the Open Moment* we could see each period both before events had been set into motion and with a retrospective view of the whole after everything had taken place.

Having recorded our Overview Statement and the Twilight Imaging that reflected the start of the Focus Period, we proceeded to work in the period with respect to the two directions of time, first drawing events together as they move sequentially *through time* and then describing events as they rest side-by-side and form the composite of each period *across time*.

To establish a chronological perspective within each Focus Period we made a listing of the Signpost Events. These are the significant events within a period whose sequence indicates the nature of the developments within the period. We could then undertake the detailed work of moving across time. At this point it was not events that we were looking for but circumstances and situations, relationships and feelings. Recognizing that these come in subjective, often insubstantial, forms in a person's experience and can easily be overlooked, we used the *Nine Questions* as a combination checklist and guideline in assembling the contents of each Focus Period. In responding to the Nine Questions one by one we were moving across time, examining the several areas of the life and recording our observations in the sub-section of the Period Log which we had marked off for this work. The result was a picture of that time in our person's life, each entry made from a different vantage point.

We made the log entries in response to the Nine Questions, one for each question. We also made feedback entries in response to many of the Nine Questions, but here we sometimes had several feedback answers placed in several different sub-sections as our response to a single question. The reason for the difference lies in the purposes of the two types of entries. With the log entries we were seeking to build a composite view of the contents of the period as they spread *across time*. With the feedback entries we were drawing out the factors that were continuously active as processes moving *through time* in the person's life. The nature of these entries is that they lead to further Journal Feedback experiences. One of the purposes of the feedback entries was to open the channels in order that these experiences could take place and be recorded.

In making the log and feedback entries in response to the Nine Questions, we were providing the materials and establishing the framework for further Journal Feedback experiences. To this degree our Journal entries in answer to the Nine Questions fulfilled the essentials of our commitment in becoming a Journal Trustee. We not only have set up a Life-Study Journal for our person but, having carried out the basic sequence of exercises, the entries we have made provide a foundation and give us a framework for further Journal work that we may do in this person's life whenever the impulse or the inspiration comes to us.

From time to time during our Life-Study, we have used the Journal Trustee Log as our private workplace where we can consider the implications of the entries we have made and can encourage twilight perceptions to come to us. We did that when we had completed our response to the Nine Questions, and we do that now. We are always free to enter our private workplace in the Journal Trustee Log to reflect on our person's life at the twilight level. In addition, as thoughts and feelings and intuitions come to us regarding our person's life we may feel the desire to share them with our person at the twilight level. We did that in the Meetings section after writing our responses to the Nine Questions and considering them in the Journal Trustee Log. We had the experience of moving from Twilight Monologue to Twilight Dialogue. Since that first experience of Meetings in the Journal we have had an open invitation to come together with our person whenever we felt it might be helpful and meaningful for us to do so. That is an invitation that we should feel free to act on from time to time.

The combination of working back and forth in the Journal Trustee Log and in Meetings can be particularly valuable to us. In both of these Journal sections we can conduct open explorations within the Journal framework in a twilight atmosphere that encourages intuitive awarenesses to come to us. At the same time we can work in these Journal sections at the level of mental consciousness drawing upon our rational intellect. There is a special benefit to us as individuals when we feel free to intermingle the procedures of monologue and dialogue at the twilight level, as we are able to do when our familiarity with the Life-Study practices has given us open access to both the Journal Trustee Log and the Meetings sections. It makes it possible for us to extend our Journal Relationship in ongoing contacts with our person, sharing concerns and exploring them together. As we do this, we are deepening a friendship that exists between the covers of the Journal and within the depths of ourselves.

Appendix A

The *Intensive Journal* Life-Study Workbook

The following pages contain a model of the Life-Study Journal that is used as the instrument for the exercises that are described in this volume.

Registered and numbered copies of the Life-Study Journal are issued to all persons who participate in Dialogue House Life-Study workshops. A full model of the Journal with the face-sheets for all its sections is printed here as a convenience for persons who wish to begin their Life-Study immediately by working directly from the descriptions presented in the chapters of this book.

The actual Life-Study Journal issued by Dialogue House is in a three-hole loose-leaf binder using note paper that is eight and a half by eleven inches in size.

The Journals issued by Dialogue House are numbered and registered both by the name of the Journal Trustee and the person whose life is being studied. Records are kept for participation in the Life-Study Research program.

It should be noted that the Life-Study Journal as used in the exercises of this volume and as printed on the following pages includes the complete *Intensive Journal* workbook with all the Journal sections currently in use including the Process Meditation sections. The latter were not part of the *Intensive Journal* workbook used and described in the exercises of *At a Journal Workshop*. These sections were, however, included in the *Intensive Journal* workbook that is described in *The Practice of Process Meditation*. The Life-Study Journal contains, in addition to the sections of the full *Intensive Journal* workbook, the three additional sections that are used only for the purposes of Life-Study.

It should be noted also that while all the sections of the *Intensive Journal* workbook are used in Life-Study, the exercises for some of them have been substantially changed for the purposes of Life-Study in order to reflect the special nature of the Life-Study subject matter.

(white)

INTENSIVE JOURNAL®
WORKBOOK

Life-Study Edition

Journal Trustee _____

Representing _____

Registered Journal # _____

The Personal Growth and Creativity Program of
Dialogue House Associates, Inc.   80 East 11th Street,
New York, N.Y. 10003

© Dialogue House Associates, Inc., 1983

Intensive Journal® is a registered trademark of Dialogue House Associates, Inc

APPENDIX A

(green)

PERIOD LOG

PERIOD LOG

(yellow)

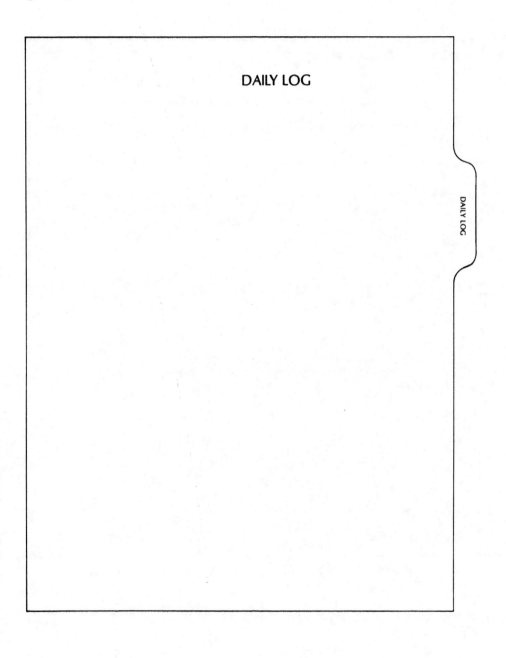

DAILY LOG

DAILY LOG

(orange)

DIALOGUE DIMENSION:
Special Personal Sections

DIALOGUE DIMENSION

(orange)

DIALOGUE WITH PERSONS

APPENDIX A

(orange)

DIALOGUE WITH WORKS

DIALOGUE WITH WORKS

(orange)

DIALOGUE WITH SOCIETY
Group Experiences

DIALOGUE WITH SOCIETY

(orange)

DIALOGUE WITH EVENTS
Situations and Circumstances

DIALOGUE WITH EVENTS

(orange)

DIALOGUE WITH THE BODY

(blue)

DEPTH DIMENSION:
Ways of Symbolic Contact

DEPTH DIMENSION

(blue)

DREAM LOG
Description, Context, Associations

DREAM LOG

(blue)

DREAM ENLARGEMENTS

DREAM ENLARGEMENTS

(blue)

TWILIGHT IMAGERY LOG

TWILIGHT IMAGERY LOG

(blue)

IMAGERY EXTENSIONS

IMAGERY EXTENSIONS

(blue)

INNER WISDOM DIALOGUE

INNER WISDOM DIALOGUE

(red)

LIFE / TIME DIMENSION:
Inner Perspectives

(red)

LIFE HISTORY LOG
Recapitulations and Rememberings

LIFE HISTORY LOG

(red)

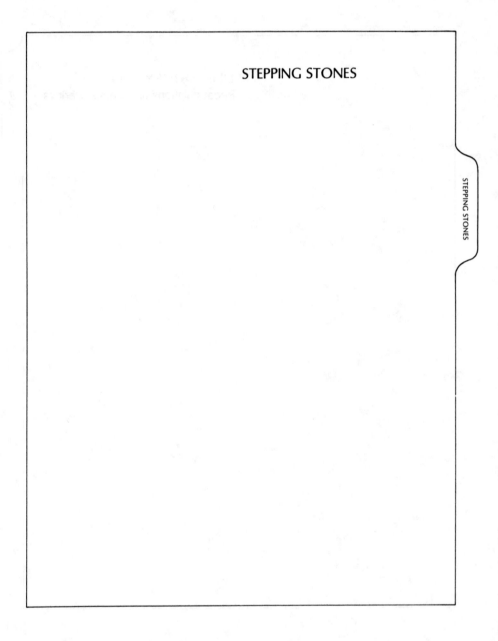

STEPPING STONES

STEPPING STONES

(red)

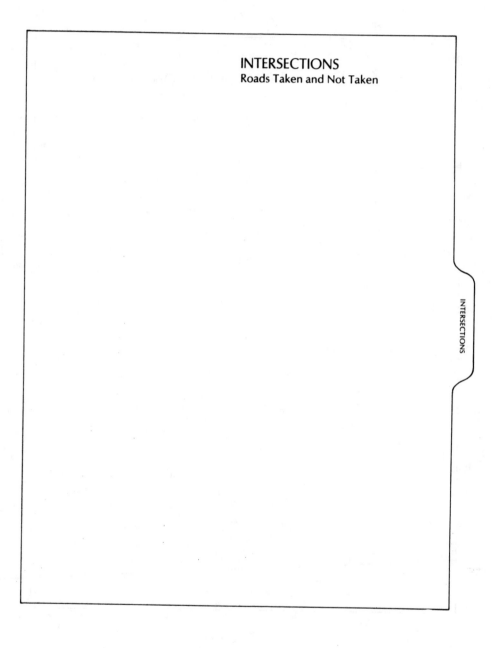

INTERSECTIONS
Roads Taken and Not Taken

INTERSECTIONS

(red)

NOW: The Open Moment

NOW:
The Open Moment

(purple)

PROCESS MEDITATION

PROCESS MEDITATION

(purple)

MEDITATION LOG
Entrance Meditations
Spiritual Positioning
Inner Process Entries

MEDITATION LOG

(purple)

CONNECTIONS
Gatherings
Spiritual Steppingstones
Re-Openings: Spiritual Roads Not Taken

CONNECTIONS

(purple)

MANTRA/CRYSTALS
Mantra/Crystal Index
Workings

MANTRA/CRYSTALS

(purple)

PEAKS, DEPTHS and
EXPLORATIONS

PEAKS, DEPTHS and
EXPLORATIONS

(purple)

TESTAMENT

TESTAMENT

(gray)

JOURNAL TRUSTEE LOG

JOURNAL
TRUSTEE LOG

(gray)

LIFE-STUDY RESEARCH

LIFE-STUDY RESEARCH

(gray)

MEETINGS

MEETINGS

Appendix B

Entrance Meditations
for Life-Study

Introductory Note

In the *Intensive Journal* program three small volumes of Entrance Meditation are used to help establish an atmosphere of stillness and depth at Journal Workshops.

The essence of Entrance Meditation is expressed in its name. It is a means of moving through the entryway of consciousness. Once we have gone through the entrance, have entered the mansion and have begun to move inward, we may experience whatever we find in the depths of ourselves. It may be pleasant. It may be exalting. It may not be pleasant at all. To this degree Entrance Meditation is a neutral procedure. It does not specify what we shall experience. It merely takes us through the doorway at the surface of consciousness, and it establishes an atmosphere that is congenial to our moving further inward.

In the pages that follow in this Appendix, a section is given from each of the three Entrance Meditation volumes. Each section was chosen for its appropriateness in relation to Life-Study. Since the purpose of the meditations is for them to serve as aids in moving inward through the entryway of consciousness, each may be used in whole or in part. Let your own experience be your guide.

THE WELL AND THE CATHEDRAL*

Sharing the Underground Stream

3.   Here in the underground stream
    We realize
    That many others
    In earlier times
    Have entered their wells
    And have gone inward
    Until they reached
    The waters beyond the well
    Where we are now.

4.   In ancient days
    Jacob went down his well,
    And where he returned
    He placed a stone
    For remembrance.
    In his way, Moses went down,
    And Isaiah and Ezekiel,
    Lao Tse and Zoroaster,
    Gotama Siddhartha,
    Jesus of Nazareth,
    Teresa and Juliana,
    Meister Eckhart,
    George Fox,
    Waldo Emerson and Walt Whitman,
    And many others
    Have gone down their well
    To the underground stream.

*Ira Progoff, *The Well and the Cathedral*, Dialogue House Library, New York, 1971, 1981, p. 117ff.

5. These and many more have been here,
    Some famous in history,
    Others unknown,
    But each by direct beholding
    Discovered
    Many marvelous things
    That were shown to them
    Or that they recognized
    And drew to themselves
    In the underground stream.

6. Those who have gone down their well
    Into the underground stream
    Have done many things
    Upon returning
    To the surface of their lives.
    Some have written books,
    Some have painted and sculpted,
    Some have made philosophies,
    Some have stated doctrines,
    Some have lived their lives
    More fully
    With inward abundance
    And with gentler wisdom
    Than was possible before.

7.   We think of them,
Those who have been here before us,
As we ourselves
Enter the underground stream.
We are not the first
Nor shall we be the last
To go
Through the center point of Self
Into the well
And beyond the well
Into the underground stream.

8.   Now we have entered the stream,
Ourselves
And more than ourselves,
Present to one another
Beyond separateness
In the unity of Being,
Accessible to everyone,
Sharing with all
In the unity of Being.

9.   Sharing the underground stream
We recognize others here,
Not only we who are entering now
But those who have been here before us.
Their quality of being,
Their atmosphere,
Still is present
In the underground stream.

10.   Those who have been here before us
Century upon century
Have left the imprint of their presence
On the waters
Of the underground stream.
Through the quality of their being
They will speak with us.
They will share with us
Their atmosphere
And their awareness,
Their lives and their knowledge,
The quality of their being
In the timeless unity.
In the timeless unity
They will share with us
As one.

11. Sharing the underground stream
    We are invited to speak,
    To ask our questions,
    To consider the answers
    And to record what is said.
    We are invited to speak,
    To share in dialogue
    Here in the underground stream,
    Listening and speaking
    With those who have entered before us
    And have left their mark
    Upon the atmosphere
    Of the underground stream.
    Their quality of being
    Is awaiting us
    In the timeless waters.

12. Gratefully
    We greet them,
    Speaking and listening,
    Our hearts open to their wisdom,
    Asking and hearing,
    Speaking of all life,
    Speaking of our life,
    With those who have been here before us.
    Their quality of being is present,
    Present for us now.
    We are speaking and listening
    In the Silence . . . In the Silence.

THE WHITE ROBED MONK [*]

The Silent Work of the Monks

1. As I stand in the silence
    Before the altar/tree
    I become aware
    That others are present
    In the underground chapel.
    I see
    Monks in brown robes
    Seated on every side.
    Their heads are bowed,
    They are in silence.

2. The monks do not raise their eyes,
    But they know I am here.
    They have permitted me to enter.
    The warmth of their silence
    Enters me
    And encourages me
    To be with them.

3. I take a place on a bench
    Beside the brown robed monks.
    Each is intent
    Upon his own work.
    No one speaks,
    But something emanates
    From each of the monks.

---

[*] Ira Progoff, *The White Robed Monk*, Dialogue House Library, New York, 1971, 1983, p. 59 ff.

4.   These emanations
From the monks
Are like sparks,
But not sparks that burn.
They are sparks
That give glistenings of light;
They are warm and bright
But they do not burn.

5.   A power
Becomes present in the silence.
It comes from something stirring
In the silence of the monks,
In the silence of the chapel.
The power is carried
By emanations of love
Coming from the monks,
Healing,
Strengthening,
Warming the air around me.

6.   An atmosphere is forming around me.
I move deeper into it,
Absorbed by it,
Drawn into
The silent work of the monks,
Each intent on his own work
And all contributing to all.
Each and all
Silently adding
His stirrings of love
To the energies of everyone.

7.   I am sitting
In the warmth of the chapel.
The silent stirrings of love
Move around me.
Carried by my breath,
They enter me,
They move around within me
And become a great warmth,
A great warmth within me
And a great warmth around me.

8.   Drawn inward by my breath,
The atmosphere enters my Self.
It circulates within me,
It moves within me,
Carried by my breath,
The outward atmosphere
Of the chapel
Becomes an inward atmosphere
Within my Self.

9.   I am sitting
In the warmth of the chapel
As we each do our inward work,
Working together,
Alone
And together . . .
Sharing the work of the monks
In the silence . . . In the Silence.

APPENDIX B

THE STAR/CROSS★

Breathing the Breath of Mankind

1.　Holding myself in stillness
　　I look into the open space
　　At the center of the Star/Cross.
　　It opens into infinity
　　In each direction.
　　The roots of the past are there
　　And the unformed future.

2.　There is an energy
　　Pulsating
　　At the center of the Star/Cross.
　　Strong,
　　The beating of many hearts,
　　Many lives
　　Brought together
　　In the course of the centuries,
　　Layers of time
　　Placed upon time
　　To form the Star/Cross.
　　The heartbeats of many lives
　　Are in the Star/Cross.

★Ira Progoff, *The Star/Cross,* Dialogue House Library, New York, 1971, 1981, p. 115 ff.

298

3.   The Star and the Cross are one,
A unity
Shaped by history,
I stand before it
Addressing it
With my mind and heart
Wondering at its message,
Wondering what it means
To meet a Star/Cross
In the forest of one's life.

4.   I seek my answers
At the center of the Star/Cross,
The place of Inward Visioning.
In time past
Inward Visioning
Has been the way of peace,
The path of the prophets of old.
Now the place of Inward Visioning
Is the center of the Star/Cross.
The gate to peace opens
At the center of the Star/Cross.

5.   I look again
      Into the open space
      At the center of the Star/Cross.
      I am drawn into it.
      My body remains where it is,
      But my inner being is placed
      At the center of the Star/Cross.
      Past and future
      Are moving through me
      At the center of the Star/Cross.

6.   My life is here
      At the center of the Star/Cross.
      I feel the past days of my life
      Come together as one day.
      I go over them in my mind.
      They are many days
      Filled with many things,
      But I feel them now
      As one day.
      I have been doing one thing,
      Becoming one life.
      Doing many things,
      I have been doing one thing,
      Becoming one life.

7.   At the center of the Star/Cross
Time is moving through.
All of time
Is one moment,
All of my life
Is one moment,
All of mankind's life
Is one moment,
So much behind,
So much ahead,
And all here
Now,
Moving through.
Moving through
This one point
Where I am,
Where mankind is.

8.   My life is here
At the center of the Star/Cross
With everyone's life.
Carried on this one breath,
Mankind and I
Together
As one.

9.   Breathing this one breath,
Myself
With everyone,
Breathing my breath
And the breath of everyone,
Breathing the breath of mankind,
Being in the open space
At the center of the Star/Cross.

10.   Being in the open space,
Breathing the breath of mankind.
Being my life,
The life of mankind within me.
Breathing,
Being,
Living my life,
The life of mankind within me,
At the center of the Star/Cross
In the Silence . . . In the Silence.

About the Author

Since the early nineteen-fifties Dr. Ira Progoff has been exploring psychological methods for creativity and spiritual experience with social applications. He is the creator of the widely accepted *Intensive Journal* method of personal development and its related approach of Process Meditation. Of his several books, *At a Journal Workshop* (1975) and *The Practice of Process Meditation* (1980) are the two textbooks that describe the techniques for using the *Intensive Journal* process. In *Life-Study*, the *Intensive Journal* method is extended to provide a means of experiencing the lives of significant individuals from past generations.

The conceptual base of Ira Progoff's *holistic* depth psychology is contained in a trilogy of earlier books. *The Death and Rebirth of Psychology* (1956) crystallizes the cumulative results of the work of Freud, Adler, Jung and Rank to build the foundation for a new psychology. *Depth Psychology and Modern Man* (1959) presents a holistic view of evolution as the foundation for a non-analytic method in depth psychology. *The Symbolic and the Real* (1963) discusses the significance of these concepts for modern society, and demonstrates the personal use of twilight imagery.

Drawing on the principles of these books, the *Intensive Journal* method emerged in 1966 as a system of non-analytic, integrative techniques for drawing out and interrelating the contents of an individual life. In 1977, as the public use of the method increased, the National *Intensive Journal* Program was formed. It now supplies the materials and trained leaders for *Intensive Journal* workshops in the United States and other countries in cooperation with local sponsoring organizations.

Dr. Progoff is currently director of the *Intensive Journal* program at its Dialogue House headquarters in New York City.